The economic theory and measurement of environmental benefits

The economic theory and measurement of environmental benefits

Per-Olov Johansson

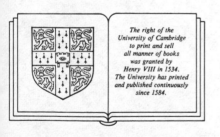

The right of the
University of Cambridge
to print and sell
all manner of books
was granted by
Henry VIII in 1534.
The University has printed
and published continuously
since 1584.

CAMBRIDGE UNIVERSITY PRESS

Cambridge
London   New York   New Rochelle
Melbourne   Sydney

Published by the Press Syndicate of the University of Cambridge
The Pitt Building, Trumpington Street, Cambridge CB2 1RP
32 East 57th Street, New York, NY 10022, USA
10 Stamford Road, Oakleigh, Melbourne 3166, Australia

First published 1987

Printed in Great Britain at the University Press, Cambridge

British Library cataloguing in publication data

Johansson, Per-Olov
The economic theory and measurement of environmental benefits.
1. Environmental policy. 2. Human ecology – Economic aspects
I. Title
333.7'1   HC79.E5

Library of Congress cataloguing in publication data

Johansson, Per-Olov, 1949–
The economic theory and measurement of environmental benefits.
Bibliography.
Includes index.
1. Consumers' surplus. 2. Consumers' surplus – Econometric models.
3. Public goods. 4. Externalities (Economics)
I. Title.
HB825.J64 1987   339.4   86-33364

ISBN 0 521 32877 2 hard covers
ISBN 0 521 34810 2 paperback

CE

Contents

v

Preface

A few years ago I applied for and obtained a position in the Department of Forest Economics at the Swedish University of Agricultural Sciences (SLU) in Umeå. In particular, my work was supposed to include evaluations of different uses of forest land. When the pressure to start undertaking research finally became irresistible, it was quite natural for me to begin by looking for surveys of available methods. I was especially interested in consumer surplus approaches to environmental problems.

It soon became apparent to me that there is a vast number of articles published within this field. In addition, a few books have recently been published which shed considerable light on the problems involved in deriving money measures of utility change. Unfortunately, these books are mainly concerned with goods that are traded in the market. Environmental economics, on the other hand, generally deals with goods and services that are not traded in the market. Moreover, time, discreteness, as well as uncertainty, are important complications in many applications of consumer surplus analysis to environmental issues.

For these reasons, I decided to collect available material on consumer surplus measures for different classes of private and public goods. In a few instances this has enabled me to derive new results, or, treating new cases that have escaped earlier investigators but nevertheless seemed worth pursuing. Throughout this book, I have aimed at presenting the theoretical properties of different consumer surplus measures as well as the practical methodologies available in calculating the measures.

I am grateful to Runar Brännlund, Bengt Kriström, Peter Lohmander, Leif Mattsson, Henry Ohlsson, Bo Ranneby, and Jon Strand for helpful discussions and comments upon parts of earlier versions of the manuscript. My special thanks must go to my friend, teacher, and colleague Karl Gustaf Löfgren who has the quite unusual quality of supporting others not only in times of success but also in times of adversity. His detailed comments on various versions of the manuscript have been of invaluable importance for the completion of this work. Alan Harkess and Chris Hudson made the manuscript readable by scrutinizing the language. I am also indebted to Solveig Edin, Barbro Gunnarsson, Marie Hammarstedt, and Cici Rüetschi for their incredible endurance and ability to decipher hieroglyphics. I also owe a great debt to the Multiple-Use Forestry Project at the SLU for providing me with research funds for all the arduous travelling around the world needed to pursue this topic. Finally, I wish to thank the Trade Union Institute for Economic Research, Stockholm, and its research staff for their hospitality and support during my extended stays there.

In spite of all the help that has been provided by outsiders, there are undoubtly errors, flaws, and 'Scandinavianisms' remaining. As a matter of good form, I remind the reader that they are the responsibility of the author.

P.O.J.

CHAPTER 1

Introduction

Scope of the study

The environment provides the economy with raw materials and energy. Ultimately these return to it as waste products. The environment also provides services directly to consumers, such as air to breath, water to drink, and recreational opportunities.

In many cases an environmental asset provides different but conflicting services. For example, a wilderness area can be left unspoiled and used for various recreational purposes *or* it can be commercially exploited by harvesting the trees. This is an example of a kind of land-use conflict that has become increasingly important during the last decade. In many countries, one would expect still more severe conflicts in the future between 'development' interests and 'conservation' interests. Similarly there is an increasing awareness of the fact that pollution, e.g. acid rain, reduces the benefits derived from recreational activities as well as the value of real estate. In addition, the health of human beings as well as the existence of some species may be threatened by various human activities. A well-known example of the latter is the blue whale stock whose growth has been insufficient to prevent the depletion of the animal almost to extinction. Besides the fact that a living stock of blue whales has a value in itself to most people, there is also the possibility that an extinction may imply the loss of some unique genetic material that may turn out to be useful in, for example, medicine sometime in the future.

Since choices concerning the environment's assets are inevitable, there must be a criterion on which selection among various, and usually conflicting, options can be made. This forces us to place some sort of value on the various service flows received and waste products returned.

Consumer surplus analysis is a very important part of the economic approach to this issue. There is a long tradition of work in this field by

1

economists. Unfortunately, there is also a long tradition of confusing and seemingly contradictory statements concerning the usefulness of the consumer surplus concept.

This study is an attempt to introduce students to some of the mysteries of consumer surplus analysis, or what Morey (1984) so strikingly calls confuser surplus. Even if the notion of 'Foggy Economics' comes to mind, recent research has undoubtly considerably increased the 'range of visibility'. The study's first goal is therefore to explain the circumstances in which a consumer surplus measure correctly ranks commodity bundles or projects. The study's second aim is to extend such measures so as to include the types of commodities which are important in environmental economics. Finally, the study attempts to present empirical approaches which can be used to calculate the consumer surplus measures of programmes that affect the environment.

The first part of this study derives consumer surplus measures to be used in a timeless world. Throughout, the emphasis is on the circumstances in which a money measure correctly ranks/measures the underlying utility change. Four major cases are to be considered: unrationed private goods, rationed private goods, public goods or 'bads' (externalities), and discrete choices. Reviews of practical methodologies are also included in order to calculate the consumer's surplus for these classes of goods. The second part of the book considers intertemporal issues. In particular, it derives consumer surplus measures, and presents practical methodologies, to be used when the consumer faces a risky rather than a perfectly certain future.

A brief review of the literature

The literature that deals with the theory and measurement of the *consumer's surplus* is both large and growing.[1] The concept of consumer surplus was first introduced by Dupuit (1844), who was concerned with the benefits and costs of constructing a bridge. Marshall (1920) introduced the concept to the English-speaking world. As a measure of consumer surplus, Marshall used the area under the demand curve less actual money expenditure on the good. At least this is a common interpretation.[2] Marshall's measure, like that of Dupuit, was an all-or-nothing measure: 'The excess of the price which he would be willing to pay rather than go without the thing, over that which he actually does pay is the economic measure of this surplus of satisfaction' (Marshall, 1920, p. 124). Later, Hicks, in a series of articles in 1940/1–1945/6, and Henderson (1940/1) demonstrated that consumer surplus could be interpreted in terms of amounts of money that must be given to/taken from a household.

An analysis of the welfare foundations of different consumer surplus measures and the conditions under which they coincide began with the work by Samuelson (1942) and Patinkin (1963). The debate centred around the interpretation of the *constancy of the marginal utility of income or money*; some kind of constancy assumption is needed for the area to the left of a demand curve to be proportional to the underlying change in utility. In recent years, much attention has been devoted to the more general question of how to evaluate consumer surpluses in the multiple price change case. Although the basic problem, which is known as the *path-dependency issue*, was introduced in 1938 by Hotelling, the main stream of papers on this issue have appeared in the 1970s and the 1980s. (See, however, Samuelson's (1950) historical survey of the integrability issue.) The basic problem is that the sum of the changes in consumer surpluses in general depends on the order in which prices are changed. However, conditions for path independency have been established, and these conditions turn out to be closely related to the aforementioned constancy of the marginal utility of income (see Burns, 1973; Harberger, 1971; Just *et al.*, 1982; McKenzie and Pearce, 1982; Morey, 1984; Silberberg, 1972; 1978; to mention just a few).

The previously mentioned literature is generally confined to situations in which the only constraint facing the consumer is the size of his budget. In many situations, however, one would expect individuals to face *quantity constraints*. For example, the government may impose price ceilings or floors which result in excess demand or supply in markets for goods and factors. Or the 'carrying capacity' of a natural area for recreation activity may be limited so that its use must be rationed.

The seminal work on utility maximization subject to quantity constraints is that of Tobin and Houthakker (1950/1). They examined a situation where constraints are just on the verge of binding at the examined point. More recently, the Tobin–Houthakker results have been generalized to situations where the rationing constraints are not optimal (see Howard, 1977; Mackay and Whitney, 1980; Neary and Roberts, 1980). There are also a few attempts to derive consumer's surpluses in quantity-constrained regimes (see, for example, Cornes and Albon, 1981; Just *et al.*, 1982; Randall and Stoll, 1980).

In the growing literature on the economics of the environment, the concepts of *public goods* and *externalities* are important. There are at least two basic characteristics that distinguish pure public goods from private goods. Firstly, the same unit of a public good can be consumed by many. Secondly, once a public good is provided for some individuals, it is impossible or at least very costly to exclude others from benefiting from it. A private good, on the other hand, once consumed by one individual cannot be consumed by others. Moreover, the buyer of the good is free to exclude other individuals from consuming it.

Discussions of externalities are often concerned with the case where one party affects the consumption or production possibilities of another. However, most important external effects concern a large number of individuals. For example, a dam may flood and destroy a valuable wilderness area which is used for hiking, fishing, hunting and bird watching, and hence affect many (groups of) individuals. Another example is pollution of the air and water. These examples also show that there is a close correspondence between public goods ('bads') and externalities. In fact, it is reasonable to view a public good or 'bad' as a special kind of externality in consumption. For further discussion on the definitions of public goods and external effects see McGuire and Aaron (1969), Musgrave (1959), Mäler (1974), Ng (1979), Samuelson (1954, 1955, 1969), and Strotz (1958). For recent surveys of the environment in economics and externalities, the reader is referred to Fisher and Peterson (1976) and Mishan (1971) respectively.

Since demand functions for public goods or 'bads' are not directly observable the central task is to overcome the *problem of preference revelation* for such goods. Different methods have been proposed in the literature. Of particular interest, in the present context, are methods which exploit the selfish interest of consumers to communicate, in the market, true signals about preferences for private goods, thereby simultaneously providing the information needed about public goods as well. By observing the effect on demand schedules for private goods one can in certain circumstances infer the value consumers place on changes in the levels of public goods or 'bads'.

There are important situations in which consumers face a *discrete* rather than a continuous set of *choices*. For example, a household cannot simultaneously visit two different recreation sites. Or quality changes, such as pollution or the development of new sites, may induce households to switch from trips to one area to another. In order to handle such discrete choice situations, the continuous choice models must be modified.

To my knowledge, no general discrete choice theory is available for use in deriving consumer surplus measures. A few authors, notably Mäler (1974) and Small and Rosen (1981), have rigorously derived surplus measures for particular classes of discrete choices. Mäler considers a good which must be purchased in a given quantity or not at all. Small and Rosen concentrate on the case when two goods are mutually exclusive, but also briefly discuss other kinds of discrete choice situations. A unified framework for formulating econometric models of such discrete/continuous choices has been formulated by Hanemann (1984a).

It is straightforward to extend single-period models to cover optimization for T-period horizons, at least provided the world is perfectly competitive. Such models have been used by, for example, Boadway and Bruce (1984) to derive overall or *lifetime consumer surplus measures*. However, such measures require huge amounts of information and may hence be difficult to calculate and estimate. Recently, Blackorby *et al.* (1984) have shown that the present value of *instantaneous consumer's surpluses* can be a sign-preserving measure of the overall utility change. These findings probably simplify calculations in many càses.

In many situations involving time, households operate under various forms of *uncertainty*. It is probably fair to say that the majority of effort in the consumer surplus field has been concentrated on analyses of situations in which prices are random but uncertainty is resolved before decisions are taken. In particular, a considerable theoretical literature has developed which focuses on the effects of stabilizing commodity prices. Most of these studies base their analysis on the concept of consumer surplus. The approach was first used by Waugh (1944) who showed that consumers facing exogenous random prices are better off than if these prices are stabilized at their arithmetic means. Later studies, e.g. Samuelson (1972) and Turnovsky *et al.* (1980), have shown that the Waugh result is not generally correct.

In a seminal paper Weisbrod (1964) argued that an individual who was unsure of whether he would visit, say, a national park would be willing to pay a sum in excess of his *expected consumer surplus* to ensure that the park would be available:

To see why, the reader need recognize the existence of people who anticipate purchasing the commodity (visiting the park) at some time in the future, but who, in fact, never will purchase (visit) it. Nevertheless, if these consumers behave as 'economic men' they will be willing to pay something for the option to consume the commodity in the future. This 'option value' should influence the decision of whether or not to close the park and turn it to an alternative use. (Weisbrod, 1964, p. 472)

This argument seemed both novel and intuitively appealing. Nevertheless, there has been much discussion about the precise definition of *option value*. There seem to be at least two different interpretations. The first interpretation links the definition to the idea of a *risk premium* arising from uncertainty as to the future value of the commodity (park) if it were preserved. This view has been advanced by Bishop (1982), Bohm (1975), Cicchetti and Freeman (1971), Freeman (1984a), Graham (1981), Plummer and Hartman (1985), and Schmalensee (1972), among others.

A second interpretation of option value focuses on the intertemporal aspects of the problem and the *irreversibility* of any decision to close the park and convert it to alternative uses. This concept, sometimes called the *quasi-option value*, was developed by Arrow and Fisher (1974) and Henry (1974). Recently Fisher and Hanemann (1983), Hanemann (1984b), and Mäler (1984) have analysed the relationship between the two different definitions of option value.

Plan of the study

The arrangement of chapters in this book is based on the above presentation of the consumer surplus issue for different classes of private and public goods. However, in pursuing the study of consumer surplus measures, we will need a few basic concepts such as the direct utility function, demand functions, the indirect utility function, the cost or expenditure function, and the compensation or money-metric function. These concepts will be defined in Chapter 2.

The basic topic of consumer surplus measures for unrationed goods is dealt with in Chapters 3 and 4. The emphasis is on path-independency conditions for consumer surplus measures with multiple price changes. Conditions under which there is an exact correspondence between the dollar gain reported by a money measure and the underlying utility change are clarified. The ordinal/cardinal properties of money measures of utility change are discussed, and the problem of aggregation across individuals is addressed. We also discuss the approaches that can be used to estimate consumer surpluses in real world situations.

Chapter 5 derives consumer surplus measures to be used in quantity-constrained situations. Path-independency conditions for ordinary or uncompensated as well as Hicksian or income compensated measures are derived. The chapter also offers an interpretation of the results in terms of virtual or market clearing prices.

The first part of Chapter 6 derives consumer surplus measures for public goods. It is a straightforward matter to interpret these measures in terms of external effects or public 'bads'. For this reason the second part of the chapter considers measures which can be calculated with market data. Chapter 7 contains a review of some of the methodologies that have actually been used to calculate consumer surpluses for non-priced commodities.

Chapter 8 shows how the methods can be modified to handle situations in which consumers face a discrete rather than a continuous set of choices. The chapter concentrates on a case intermediate to those dealt with by Mäler (1974) and Small and Rosen (1981), but the analysis is much inspired by the work of these authors. A household is assumed to have the option to visit a particular recreation site. This is the discrete part of the choice. However, if the household decides to visit the site it is free to choose the on-site time subject to budget and time constraints. Later, the option to choose among several different sites is introduced. Finally, we discuss the application of discrete choice models and present a recent attempt to estimate the value of a hunting permit from discrete, i.e. 'yes' and 'no', response data.

Chapter 9 extends the single-period model of Chapters 3 and 4 to cover optimization for *T*-period horizons. Overall as well as instantaneous consumer surplus measures are introduced. In some applications, e.g. fishing and hunting, the size of the stock of a natural resource is of importance. For this reason the second part of the chapter focuses on models with renewable natural resources. In particular, we introduce a model used by Hammack and Brown (1974) to analyse the optimal allocation of prairie wetlands in the north-central U.S. and southern Canada. The chapter also presents different frameworks which have been suggested for the aggregation of intergenerational welfares. Obviously this is an important issue since environmental programmes often affect not only the present but also future generations.

The assumption that agents face no uncertainty is relaxed in Chapter 10. The first section of the chapter is devoted to exploring some basic concepts, e.g. risk attitudes, cardinal properties of preferences and concavity/convexity of a function. Then the welfare measures are modified so as to be able to cope with cases of uncertainty where certain decisions must be made before prices are known. This is done in the context of simple two-commodity models as well as in the context of more complex intertemporal models. The chapter also illustrates the practical use of such models by presenting an empirical study involving discrete choices as well as uncertain prices.

Finally, in Chapter 11 the tools developed in the previous chapters are put together in an analysis of the total benefits of an environmental asset in a certain as well as in a risky world. The concepts of existence value, supply-side option value, access value, and quasi-option value are defined and illustrated. The chapter also presents the Brookshire *et al.* (1983) study, which is concerned with two wildlife populations, grizzly bear and bighorn sheep in Wyoming, whose future availability is uncertain. The chapter ends with brief discussions of the choice of money measure in situations involving risks and some possible directions for future research.

CHAPTER 2

Some basic concepts

In order to be able to derive consumer surplus measures a number of essential tools and definitions are required. Instead of waiting until those different concepts arise in the text before introducing them, this chapter presents the basic tools used in the subsequent chapters. For this reason, the chapter serves as a basic point of reference for the analysis in the remainder of this volume.

Section 1 considers the properties of the *direct utility function*. Equipped with this function, we then turn to the consumer's utility maximization problem. Necessary and sufficient conditions for utility maximization are stated in Section 2, while the *demand functions* for commodities are derived and examined in Section 3. The rest of the chapter is devoted to a presentation of the *indirect utility function*, the *expenditure function*, and the *compensation or money-metric function*. These concepts will turn out to be extremely useful in derivations of consumer surplus measures.

By necessity, the presentation of different concepts must be brief. The main sources used in this chapter are Barten and Böhm (1982), Deaton and Muellbauer (1983), Diewert (1982), Katzner (1970), and Varian (1978). The reader interested in more details, as well as heavier and more precise mathematical artillery, is referred to one or other of the books listed above.

1 *The utility function*

Let us assume that the consumer possesses a continuous and increasing[1] utility function $U = U(\mathbf{x})$, where $\mathbf{x} = (x_1, \ldots, x_n)$ is a vector, or bundle, of goods consumed. The existence of such a function is taken for granted, i.e. a set of axioms of choice, which represent sufficient conditions for the existence of the above utility function, is not presented. Instead, we will

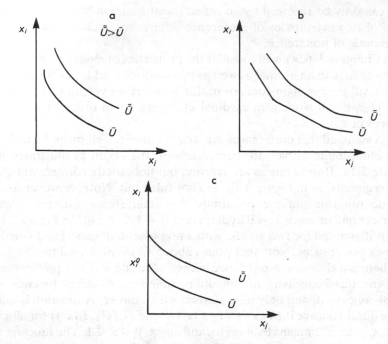

Figure 2.1 (a) Strictly convex preferences, (b) convex preferences, and (c) strictly convex preferences generating corner solutions

concentrate on a few properties of the utility function which are essential for the analysis to be carried out in the subsequent chapters.

First of all, it is important to note that the function $U(\mathbf{x})$ is not unique in an ordinal world. Any other function that produces the same ordering of commodity bundles must be just as good. If $U=U(\mathbf{x})$ is a utility function representing a preference ordering, any other increasing function or monotonic transformation of $U(\mathbf{x})$, say $F(\mathbf{x})=f(U(\mathbf{x}))$ with $\partial f/\partial U > 0$, will represent exactly the same preferences. This is so since $f(U(\mathbf{x}^1)) \geqslant f(U(\mathbf{x}^2))$ if and only if $U(\mathbf{x}^1) \geqslant U(\mathbf{x}^2)$, where $\mathbf{x}^1$ and $\mathbf{x}^2$ are any two bundles in the consumption set X, which is taken to be the non-negative orthant of Euclidean n-space.[2] The purpose of the utility function is to order commodity bundles. The actual values taken by the function are not in themselves meaningful in an ordinal world.

A much more stringent requirement would be that the relative magnitude of the intervals between different levels of utility have some definite meaning. In order to meet this requirement, we would need to restrict f( ) to be a positive affine transformation, such as $G(\mathbf{x})=a+bU(\mathbf{x})$ with the constant $b > 0$. A utility function is said to be (strongly) cardinal if it can only be replaced by an affine transformation of itself, and the ratio of two magnitudes of preference differences is also a meaningful magnitude of preference.

In Chapters 3–6, we will consider the properties of money measures of utility change in an ordinal as well as in a cardinal world, but the ordinal world will be our main concern in this book. However, in Chapters 10 and 11, we will work with cardinal utility theory in order to examine choices in a risky world.

It is assumed that preferences are strictly convex. This property means that indifference curves are curved toward the origin as illustrated in Figure 2.1a. If preferences are convex, but not strictly convex, straight line segments, as in Figure 2.1b, are not ruled out. Note, however, that we do not rule out the possibility that indifference surfaces might intersect one or more $x_j = 0$ hyperplanes ($j = 1, \ldots, n$). In Figure 2.1c this is illustrated for two goods, with a non-essential[3] good j and strictly convex preferences. Note that points above x_1^0 are preferred to x_1^0.

There is a close correspondence between the convexity of preferences and the quasi-concavity of the utility function. A utility function is quasi-concave if, and only if, preferences are convex. A function is said to be quasi-concave if $U(\pi \mathbf{x}^1 + (1-\pi)\mathbf{x}^2) \geq \min \{U(\mathbf{x}^1), U(\mathbf{x}^2)\}$ for all $\mathbf{x}^1$, $\mathbf{x}^2 \in X$, where $\in$ means belongs to, and any π, $0 \leq \pi \leq 1$. The function is strictly quasi-concave (and preferences strictly convex) if the strict inequality holds for $0 < \pi < 1$. It should be noted that quasi-concavity is a property which relates directly to the preference ordering. This property is preserved under increasing transformations, i.e. it is an ordinal property. (Concavity of a function, on the other hand, is a cardinal property (see Kannai, 1977).)

The above technical restrictions on the utility function may seem too strong. Indeed, some of the assumptions are not needed at all or can be weakened in certain analyses of consumer behaviour. However, in deriving money measures of utility change, the above set of assumptions will turn out to be convenient. In point of fact, we will frequently need an additional assumption, namely that the utility function is thrice continuously differentiable on the interior of X.

In the theory of demand, it is usually assumed that the utility function has well-defined first and second derivatives. This assumption eliminates kinks in the indifference curves. The assumption also (almost) ensures that the demand functions are differentiable. However, in consumer surplus analysis, one sometimes makes assumptions about the second derivatives of the demand functions and the 'marginal utility of income function'. Hence, we might as well assume that the utility function is thrice continuously differentiable. In point of fact, we will sometimes use the expression 'a smooth function'. This is taken to mean a function which has well-defined derivatives of all orders, i.e. first, second, third, fourth, and nth derivatives.

However, in most cases we will speak of a well-behaved utility function. The following definition is introduced.

Definition: A utility function $U(\mathbf{x})$ is said to be *well-behaved* if (i) it is continuous where finite on X, (ii) it is increasing (and $\partial U(\mathbf{x})/\partial x_i > 0$ for all i), (iii) it is strictly quasi-concave on X, and (iv) it generates at least twice continuously differentiable demand functions (on a set, say Ω_1, of strictly positive prices and income; this set will be discussed further in Section 3).

2 *Utility maximization*

Having established a convenient form of the representation of preferences, a start can now be made with the investigation of consumer behaviour. Let us assume that the consumer has an exogenous budget y, which is to be spent on some or all of n commodities. These can be bought in non-negative quantities at given, fixed, strictly positive prices p_i. Because of our assumption that the household is not satiated, the best choice lies on, rather than inside, the budget constraint.

The problem of utility maximization can then be written as

$$\left. \begin{aligned} &\max U(\mathbf{x}) \\ &\text{s.t. } y - \mathbf{p}\mathbf{x}' = 0 \\ &\mathbf{x} \text{ is in } X \end{aligned} \right\} \tag{2.1}$$

where $\mathbf{x} = (x_1, \ldots, x_n)$ is a vector of commodities, $\mathbf{p} = (p_1, \ldots, p_n)$ is a vector of strictly positive prices ($\mathbf{p} \gg 0$), $y > 0$ is income, and a prime denotes a transposed vector. In order to simplify notation this prime is suppressed hereafter.

According to (2.1), the consumer is assumed to act as if he/she maximizes a well-behaved ordinal utility function subject to his budget constraint. The first-order conditions for an interior solution (i.e. $\mathbf{x} \gg 0$) to (2.1) are

$$\left. \begin{aligned} &\frac{\partial U(\mathbf{x})}{\partial \mathbf{x}} - \lambda \mathbf{p} = 0 \\ &y - \mathbf{p}\mathbf{x} = 0 \end{aligned} \right\} \tag{2.2}$$

where λ is the Lagrange multiplier of the budget constraint, and $\partial U(\mathbf{x})/\partial \mathbf{x}$ is a vector of order $n \times 1$ whose elements are given by $\partial U(\mathbf{x})/\partial x_i > 0$ for $i = 1, \ldots, n$.

The consumer wants to find the point on the budget plane that achieves

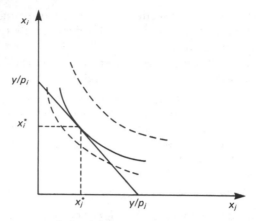

Figure 2.2 Preference maximization

highest satisfaction. Consider the two goods case in Figure 2.2. Here, the budget line is tanget to a smoothly convex indifference curve at a single point, and both goods are bought. This means that an interior solution requires that the marginal rate of substitution $(\partial U/\partial x_i)/(\partial U/\partial x_j)$ between goods must be equal to the price ratio p_i/p_j. This can be verified by rearranging the equations in (2.2).

Under strict quasi-concavity of the utility function, the necessary second-order condition for a relative maximum is satisfied. Geometrically, the second-order condition means that the set of all bundles $\mathbf{x}$ that are at least as good as $\mathbf{x}^*$ (the upper contour set) must lie above the budget hyperplane at $\mathbf{x}^*$, as in Figure 2.2 (see, for example, Varian, 1978).

3 Demand functions

The first-order conditions (2.2) can be solved for the n unknown variables x_i (and the Lagrange multiplier λ) in terms of prices and income

$$\mathbf{x} = \mathbf{x}(\mathbf{p}, y) \quad (=[x_1(\mathbf{p}, y), \ldots \ldots \ldots, x_n(\mathbf{p}, y)]') \tag{2.3}$$

with the quantity demanded being a function of prices and income.

In this book, it will be generally assumed that the demand functions are twice continuously differentiable. This means that attention is restricted to a dense, open subset, denoted by Ω, of the set of strictly positive prices and incomes. This subset Ω contains all $\mathbf{p} \gg 0$, $y > 0$ for which the demand functions are twice continuously differentiable. However, corner solutions are not excluded, i.e. utility maximizing commodity bundles may lie on the boundary of the commodity space X. For example, the quasi-linear utility function $U = f(x_1, \ldots, x_{n-1}) + ax_n$, where $a > 0$, which is frequently used in the subsequent chapters, may generate corner solutions.

This complication can be handled by partitioning Ω into subsets corresponding to interior solutions and corner solutions respectively. The demand functions have the appropriate properties on the interiors of these subsets. An example which will help to clarify these matters can be found in the appendix to Chapter 2. However, unless otherwise stated, we hereafter only consider a set, say Ω_I, of prices and incomes which generates both interior solutions ($\mathbf{x} \gg 0$) and twice continuously differentiable demand functions. Analyses involving corner solutions can be found in Chapters 6 and 8.

Several important properties of the demand functions can be deduced. Firstly, the demand for any commodity is a single-valued function of prices and income (on Ω_I). This follows from the strict convexity of preferences, i.e. indifference curves are curved towards the origin so that a single commodity combination corresponds to a given configuration of prices and income.

Secondly, the fact that the demand functions satisfy the budget constraint ($\mathbf{px} = y$), places a set of restrictions on the functions which is referred to as the adding-up restriction. For example, the sum of the income effects equals unity ($\mathbf{p}\partial\mathbf{x}/\partial y = 1$) (see, for example, Deaton and Muellbauer (1983) Chapter 3 for details).

Thirdly, demand functions are homogeneous of degree zero in prices and income. If all prices and income change in the same proportion, the quantities demanded remain unchanged. Intuitively, multiplying all prices and income by some positive number does not change the budget set and thus cannot affect the solution to the utility maximization problem. This can be checked by multiplying $\mathbf{p}$ and y in the first-order conditions (2.2) by a positive constant π. As a consequence, we can write the demand functions as $\mathbf{x}(\mathbf{p}, y) = \mathbf{x}(\pi\mathbf{p}, \pi y)$. Next, π is set equal to the (inverted) price of an arbitrarily selected commodity, say x_n, generally called the *numéraire*. This procedure illustrates that only relative prices, i.e. p_i/p_n, matter for a rational consumer. Alternatively, income is used as the *numéraire* ($\pi = 1/y$). Both these approaches are common in consumer surplus analysis, as we shall see in the next chapter.

It can also be shown that the change in demand for commodity i resulting from a change in the price of commodity j can be written as

$$\frac{\partial x_i}{\partial p_j} = \frac{\partial \tilde{x}_i}{\partial p_j} - x_j \frac{\partial x_i}{\partial y} \quad \text{for all } i, j \tag{2.4}$$

The first term on the right-hand side describes the change in demand in response to the price change assuming that utility is kept constant. This is the (cross-) substitution effect. The second term on the right is known as the income effect, which states the rate at which the consumer's purchases of the commodity would change with changes in his income, prices remaining constant. The sum of the two terms gives the total effect on demand for good i of small changes in the jth price.

In general, the terms in (2.4) may be of either sign. If commodity i is a superior (inferior) good, the income effect is positive (negative). The signs of the cross-substitution effects are not known in general. However, as is demonstrated in Section 5, the substitution effect on the ith commodity resulting from a change in the jth price is equal to the substitution effect on the jth commodity resulting from a change in the ith price. Moreover, it is possible to show that the own-price substitution effect is negative if the utility function is strongly quasi-concave. For the moment, this concludes our examination of the properties of the demand functions, but we will return to these issues in Section 5.

4 *The indirect utility function*

An alternative approach, using the notion of an indirect utility function, has become an important tool of demand analysis. In particular, the indirect utility function arises in a variety of places in welfare economics. Apart from this, it also provides a simple technique for computing demand functions.

In order to obtain the indirect utility function, substitute the demand functions (2.3) into the direct utility function

$$U(\mathbf{x}(\mathbf{p}, y)) = V(\mathbf{p}, y) \tag{2.5}$$

Due to the assumed properties of the direct utility function and the demand functions, the indirect utility function is: (i) continuous, (ii) strictly quasi-convex, i.e. $-V(\mathbf{p}, y)$ is strictly quasi-concave, (iii) homogeneous of degree zero in prices and income, (iv) decreasing in prices, (v) increasing in income, and (vi) thrice continuously differentiable in all arguments (on Ω_I).

We shall not attempt to provide proofs here. Detailed proofs can be found in Diewert (1982) and Varian (1978, Ch. 3). Most of the properties listed above, however, follow straightforwardly from our earlier discussion.

We now examine the differential properties of the indirect utility function. Differentiating (2.5) with respect to the ith price and invoking the envelope theorem yields

$$\frac{\partial V}{\partial p_i} = -\lambda x_i(\mathbf{p}, y) < 0 \quad \text{for all } i \tag{2.6}$$

as is shown in the appendix to this chapter. Thus, the partial derivatives of the indirect utility function with respect to prices are the demand functions multiplied by $(-\lambda)$. In turn, it is easily demonstrated that λ, the Lagrange multiplier associated with the budget constraint, is the derivative of the indirect utility function with respect to income

$$\frac{\partial V}{\partial y} = \lambda(\mathbf{p}, y) \tag{2.7}$$

In the light of this result, it is not surprising that λ is frequently referred to as the marginal utility of income.

Dividing (2.6) by (2.7) one obtains the demand function for the ith good. This result, arrived at by Roy (1942), is known as Roy's identity. It suggests that a theory of demand may be constructed by making assumptions on the indirect utility function instead of on the direct utility function. Moreover, the second (and third) derivatives of the indirect utility function can be used to examine the properties of both the demand functions and $\lambda(\mathbf{p}, y)$, as well as the relationship between changes in utility and changes in $\mathbf{x}$ and λ.

It is important to describe two additional results. These relate to the properties of λ, which is used in subsequent chapters to transform unobservable utility changes to observable money measures. For this reason, the properties of the function $\lambda(\mathbf{p}, y)$ are of the vital importance to us.

In the previous section, it was shown that the demand functions for commodities are homogeneous of degree zero in prices and income. The 'marginal utility of income function' does not have this property. This may be illustrated by multiplying prices and income in the first-order conditions (2.2) by a positive scalar π to obtain

$$\frac{\partial U(\mathbf{x}(\mathbf{p}, y))}{\partial \mathbf{x}} = \lambda \mathbf{p} = \frac{\partial U(\mathbf{x}(\pi\mathbf{p}, \pi y))}{\partial \mathbf{x}} = \lambda^* \pi\mathbf{p} \tag{2.8}$$

where the derivatives are evaluated at the same $\mathbf{x}$, since $\mathbf{x}(\mathbf{p}, y) = \mathbf{x}(\pi\mathbf{p}, \pi y)$ for $\pi > 0$. In order to preserve the equalities in (3.8), λ^* must be equal to λ/π. This finding implies that the marginal utility of income is homogeneous of degree minus one in prices and income. If prices and income double, λ must halve.

It is also important to note that λ is not invariant under increasing transformations of the utility function. To show this, we use the fact that the ordinal indirect utility function, as well as the direct utility function, is unique except for a monotonic transformation. Hence, $f[V(\mathbf{p}, y)] = f[U(\mathbf{x}(\mathbf{p}, y))]$. Differentiation with respect to income establishes that the new marginal utility of income is $(\partial f/\partial V)\lambda$. It is easily verified that the demand functions are left unchanged by such transformations since $\partial f/\partial V$ appears in both the numerator and the denominator when dividing (2.6) by (2.7) in order to obtain the demand function for the ith good.

5 *The expenditure function*

We now turn to an alternative approach which is based on the concept of an expenditure or cost function. Given an attainable utility level, $\bar{U}$ say, the expenditure function is the minimum amount of expenditure necessary to attain a utility level at least as high as $\bar{U}$ at given prices $\mathbf{p}$.

Hence, the expenditure function is defined as

$$e(\mathbf{p}, \bar{U}) = \min_{\mathbf{x}} \{\mathbf{px}|U(\mathbf{x})\geqslant\bar{U}\}$$
$$= \mathbf{px}(\mathbf{p}, \bar{U})$$

(2.9)

where a tilde denotes a compensated demand function. (See the appendix to this chapter for a derivation of these demand functions.)

If the utility function is well-behaved, then the expenditure function is: (i) jointly continuous in $(U, \mathbf{p})$, (ii) concave in prices, (iii) positively linearly homogeneous in prices, (iv) increasing in prices, (v) increasing in utility, and (vi) thrice continuously differentiable in all of its arguments (on Ω_I).

The partial derivatives of the cost function with respect to prices are the cost-minimizing demand functions, $\partial e/\partial p_i=\tilde{x}_i$ as is shown in the appendix to Chapter 2. These cost-minimizing demand functions are known as Hicksian or compensated demand functions. They tell us how demand is affected by prices when income is adjusted in such a way as to leave utility unchanged. Hence, the properties of these demand functions differ from the ordinary or Marshallian demand functions considered in the previous sections, where income remained fixed when prices were changed.

However, the utility maximization and expenditure minimization problems are 'dual' problems. Suppose the price–income vector is such that utility maximization produces the utility level $\bar{U}$. We can then reformulate the problem as one of selecting goods to minimize the expenditure or income necessary to attain $\bar{U}$ at the given price vector. Clearly, both problems generate the same optimal commodity bundle, i.e.

$$y=\mathbf{px}(\mathbf{p}, y)=\mathbf{p\tilde{x}}(\mathbf{p}, \bar{U})=e(\mathbf{p}, \bar{U})$$

(2.10)

Although we refrain from stating a formal proof, inspection of Figure 2.3 should convince the reader that $x_i=\tilde{x}_i$ for all i in optimum.

However, in general, a change in a price affects ordinary and compen-

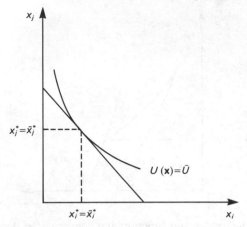

Figure 2.3 The utility maximizing bundle $\mathbf{x}^*$ is equal to the cost-minimizing bundle $\bar{\mathbf{x}}^*$

sated demands in different ways. Let us use (2.10) to write the compensated demand function for commodity i in terms of its ordinary demand function, i.e. $\bar{x}_i = x_i(\mathbf{p}, e(\mathbf{p}, \bar{U}))$. That is, if a price is changed, expenditure (income) is adjusted so as to leave utility unchanged. Differentiating this expression with respect to p_j yields

$$\frac{\partial \bar{x}_i}{\partial p_j} = \frac{\partial x_i}{\partial p_j} + \frac{\partial x_i}{\partial y} \bar{x}_j \qquad (2.11)$$

where $\bar{x}_j = \partial e / \partial p_j$. The first term on the right of (2.11) gives the change in ordinary demand with respect to changes in the jth price. The second term is an income effect.

From the Slutsky equation (2.11) it can be seen that the compensated demand functions have the property that a price change has a substitution effect, but not an income effect. Therefore, in general, the slope of a compensated demand curve is different from the slope of an ordinary demand curve. As is illustrated in Figure 2.4, the compensated demand curve is steeper than the ordinary demand curve in the case of a normal good. Only in the case of zero income effects do the curves coincide.

Next we illustrate a result which will turn out to have far-reaching consequences in the subsequent chapters. According to Young's theorem, the cross derivatives of a twice continuously differentiable function are symmetric. Applying this property to the expenditure function (2.9), it follows that $\partial \bar{x}_i / \partial p_j = \partial \bar{x}_j / \partial p_i$. Hence, Young's theorem implies that the cross-price derivatives of the Hicksian demands are symmetric. In the appendix to this chapter, it is demonstrated that Young's theorem does not imply that the cross-price derivatives of the

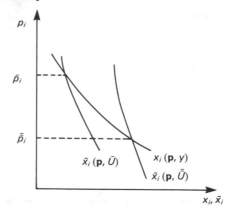

Figure 2.4 An ordinary demand function and compensated demand functions associated with utility levels $\bar{U}$ and $\bar{\bar{U}}$ respectively ($\bar{\bar{U}} > \bar{U}$)

ordinary or Marshallian demand functions are symmetric. It is the presence of income effects which causes the asymmetry. In point of fact, this asymmetry is the source of the problems which will confront us when deriving ordinary consumer surplus measures in the next chapter.

Finally, we indicate the properties of the behaviour functions with respect to monotonic transformations of the utility function. We have already argued that $x_i(\mathbf{p}, y) = \bar{x}_i(\mathbf{p}, \bar{U})$ for any $\bar{U}$, provided $y = e(\mathbf{p}, \bar{U})$, and that x_i is left unaffected by a monotonic transformation of the utility function. In order for the equality to be preserved, the compensated demand functions must also be unaffected by such a transformation. Intuitively, indifference surfaces are unaffected by the transformation; they are simply relabelled. Therefore, the minimum cost of reaching any given indifference surface (commodity bundle) remains unchanged.

On the other hand, $\partial e/\partial U$ or the marginal cost of utility is affected by the transformation. As is shown in the appendix, the marginal cost of utility is the reciprocal of the marginal utility of income, and we have already demonstrated that the marginal utility of income cannot remain unaffected by the considered transformation.

6 *The compensation function*

The expenditure function can be used to introduce a construction, the compensation function or money-metric function, which has received considerable attention in welfare economics. The fact that the expenditure function, is, by assumption, increasing in utility, enables us to make the following construction:

$$f(\mathbf{p}; \mathbf{p}^c, y) = e(\mathbf{p}, V(\mathbf{p}^c, y)) \tag{2.12}$$

where $\mathbf{p}$ is a vector of reference prices. This is the (indirect) compensation function.

If the utility level is fixed, say $V(\mathbf{p}^c, y) = \bar{U}$, (2.12) is an expenditure function. Hence, partial derivatives can be taken of $e(\quad)$ with respect to prices $\mathbf{p}$ to obtain the Hicksian demand functions $\bar{\mathbf{x}}(\mathbf{p}, \bar{U})$.

On the other hand, with respect to changes in utility, via $\mathbf{p}^c$ or y with $\mathbf{p}$ fixed, the compensation function behaves like a utility function since, by assumption, $\partial e/\partial U > 0$. In fact, for any fixed $\mathbf{p}$, the compensation function is, itself, a utility function, i.e. it is a monotonic transform of the (direct or) indirect utility function. In other words, the compensation function ranks commodity bundles in the same order as the utility function (and only the ranking, not the values a function takes, make sense in an ordinal world). The reader interested in a detailed analysis of the properties of compensation functions is referred to Weymark (1985).

Appendix

On the properties of the indirect utility function

In order to examine the partial derivative of the indirect utility function (2.5) with respect to the ith price we use the first-order conditions (2.2) to obtain

$$V_i = \frac{\partial V(\mathbf{p}, y)}{\partial p_i} = \sum_{j=1}^{n} \frac{\partial U}{\partial x_j} \frac{\partial x_j}{\partial p_i} = \Sigma \lambda p_j \frac{\partial x_j}{\partial p_i} \tag{A2.1}$$

Differentiating the budget constraint $y = \mathbf{p}\mathbf{x}$ with respect to p_i we obtain

$$0 = \Sigma p_j \frac{\partial x_j}{\partial p_i} + x_i \tag{A2.2}$$

Inserting (A2.2) into (A2.1) we find that

$$V_i = \frac{\partial V(\mathbf{p}, y)}{\partial p_i} = -\lambda x_i \quad \text{for all } i \tag{A2.3}$$

which is the expression stated in equation (2.6). Using the same approach as above, it is a straightforward matter to show that $\partial V/\partial y = \lambda$.

In Section 5, it was argued that the cross-price derivatives of the ordinary demand functions are not generally symmetrical. If the indirect utility function is twice continuously differentiable, then according to Young's theorem

$$V_{ij} = V_{ji} \quad \text{for all } i, j \tag{A2.4}$$

where $V_{ij} = \partial^2 V/\partial p_i \partial p_j = -\lambda \partial x_i/\partial p_j - x_i \partial \lambda/\partial p_j$ from (A2.3). Thus, $\partial x_i/\partial p_j \neq \partial x_j/\partial p_i$ unless $x_i \partial \lambda/\partial p_j = x_j \partial \lambda/\partial p_i$. This shows that the cross-price derivatives are not generally symmetrical.

The expenditure function

The first-order conditions of the expenditure minimization problem (2.9) can be written as

$$
\left.
\begin{aligned}
&\mathbf{p} - \frac{\mu \partial U}{\partial \bar{\mathbf{x}}} = 0 \\[2mm]
&\bar{U} - U(\bar{\mathbf{x}}) = 0
\end{aligned}
\right\}
\tag{A2.5}
$$

where μ is the Lagrange multiplier associated with the constraint $\bar{U} - U(x) = 0$. Solving this system we obtain the compensated demand functions $\bar{\mathbf{x}} = \bar{\mathbf{x}}(\mathbf{p}, \bar{U})$.

Next, differentiating the expenditure function (2.9) with respect to p_i yields

$$
\begin{aligned}
\frac{\partial e}{\partial p_i} &= \sum_{j=1}^{n} p_j \frac{\partial \bar{x}_j}{\partial p_i} + \bar{x}_i \\[2mm]
&= \frac{\mu \partial U}{\partial p_i} + \bar{x}_i = \bar{x}_i \quad \text{for all } i
\end{aligned}
\tag{A2.6}
$$

i.e. the partial derivatives of the expenditure function with respect to prices are the Hicksian demand functions. In order to show that $\mu \partial U/\partial p_i = \Sigma p_j \partial \bar{x}_j/\partial p_i = 0$, use the first-order conditions (A2.5), and the fact that the utility level is fixed, i.e. $U(\mathbf{x}) = \bar{U}$.

Let us examine the effect on expenditure of changes in the utility level:

$$
\frac{\partial e}{\partial U} = \Sigma p_i \frac{\partial \bar{x}_i}{\partial U} = \mu \Sigma \frac{\partial U}{\partial \bar{x}_i} \frac{\partial \bar{x}_i}{\partial U} = \mu
\tag{A2.7}
$$

where we interpret μ as the marginal cost of utility. In other words, μ is the reciprocal of the marginal utility λ of income. To demonstrate this, fix the utility level at an arbitrarily chosen level $\bar{U}$, say, and insert the corresponding expenditure function into the indirect utility function to obtain $\bar{U} = V(\mathbf{p}, e(\mathbf{p}, \bar{U}))$. Differentiating this expression with respect to U yields

$$
1 = \frac{\partial V}{\partial y} \frac{\partial e}{\partial U} = \lambda \mu
\tag{A2.8}
$$

i.e. $\mu = 1/\lambda$.

Finally, if the expenditure function is twice continuously differentiable, then it holds that

$$\frac{\partial^2 e}{\partial p_i \partial p_j} = \frac{\partial \bar{x}_i}{\partial p_j} = \frac{\partial \bar{x}_j}{\partial p_i} = \frac{\partial^2 e}{\partial p_j \partial p_i} \qquad (A2.9)$$

Thus, the cross-price derivatives of the compensated demands are symmetrical. Compare the discussion in Section 5; see Diamond and McFadden (1974) for a comprehensive discussion.

Corner solutions

In Section 3 we discussed the implications of corner solutions. The following example is adapted from Katzner (1970).

The utility function is

$$U = (x_1 + 1)(x_2 + 1)x_3 \qquad (A2.10)$$

From utility maximization we obtain (for x_1)

$$
\left.
\begin{aligned}
x_1 &= \frac{y - 2p_1 + p_2}{3p_3} & \text{on } \Omega^1 \\[4pt]
x_1 &= \frac{y - p_1}{2p_1} & \text{on } \Omega^2 \\[4pt]
x_1 &= 0 & \text{on } \Omega^3 \cup \Omega^4
\end{aligned}
\right\}
\qquad (A2.11)
$$

where

$$
\begin{aligned}
\Omega^1 &= \{(\mathbf{p}, y) \mid y - 2p_1 + p_2 > 0, \; y - 2p_2 + p_1 > 0\} \\
\Omega^2 &= \{(\mathbf{p}, y) \mid y - 2p_2 + p_1 \leq 0, \; y > p_1\} \\
\Omega^3 &= \{(\mathbf{p}, y) \mid y - 2p_1 + p_2 \leq 0, \; y > p_2\} \\
\Omega^4 &= \{(\mathbf{p}, y) \mid y \leq p_1, \; y \leq p_2\}
\end{aligned}
$$

It is easily verified that the demand functions are everywhere continuous and the Slutsky equations have the appropriate properties on the interiors of Ω^i for $i = 1, \dots, 4$.

CHAPTER 3

The concept of consumer surplus

This chapter, which is inspired by the analysis in Just *et al.* (1982), deals with the measurement of consumer surplus under multiple price changes. Section 1 considers the relationship between a change in utility and areas to the left of ordinary or Marshallian demand curves. In particular, it is shown that the sum of the changes in consumer surpluses in general depends on the order in which prices are changed. Conditions under which there is a unique or path-independent ordinary money measure are investigated in Section 2. Section 3 introduces two of the measures (the compensating and equivalent variations) suggested by Sir John R. Hicks. In order to appreciate the results, it is useful to illustrate them by means of a few straightforward examples. Section 4, which ends this chapter, introduces two simple preference functions which are used as a basis for deriving consumer surplus measures.

1 *Money measures and areas under ordinary demand curves*

Consider a household that derives satisfaction from consuming n different commodities. The household is assumed to act as if it maximizes a well-behaved utility function subject to its budget constraint. The indirect utility function of this household is written as $V(\mathbf{p}, y)$, where $\mathbf{p}$ is a vector of prices and y is income.

Taking partial derivatives of the indirect utility function with respect to p_i and y, and invoking the envelope theorem, it can be shown that

$$\left.\begin{aligned} V_i &= \frac{\partial V(\mathbf{p}, y)}{\partial p_i} = -x_i(\mathbf{p}, y)\, \lambda\,(\mathbf{p}, y) \quad \text{for all } i \\[2mm] V_y &= \frac{\partial V(\mathbf{p}, y)}{\partial y} = \lambda(\mathbf{p}, y) \end{aligned}\right\} \tag{3.1}$$

as was demonstrated in Chapter 2. Thus, by taking the partial derivative

22

of the indirect utility function with respect to the ith price, we can obtain the demand function for that good multiplied by the Lagrange multiplier λ. From the bottom line of (3.1) it is seen that λ gives the marginal utility of income. λ has been written as a function of prices and income to highlight the fact that λ is not a constant.

Armed with these expressions, we can examine the impact on utility of *infinitesimal* changes in prices and/or income. Totally differentiating the indirect utility function, using (3.1), we obtain

$$dV = \sum_{i=1}^{n} \frac{\partial V}{\partial p_i} dp_i + \frac{\partial V}{\partial y} dy$$

$$= -\lambda \Sigma x_i dp_i + \lambda dy \tag{3.2}$$

$$= -\lambda(\mathbf{x}d\mathbf{p} - dy)$$

where $d\mathbf{p} = (dp_1, \ldots, dp_n)'$.

This is a type of marginal cost-benefit rule, where the changes are assumed to be so small that the marginal utility of income can be treated as a constant (see, for example, Boadway, 1975). Therefore, the benefit/loss of a marginal change in a price can be obtained by simply observing the quantity x_i purchased. It should be recalled that $\partial V/\partial p_i = -\lambda x_i$, and λ can be set equal to one. If many, possibly all, prices and/or income are changed, the simple addition of these effects will yield the total impact on welfare. That is the essential meaning of the marginal welfare change criterion.

Consider now a *discrete* change in prices and income. The change in utility associated with a change in prices and income from $\mathbf{p}^0, y^0$ to $\mathbf{p}^1, y^1$ can be represented as a line integral

$$\triangle U = V(\mathbf{p}^1, y^1) - V(\mathbf{p}^0, y^0)$$

$$= \int_c (\sum_{i=1}^{n} V_i dp_i + V_y dy) \tag{3.3}$$

$$= -\int_c \lambda(\mathbf{p}, y)[\mathbf{x}(\mathbf{p}, y)d\mathbf{p} - dy]$$

where c is some path of prices and income between initial and final price–income vectors. Loosely speaking, the first term within brackets in the last line of (3.3) gives the sum of the areas under ordinary uncompensated or Marshallian demand curves for a change in prices from $\mathbf{p}^0$ to $\mathbf{p}^1$. The second term within brackets represents a change in lump-sum income. The marginal utility of income, λ, is there to convert the changes from dollars to units of utility. These concepts will be further discussed and interpreted below.

The exact welfare change measure (3.3) requires information on the

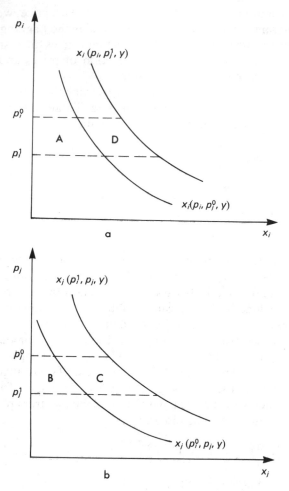

Figure 3.1 Consumer surpluses when two prices change (with all other prices and income fixed)

marginal utility of income, a variable which is, in general, unobservable. Economists have therefore tried to convert (3.3) to a money measure by eliminating λ from the expression. Then, we obtain

$$S = \int_c [\mathbf{x}(\mathbf{p}, y)d\mathbf{p} - dy] = y^1 - y^0 - \int_c [\mathbf{x}(\mathbf{p}, y)d\mathbf{p}] \qquad (3.4)$$

In words: a money measure S of utility change is obtained by adding to the change in income all the changes in consumer surpluses in the markets where prices change. Unfortunately, the order in which prices and income are changed may affect the magnitude as well as the sign of S.

The argument is illustrated in Figure 3.1. Assume p_i is lowered from p_i^0 to p_i^1 with all other prices and income fixed. The change in consumer surplus in the ith market is given by area A in Figure 3.1a. The change in p_i shifts the position of the demand curve in the jth market to the right (left) if goods i and j are complements (substitutes). However, if income and all prices but the ith price are fixed, the total change in consumer surplus is still given by area A in the figure. Recall that $\mathbf{x}d\mathbf{p} = x_i dp_i$ in (3.4) if $dp_j = 0$ for all $j \neq i$, implying that we need only bother about the ith market. Thus, the shift in the demand curve of the jth good in Figure 3.1b does not have any significance *per se* when calculating a money measure of the utility change associated with a change in the price of good i. This can also be verified by using Roy's identity discussed in Chapter 2.

Next, lower the price of the jth good. The change in consumer surplus in the market for this good must be evaluated given the fact that we have already reduced the price of the ith good. Thus, the relevant change in consumer surplus in the market for the jth good is equal to area B+C in Figure 3.1b. The money measure S of the utility change caused by the combined fall in p_i and p_j is equal to area A+B+C in the figure.

Assume that we instead lower p_j before p_i. The change in consumer surplus in the jth market is now measured to the left of the demand curve drawn for $p_i = p_i^0$, i.e. is equal to area B in Figure 3.1b. As the price of good j is lowered, the demand curve for the ith good may move leftward or rightward. In any case, the change in consumer surplus in market i must be evaluated to the left of the 'final' demand curve obtained for $p_j = p_j^1$, i.e. is equal to area A+D in Figure 3.1a.

In general, the considered paths of price adjustment impute different dollar gains or total consumer surpluses to the underlying unique change in utility, i.e. area A+B+C need not be equal to area B+A+D. In addition, it should be noted that these areas are obtained by considering just two out of possibly an infinite number of paths between initial and final prices since we could proceed by alternate, small changes in p_i and p_j. However, if the cross-price effects are equal ($\partial x_i/\partial p_j = \partial x_j/\partial p_i$), the change in total consumer surplus will not depend on which procedure or path we take, i.e. area A+B+C = area B+A+D in Figure 3.1. Intuitively, the shift in the demand curve for good i as the price of good j is changed is equal to the shift in the demand curve for good j as p_i is changed, implying that area D is equal to area C in the figure. As will be demonstrated below, a sufficient condition for the cross-price effects to be equal is that the marginal utility of income is constant with respect to those parameters (prices and/or income) which are changed. Nevertheless, if the path-independency conditions hold, the money measure depends only on the terminal values of the considered path, and not on the path itself.

2 *Path-independency conditions and the constancy of the marginal utility of income*

It remains to investigate under what conditions the line integral in (3.4) is independent of the path of adjustment. Consider a line integral

$$\int_{\bar{c}} \sum_{i=1}^{n} f_i(q_1, \ldots, q_n) dq_i \tag{3.5}$$

where $\bar{c}$ is some path between initial and final q-vectors, and assume that all f_i have continuous first derivatives in a (pathwise) simply-connected open set R of space. Accordingly, a set, for example a convex set, where any two points can be joined by a path lying in R, and any two paths in R with the same end points can be deformed into each other without moving the end points and without leaving R.

Then, the value of the line integral (3.5) is independent of the particular choice of path $\bar{c}$, as defined in the appendix to this chapter, in R and determined solely by the end points of $\bar{c}$ if and only if (iff) the mixed derivatives are symmetric, i.e.

$$\frac{\partial f_i}{\partial q_j} = \frac{\partial f_j}{\partial q_i} \quad \text{for all } i, j \tag{3.6}$$

It is important to notice that conditions (3.6) are necessary for, and almost suffice to ensure, path independency. They become sufficient if we add the assumption, stated above, concerning the geometrical properties of the region in space in which (3.5) is considered (see Courant and John, 1974, pp. 95–106). This assumption is assumed to hold throughout, thus we only refer to conditions (3.6) in the remainder of this volume.

Applying (3.6), it follows that the money measure

$$S = \int_c [-\mathbf{x}(\mathbf{p}, y) \cdot d\mathbf{p} + 1 \cdot dy] \tag{3.4a}$$

is path independent if it satisfies the conditions

$$\frac{\partial x_i}{\partial p_j} = \frac{\partial x_j}{\partial p_i} \quad \text{for all } i, j \tag{3.7'}$$

$$\partial x_i/\partial y = \partial(1)/\partial p_i = 0 \quad \text{for all } i, j \tag{3.7''}$$

All of these conditions cannot hold simultaneously. Zero income effects for all goods means that the budget constraint is violated. At most, demand for $n-1$ goods can be independent of the level of income y, implying that if y is changed, all additional income is spent on the nth good.

To further interpret these results and investigate their relationship to the marginal utility of income, it is useful to consider the path-independency conditions for equation (3.3)

$$\left. \begin{array}{l} \dfrac{\partial(\lambda x_i)}{\partial p_j} = \dfrac{\partial(\lambda x_j)}{\partial p_i} \\[4mm] \dfrac{\partial(\lambda x_i)}{\partial y} = \dfrac{\partial \lambda}{\partial p_i} \end{array} \right\} \quad \text{for all } i, j \qquad (3.8)$$

where $\partial(\lambda x_i)/\partial p_j = x_i \partial \lambda/\partial p_j + \lambda \partial x_i/\partial p_j = -V_{ij}$. Conditions (3.8) hold by construction since the integrand of (3.3), denoted by L here, is an exact, i.e. the total, differential of the indirect utility function. The latter condition is both necessary and sufficient for path independency since a line integral $\int L$, i.e. (3.3), taken over a path c in an open set R of space ($R \subseteq \Omega_1$) is independent of the particular choice of path and determined solely by the initial and final point of c iff L is the total differential of a function $f(p, y)$ in R, assuming x, λ, V_p and V_y are continuous functions of $\mathbf{p}$ and y in R (Courant and John, 1974, p. 97). Clearly, there exists a function, namely the indirect utility function $V(\mathbf{p}, y)$, for which $dV = L$. However, in many cases it may be difficult to ascertain whether a given differential is a total differential or not. In general it turns out to be easier to use the necessary and (almost) sufficient conditions (3.6). The reader should also recall the discussion of Young's theorem in Section 5 of Chapter 2. According to Young's theorem, the cross derivatives are symmetric, i.e. $V_{ij} = V_{ji}$, provided the indirect utility function is twice continuously differentiable. Using (3.1), the reader can easily verify that these symmetry conditions coincide with those stated in (3.8) (see also the appendix to this chapter).

If λ is independent of all prices and income, conditions (3.8) reduce to conditions (3.7). However, from (3.8) and the first-order conditions for utility maximization, it follows that λ cannot be independent of all prices and income. In Section 4 of Chapter 2, it was shown that if all prices and income double, λ must halve; λ is homogeneous of degree minus one in prices and income. This result implies that λ, at most, can be independent of all n prices but not of income, or independent of $n-1$ prices and income.

Equations (3.7) and (3.8) clarify the relationship between the money measure (3.4a) and the constancy of the marginal utility of income. Consider a change in all prices with income fixed (i.e. let income serve as the *numéraire*). If $\partial x_i/\partial p_j = \partial x_j/\partial p_i$ for all i, j, then $x_i \partial\lambda/\partial p_j = x_j \partial\lambda/\partial p_i$ from (3.8). Hence, path independency of the money measure (3.4a) does not imply that λ is constant with respect to all prices, but rather that λ changes at the same rate for each price change. Clearly, however, if $\partial\lambda/\partial p_i = 0$ for all i in (3.8), then the path independency conditions (3.7') must hold. This case, i.e. $\lambda = \lambda(y)$, represents the first interpretation of constancy of the marginal utility of income put forward by Samuelson (1942). Thus, if $\lambda = \lambda(y)$, the money measure (3.4a) gives an exact or at least a proportional measure of utility change, i.e. $S = \triangle U/\lambda$, when prices vary with income fixed.[1]

It has been demonstrated (see, for example, Silberberg, 1972) that conditions (3.7') require that the utility function is homothetic. A function is homothetic if all contours are radial scale replicas of each other. It is not required that the value of the function increases in the same proportion along these contours. However, there is a close connection between homotheticity and homogeneity. A utility function is said to be homothetic if $W(\mathbf{x})$ can be written as $f(U(\mathbf{x}))$ where f is a positive, finite, continuous and strictly monotonically increasing function of one variable with $f(0) = 0$, and U is a positively homogeneous function of n variables (Lau, 1969, p. 375). In the case of a homothetic utility function, the demand functions take the form $\mathbf{x} = g'(\mathbf{p})y$ with $g'(\mathbf{p})$ homogeneous of degree -1, as is shown in, for example, Lau (1969), which implies that the income elasticities are equal to one. This property means that the income expansion paths are straight lines emanating from the origin. The reader is invited to use the homothetic indirect utility function $V(\mathbf{p}, y) = -g(\mathbf{p}) + \ell n\, y$ to check (i) that such a function generates demand functions that have the above stated income elasticity property, and (ii) that the path independency conditions stated in (3.7') hold. The latter result is easily obtained by comparing the second derivatives of the indirect utility function and the cross-price derivatives of the demand functions. The reader is also referred to Section 4 where a simple example of a homothetic utility function can be found.

The assumption of homothetic utility functions is very restrictive. It should be stressed, however, that if only a subset of prices change, then conditions (3.7') need only be satisfied for that particular subset of prices, implying that the indirect utility function can be written as $V(\mathbf{p}, y) = f(\mathbf{p}) + g(\mathbf{p}^s, y)$, where $\mathbf{p}^s$ denotes the prices that remain fixed throughout the movement. Finally, if only a single price, say p_1 changes, the money measure can be written as

$$S_1 = -\int_{p_1^0}^{p_1^1} x_1\,(p_1, p_2^0, \ldots, y^0)\,dp_1 \tag{3.9}$$

Note that the area to the left of the demand curve between the initial and the final price is unique in the single-price-change case. If only one price is changed, holding all other prices and income constant throughout the movement, there can hardly be a path dependency problem, but, of course, the size of the area is determined by the levels of the fixed prices and income, since demand is a function of all prices and income.

Thus far, income has been assumed to be fixed. Consider now the case where income and $n-1$ prices are free to vary. The remaining good, say x_n, is used as *numéraire*. It is seen from (3.7) that the corresponding path independency conditions are

$$\left.\begin{array}{l} \dfrac{\partial x_i}{\partial p_j} = \dfrac{\partial x_j}{\partial p_i} \\[2ex] \dfrac{\partial x_i}{\partial y} = 0 \end{array}\right\} \quad i, j = 1,\ldots,n-1 \tag{3.10}$$

i.e. they require zero income effects for $n-1$ goods, implying a vertical income-consumption path; if income is changed, all additional income is spent on the nth good. In other words, $n-1$ demand functions must have the property that a price change has a substitution effect, but not an income effect (on the set Ω_I of prices and income). A necessary and sufficient condition for this to be the case is that the utility function is quasi-linear, i.e. takes the form $U=u(x_1,\ldots,x_{n-1}) + ax_n$, where $a>0$ is a constant. A detailed discussion of the properties of quasi-linear utility functions is found in Katzner (1970, Ch. 5). Also note that the second interpretation of the constancy of the marginal utility of income (money), discussed by Samuelson (1942), assumes that $\lambda=\lambda(p_n)$. It is seen from (3.8) that the path independency conditions (3.10) are implied by this constancy assumption.

It is easily checked that the following money measure satisfies conditions (3.10)

$$\frac{\triangle U}{\lambda(p_n)} = S_b = -\sum_{i=1}^{n-1} \int_{p_i^0}^{p_i^1} x_i(\mathbf{p})dp_i + \triangle y \tag{3.11}$$

This measure states: Add the changes in consumer surpluses in markets where prices change. The way in which prices are changed makes no difference, but the change in consumer surplus in a given market must be evaluated subject to all previously considered price changes. See Figure 3.2 and equation (3.24) for illustrations of the procedure.

If only a subset of prices and/or income is changed, the 'constancy' condition can be weakened. Hence the only requirement is that λ is independent of the prices (income) which are changed. This is a much

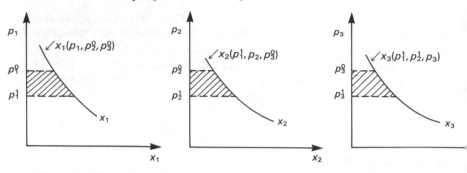

Figure 3.2 Illustration of consumer surpluses when three prices are lowered and the underlying utility function is quasi-linear; x_4 is the *numéraire* good whose price is set equal to unity

less restrictive assumption than the one employed in (3.11), at least if only a few prices are changed. Nevertheless, any constancy assumption imposes severe restrictions on the properties of the consumer's preference ordering.

3 *The compensating and equivalent variations*

If the path independency conditions (3.7) hold,[2] a unique measure of consumer surplus exists, i.e. a measure which depends only on the terminal values of the considered path, and not on the path itself. On the other hand, if the path independency conditions do not hold, there is possibly an infinite number of money measures S of a unique change in utility. In particular, this means that one can find paths such that $S<0$ even if $\triangle U>0$, and vice versa (compare Chipman and Moore, 1980).

The deficiencies of money measures based on ordinary demand functions have led economists to search for other and, hopefully, less restrictive money measures of utility change. A second reason is that many economists want to get rid of the cardinal interpretation of the utility function which seems to be implied by concepts like marginal utility of income or money (see, for example, Ng, 1979).

Although a great number of measures have been proposed in the literature, attention is focused here on the concepts of compensating and equivalent variation. The reader interested in other, less frequently used, measures is referred to McKenzie and Pearce (1982), McKenzie (1983), Ng (1979), and Stahl (1983a).

The concepts of compensating and equivalent variations were originally introduced by Sir John R. Hicks in a series of articles in the *Review of Economic Studies* (1940/1–1945/6). The compensating variation gives

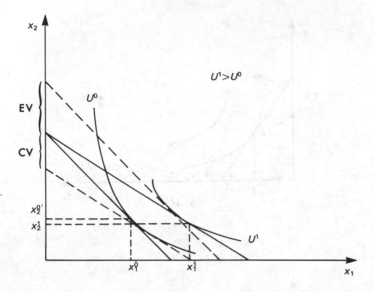

Figure 3.3 Compensating (CV) and equivalent (EV) variations when p_1 falls.
Note: CV of a price fall is equal to $-$EV of the reversed price rise

the maximum (minimum) amount of money that can be taken from
(must be given to) a household while leaving it just as well off as it was
before a fall (rise) in prices. The equivalent variation gives the minimum
(maximum) amount of money that must be given to (taken from) a
household to make it as well off as it would have been after a fall (rise) in
prices. These concepts are illustrated in Figure 3.3, where the price of the
first good falls while the price of the second good remains fixed.

In order to derive concepts of compensating and equivalent variation,
it is useful to introduce the expenditure function

$$e(\mathbf{p}, \bar{U}) = \min_{\mathbf{x}} \{\mathbf{px} | U(\mathbf{x}) \geq \bar{U}\} = \mathbf{p\tilde{x}}(\mathbf{p}, \bar{U}) \qquad (3.12)$$

This function gives the minimal expenditure necessary to reach, at most,
a pre-specified utility level $\bar{U}$. The compensated or Hicksian demand
functions, denoted by a tilde, are obtained by taking the partial derivatives of the expenditure function with respect to prices. The Hicksian
demand functions, like the Marshallian demand functions, are assumed
to be twice continuously differentiable. A compensated demand function
has the property that a change in the own price has a substitution effect,
but not an income effect. Moreover, the cross-price effects, the matrix of
substitution effects, are symmetric. For a discussion of these claims,

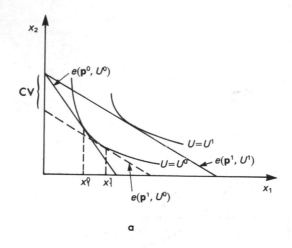

a

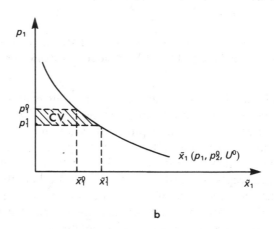

b

Figure 3.4 Compensating variations in income when only the price of one good changes: p_1 falls from p_1^0 to p_1^1

including necessary assumptions regarding the properties of the underlying direct utility function, the reader is referred to Section 5 of Chapter 2.

The compensating variation

Using the expenditure function, the compensating variation (CV) in income associated with a change in prices and income from $\mathbf{p}^0, y^0$ to $\mathbf{p}^1, y^1$ is written as

$$CV = y^1 - y^0 + e(\mathbf{p}^0, U^0) - e(\mathbf{p}^1, U^0)$$

$$= \triangle y - \int_c \tilde{\mathbf{x}}(\mathbf{p}, U^0) d\mathbf{p} \qquad (3.13)$$

where c is some path between initial and final price–income vectors to be discussed below. Note that $y^0 = e(\mathbf{p}^0, U^0)$ and $y^1 = e(\mathbf{p}^1, U^1)$, where U^1 is the final utility level. These results are obtained from equation (2.10); see also Figure 3.4. The reader should observe that this definition of CV (and the one of EV below) gives the opposite sign from the definition used by some economists.

In interpreting (3.13) it is useful to consider the following sequence of changes in income–price space. Assume income changes from y^0 to y^1 with all prices fixed at $\mathbf{p}^0$. The corresponding compensating variation, i.e. the sum of money that must be taken from/given to the household to hold it at the initial utility level U^0, equals the actual change in income $\triangle y$; in the middle term of (3.13) $e(\mathbf{p}^0, U^0)$ and $e(\mathbf{p}^1, U^0)$ are equal and cancel when $\mathbf{p}^0 = \mathbf{p}^1$. Equivalently, the integral in (3.13) is equal to zero when $d\mathbf{p} = 0$.

Consider next a change in prices from $\mathbf{p}^0$ to $\mathbf{p}^1$ with income fixed at, say y^0. Then

$$CV = e(\mathbf{p}^0, U^0) - e(\mathbf{p}^1, U^0) = -\int_c \tilde{\mathbf{x}}(\mathbf{p}, U^0) d\mathbf{p} \qquad (3.14)$$

Equation (3.14) gives the minimal expenditure necessary to reach the utility level U^0 when $\mathbf{p} = \mathbf{p}^0$ less the minimal expenditure required to reach U^0 when prices are changed to $\mathbf{p} = \mathbf{p}^1$. In Figure 3.4a, which depicts the single price change case, the two levels of expenditure are indicated by 'budget lines'. In order to arrive at the integral in (3.14) note that

$$\frac{\partial e(\mathbf{p}, U^0)}{\partial \mathbf{p}} = \tilde{\mathbf{x}}(\mathbf{p}, U^0) \qquad (3.15)$$

for infinitesimal price changes as was discussed in Chapter 2. Integrating (3.15) over some path between $\mathbf{p}^0$ and $\mathbf{p}^1$ yields $-CV$; due to the order in which prices appear in (3.14), the order of integration must be reversed to arrive at (3.14). Hence, (3.14) gives the sum of areas to the left of compensated demand curves between $\mathbf{p}^0$ and $\mathbf{p}^1$. See Figure 3.4b for an illustration of the single price change case.

The choice of adjustment path c has not yet been discussed. Consider the condition for path independence of (3.13)

$$\frac{\partial \tilde{x}_i}{\partial p_j} = \frac{\partial \tilde{x}_j}{\partial p_i} \quad \text{for all } i, j \qquad (3.16)$$

By construction, this condition is fulfilled for compensated demand functions; recall that the cross-price effects are symmetric. Hence, the

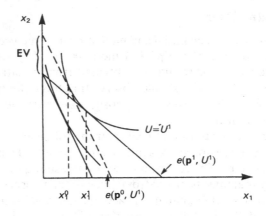

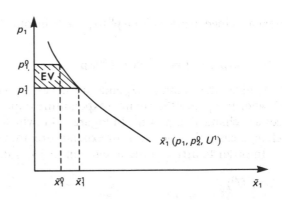

Figure 3.5 The equivalent variation in income when p_1 falls from p_1^0 to p_1^1

integrand of (3.13) is an exact differential and one may arbitrarily choose the order in which prices (and income) are changed. The area to the left of the compensated demand curve for a particular good between its initial and final price, however, must be evaluated subject to all previously considered price changes in other markets; recall Figures 3.1 and 3.2.

The equivalent variation

Equivalent variation (EV) is the amount of money that must be given to (taken from) the household at initial prices and income $\mathbf{p}^0, y^0$ to make the household as well off as it would be at final prices and income $\mathbf{p}^1, y^1$

$$\text{EV} = y^1 - y^0 + e(\mathbf{p}^0, U^1) - e(\mathbf{p}^1, U^1)$$

$$= \triangle y - \int_c \tilde{\mathbf{x}}(\mathbf{p}, U^1) d\mathbf{p} \tag{3.17}$$

where U^1 is the fixed (final) utility level.

The equivalent variation is equal to the sum of the change in income plus all the changes in consumer surpluses in the markets where prices change. The changes in consumer surpluses are evaluated to the left of compensated demands, where the demand functions are evaluated at the final utility level. Since the path independency conditions hold (see 3.16), the order in which prices are changed makes no difference. Nevertheless the change in consumer surplus in the ith market must be evaluated conditional on all previously considered price changes in other markets. The single-price-change case is depicted in Figure 3.5.

We have shown that the CV and EV measures are path independent. It has also been demonstrated that in general this is not true for the ordinary consumer surplus measure. Unfortunately, these results are not sufficient as a basis on which to choose a money measure of utility change. For example, we have not shown that there is a money measure, if any, which ranks commodity bundles in the same order as the consumer would have done. Nor have we addressed the problem of a multihousehold economy. In real world applications, one often faces the problem that some consumers gain while others lose from a proposed project. Thus we need a rule for aggregating individual welfare changes. Even if we find more or less satisfactory theoretical solutions to these issues, there remains the problem of figuring out how to calculate consumer surplus changes.

However, before turning to a discussion of these important questions, two examples of the path independency results derived in this chapter are given.

4 *Two examples*

In order to appreciate the results derived in the previous sections, it is useful to illustrate them by a few examples. Consider first the utility function

$$U = \ell n \, x_1^{\alpha} x_2^{1-\alpha} = \alpha \ell n \, x_1 + (1-\alpha) \ell n \, x_2 \tag{3.18}$$

This homothetic function can be interpreted as a monotone transformation of a function, the Cobb–Douglas function, which is homogeneous of degree one.

Maximization of (3.18) subject to the usual budget constraint yields demand functions for goods and the 'marginal utility of income' function

$$x_1 = \frac{\alpha y}{p_1}$$

$$x_2 = \frac{(1-\alpha)y}{p_2} \qquad\qquad \left.\begin{matrix} \\ \\ \\ \\ \end{matrix}\right\} \quad (3.19)$$

$$\lambda = \frac{1}{y}$$

Substituting the first two lines of (3.19) into (3.18), rearranging and suppressing constants yields an indirect utility function of the form

$$V(p_1, p_2, y) = -\alpha\ell n\, p_1 - (1-\alpha)\ell n\, p_2 + \ell n\, y \qquad (3.20)$$

It can easily be checked that taking partial derivatives of (3.20) with respect to prices and income after a few calculations, yields (3.19).

The path independency conditions (3.7′) require that $\partial x_1/\partial p_2 = \partial x_2/\partial p_1$. Obviously, this holds for the demand functions in (3.19). Hence, if p_1 and p_2 are changed, with income fixed, the order in which prices are changed makes no difference. It is also clear that the change in consumer surplus associated with a price change is proportional to the underlying utility change. This is because the marginal utility of income λ is independent of prices, i.e. $\lambda = 1/y$. Thus, the change in utility associated with a change in prices from $\mathbf{p}^0$ to $\mathbf{p}^1$ is

$$\triangle V = -\lambda[\textstyle\int_a x_1 dp_1 + \int_b x_2 dp_2]$$

$$= -(\frac{1}{y})\, [\textstyle\int_a \frac{\alpha y}{p_1}\, dp_1 + \int_b \frac{(1-\alpha)y}{p_2}\, dp_2] = \frac{1}{y}\, S \qquad (3.21)$$

where $a = (p_1^1, p_1^0)'$ and $b = (p_2^1, p_2^0)'$. Note that the sum of the terms within brackets gives the sum of changes in consumer surpluses evaluated to the left of ordinary demand curves. The practical method of evaluating an integral depends on finding a function with the function to be integrated as its derivative. Thus, the integrals in (3.21) can be evaluated in terms of the functions $\ell n\, p_i$. The reader, however, is recommended not to integrate over a range from $\mathbf{p}^i \rightarrow \infty$ to some finite price vector, since utility tends to infinity. We avoid such paths throughout this volume unless otherwise stated. See the appendix to Chapter 6 for a discussion concerning the convergence/divergence of integrals that are improper by virtue of an infinite limit of integration.

The proportionality between the money measure S and the change in utility in (3.21) vanishes if the utility function (3.18) is replaced by the (homothetic and homogeneous) Cobb–Douglas utility function, denoted by u. The reason being that $\lambda = \lambda(y)$ is replaced by $\lambda = \lambda(\mathbf{p})$; and in (3.21) all prices change while income is fixed. The indirect utility functions corresponding to U and u can be written as $V(\mathbf{p}, y) = \ell n[y/h(\mathbf{p})]$ and $G(\mathbf{p}, y) = y/h(\mathbf{p})$, respectively. Taking partial derivatives with respect to y yields the stated properties of λ. Nevertheless, the two utility functions produce the same ordering of commodity bundles (price vectors), implying that $\mathrm{sgn}(\triangle U) = \mathrm{sgn}(\triangle u)$. Moreover, the demand functions and hence also S are unaffected by the considered monotonic transformation of the utility function. Hence, $\mathrm{sgn}(\triangle u) = \mathrm{sgn}(S) = \mathrm{sgn}(\triangle U)$. Compare equations (4.3) in Chapter 4.

Turning next to CV and EV measures, we first derive the expenditure function. This function can be obtained by minimizing expenditure subject to a pre-specified utility level. Alternatively, the indirect utility function (3.20) can be used and the level of utility fixed for example at $\bar{U}$. Income y can then be replaced by the expenditure function $e(p_1, p_2, \bar{U})$ to obtain

$$e(p_1, p_2, \bar{U}) = \exp \{\bar{U} + \alpha\ell n\, p_1 + (1-\alpha)\ell n\, p_2\} = y \qquad (3.22)$$

Taking partial derivatives with respect to prices and the utility level yields

$$\left.\begin{array}{l} \dfrac{\partial e}{\partial p_1} = \tilde{x}_1 = \dfrac{\alpha}{p_1} \exp \{\bar{U} + \alpha\ell n\, p_1 + (1-\alpha)\ell n\, p_2\} \\[2ex] \dfrac{\partial e}{\partial p_2} = \tilde{x}_2 = \dfrac{1-\alpha}{p_2} \exp \{\bar{U} + \alpha\ell n\, p_1 + (1-\alpha)\ell n\, p_2\} \\[2ex] \dfrac{\partial e}{\partial U} = \Sigma p_i \tilde{x}_i = \exp \{\bar{U} + \alpha\ell n\, p_1 + (1-\alpha)\ell n\, p_2\} \end{array}\right\} \qquad (3.23)$$

Using (3.23), the compensating variation of a change in prices from $\mathbf{p}^0$ to $\mathbf{p}^1$ can be written as

$$\mathrm{CV} = -\int_a [\frac{\alpha}{p_1} \exp \{U^0 + \alpha\ell n\, p_1 + (1-\alpha)\ell n\, p_2^0\}]\, dp_1$$

$$\qquad - \int_b [\frac{1-\alpha}{p_2} \exp \{U^0 + \alpha\ell n\, p_1^1 + (1-\alpha)\ell n\, p_2\}]\, dp_2 \qquad (3.24)$$

Note that the compensating variation in the second market is evaluated subject to the price change in the first market. However, since the path independency condition holds, i.e. $\partial\tilde{x}_i/\partial p_j = \partial\tilde{x}_j/\partial p_i$ in (3.23), the order in which prices are changed makes no difference. For example, we could change p_2 before p_1. Then, p_2^0 is replaced by p_2^1 and p_1^1 by p_1^0 in (3.24). However, this does not affect the value of CV since this value is determined solely by the end points of the paths.

An EV measure is obtained by fixing utility at its final level, not at the initial level as in (3.24).

A second example of an interesting preference function is

$$U = \sum_{i=1}^{n-1} \beta_i \, \ell n \, x_i + \beta_n \, x_n \qquad (3.25)$$

where the constants β will be suppressed in what follows. It can easily be verified that the demand functions corresponding to this quasi-linear utility function can be written as

$$\left. \begin{array}{l} x_i = \dfrac{p_n}{p_i} \\[2ex] x_n = \dfrac{y}{p_n} - (n-1) \end{array} \right\} \qquad (3.26)$$

where x_n is assumed to be positive. Moreover, since it can be shown that $\lambda = 1/p_n$, the utility function (3.25) corresponds to Samuelson's second interpretation of the constancy of the marginal utility of income.

In this case, ordinary and compensated demand functions coincide. Substituting (3.26) into (3.25) and replacing y by $e(p_1, p_2, \bar{U})$ we obtain the expenditure function

$$e(p_1, p_2, \bar{U}) = p_n \bar{U} + p_n \, \Sigma \, \ell n \, p_i \qquad (3.27)$$

where constants are suppressed. Taking the partial derivative of (3.27) with respect to the price of the ith good yields the compensated demand for that good. It follows that $\tilde{x}_i = p_n/p_i = x_i$ which establishes the claim.

Hence, given a utility function of the form specified in (3.25), all three consumer surplus measures considered coincide. This result is not obtained by a mere chance. It holds for all quasi-linear utility functions (defined below equation (3.10) in Section 2). On the other hand, a homothetic utility function, such as (3.18), does not generate measures of equal size, i.e. $S \neq CV \neq EV$. The marginal utility of income depends on income and the level of utility. Some inspection of equations (3.21) and (3.24) should make this clear. These claims will be discussed in Chapter 4.

Appendix

Definition of a path

By a path (a 'simple oriented arc' or a 'regular curve') $\bar{c} = (\mathbf{q}^b, \mathbf{q}^a)' = \mathbf{q}^a \widehat{\mathbf{q}^b}$ in R joining two points $\mathbf{q}^a = (q_1^a, \dots, q_n^a)$ and

$\mathbf{q}^b = (q_1^b, \ldots, q_n^b)$, we mean n continuous functions $q_i = g_i(t)$ defined in the interval $0 \leqslant t \leqslant 1$ (say) such that the point $\mathbf{q}^t = (g_1(t), \ldots, g_n(t))$ lies in R for all t of the interval, different t in the interval correspond to different points $\mathbf{q}$, and coincides with $\mathbf{q}^a$ for $t = 0$ and $\mathbf{q}^b$ for $t = 1$. Ordering points according to either increasing or decreasing t converts a simple arc into an oriented simple arc (denoted by '$\frown$'). Finally, attention is restricted to paths or arcs that are continuously differentiable or at least sectionally smooth, e.g. simple polygonal arcs; the latter kind of arcs can always be approximated by smooth (differentiable) ones in R with the same end points. (see Courant and John, 1974, Ch. 1; Widder, 1961, Ch. 7).

Line integrals

Suppose $dV = V_p dp + V_y dy$ is the total differential of $V(\mathbf{p}, y)$. Consider the line integral

$$\int_c L = \int_c (V_p \, d\mathbf{p} + V_y dy) = \int_c (\Sigma V_i dp_i + V_y dy) \qquad (A3.1)$$

where $V_i = \partial V / \partial p_i$ for all i, $c = \overset{\frown}{AB}$ with $A = \mathbf{p}^0, y^0, B = \mathbf{p}^1, y^1$, and $c \in \Omega_I$. We take the set Ω_I, as defined in Chapter 2, as our domain. The line integral (A3.1) exists if all functions V_p, V_y are continuous on c. This is clearly valid since $V \in C^3$, i.e. thrice continuously differentiable, in Ω_I by assumption (see Chapter 2).

Using the definition of a path given above, (A3.1) can also be written as

$$\int_c L = \int_0^1 (\Sigma V_i \frac{dp_i}{dt} + V_y \frac{dy}{dt}) dt \qquad (A3.2)$$

where $p_i = g_i(t), y = g_y(t)$, and we have used the fact that $(dp_i/dt)dt = (\partial g_i/\partial t)dt$, $(dy/dt)dt = (\partial g_y/\partial t)dt$.

By the chain rule of differentiation, we then have

$$\int_c L = \int_0^1 [\frac{dV(\mathbf{g}(t))}{dt}] dt = V|_0^1 = V(\mathbf{p}^1, y^1) - V(\mathbf{p}^0, y^0) \qquad (A3.3)$$

where $\mathbf{g}(t) = (g_1(t), \ldots, g_n(t), g_y(t))$, and $p_i^s = g_i(s), y^s = g_y(s)$ for $s = 0,1$. Since the final expression in (A3.3) does not depend on $g_i(t)$ or $g_y(t)$, the integral extended over c is independent of c. This result can be proved by invoking Theorem II below.

Moreover, line integrals are additive, implying that

$$\int_c L = \sum_{i=1}^n \int_{c_i} V_i dp_i + \int_{c_{n+1}} V_y dy \qquad (A3.4)$$

where $c_i = p_i^0 p_i^1$ for all i, $c_{n+1} = y^0 y^1$, and $V_i = V_i(p_1^1, \ldots, p_{i-1}^1, p_i, p_{i+1}^0, \ldots, p_n^0, y^0)$, assuming that the prices are changed in order from initial to final values, and that each Riemann integral in the right-hand expression of (A3.4) exists.

The following definitions and theorems, which are proved in Fleming (1965), are useful.

Definition: A differential form of degree 1 (a 1-form)
$f = \Sigma f_i(\mathbf{p}, y)dp_i + f_y(\mathbf{p}, y)dy$ is *exact* if there is
a function $F(\mathbf{p}, y)$ such that $f = dF$.

Definition: A 1-form f of class C^1 which satisfies

$$\left. \begin{array}{l} \dfrac{\partial f_i}{\partial p_j} = \dfrac{\partial f_j}{\partial p_i} \quad \left(= \dfrac{\partial^2 F}{\partial p_i \partial p_j} = \dfrac{\partial^2 F}{\partial p_j \partial p_i} \right) \\[4mm] \dfrac{\partial f_i}{\partial y} = \dfrac{\partial f_y}{\partial p_i} \quad \left(= \dfrac{\partial^2 F}{\partial p_i \partial y} = \dfrac{\partial^2 F}{\partial y \partial p_i} \right) \end{array} \right\} \quad \forall i, j$$

is called a *closed* 1-form.

Theorem I: If Ω_I is a simply-connected open subset of non-negative Euclidean $(n+1)$-space, then every closed 1-form with domain Ω_I is exact.

Theorem II: Let Ω_I be open, and f a continuous 1-form with domain Ω_I. The following statements are equivalent:

(i) f is exact.

(ii) If c_1 and c_2 are any two piecewise smooth curves lying in Ω_I, then $\int_{c_1} f = \int_{c_2} f$.

Corollary: If Ω_I is simply connected and f is of class C^1, then each of the statements (i) and (ii) of Theorem II is equivalent to the statement that f is closed.

CHAPTER 4

Topics in the theory of consumer surplus measures

This chapter is a natural sequel to Chapter 3 in that it is essentially a comparison of the three different consumer surplus measures presented there. We begin in Section 1 with an analysis of the conditions under which the different consumer surplus measures coincide. As the measures in general impute different dollar gains to a unique utility change, the question naturally arises as to whether any of the measures rank commodity bundles correctly, i.e. in the same way as the consumer would. The ordinal/cardinal properties of money measures of utility change are also briefly discussed. Section 2 is devoted to the problem of aggregation over individuals, and the chapter ends with a presentation of different techniques for determining consumer surpluses in empirical situations.

1 A comparison of different money measures of utility change

Three different money measures of utility change were introduced in Chapter 3. Unfortunately, these measures need not coincide. This was demonstrated by means of two examples in the final section of the chapter. What is the relationship between these measures?

There is a simple case in which the three considered measures (CV, EV and the ordinary consumer surplus measure S) coincide. If the utility function is quasi-linear, then demand for $n-1$ goods are independent of the level of income, implying that all additional income is spent on the nth good. Thus, the ordinary and compensated demand function for any good (but the nth) must coincide.[1] Consequently, $S=CV=EV$ and must equal the measure given by equation (3.11). If only a restricted number of prices are changed, the three measures still coincide provided the demands for those goods whose prices are changed are independent of the level of income.

41

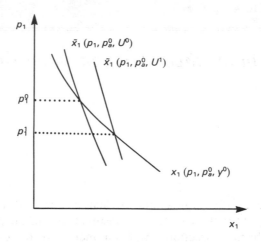

Figure 4.1 Ordinary and compensated demand curves

If income elasticities differ from zero, our money measures impute three different values to a unique utility change. Consider the case where income elasticities are positive over the entire adjustment path. Then, $EV > CV$ for a fall in a single price since $\partial \tilde{x} / \partial U > 0$ and $U^1 > U^0$; recall that CV is defined for $U = U^0$ and EV for $U = U^1$. This means that the EV is evaluated left of a curve which is situated outside that one used in evaluating the CV.[2] Moreover, since an ordinary demand curve connects the compensated demand curves, the consumer surplus evaluated to the left of the ordinary demand must exceed (fall short of) the corresponding compensating variation (equivalent variation), i.e. $CV < S < EV$ (see Figure 4.1). Unfortunately, this result does not hold in the multiple price change case unless the path independency conditions (3.7′) hold for the goods whose prices are changed or the set of paths is restricted. This is shown in Dixit and Weller (1979) and Stahl (1983b; 1984) respectively. Also note that our definition of the money measures yields the opposite signs and hence the variation from the definition used by some economists.

Since $S \neq CV \neq EV$ in general, the question naturally arises as to whether all three measures rank commodity bundles correctly, i.e. in the same order as that chosen by the consumer. From equation (3.21) it can be seen that if the utility function is homothetic and income is fixed, then the ordinary money measure S ranks any number of bundles (price vectors) correctly. Recall that by subjecting a homothetic utility function to a suitable monotonic transformation, $S = \Delta U / \lambda$ is obtained. Obviously, S is a sign-preserving measure of utility change also in the case of a quasi-linear utility function, provided one price is fixed. If the utility function does not belong to one or other of these classes of functions or if all prices *and* income are free to vary (including the special case in which, say, income is not constant throughout the movement although the initial and final levels coincide), then there is no money measure S such that S is both unique and a sign-preserving measure of utility change. Recall that all of the path-independency conditions (3.7) cannot hold simultaneously, and that conditions (3.7′) hold iff the utility function is homothetic while conditions (3.10) hold iff the utility function is quasi-linear. (If only a few prices and/or income are changed, these conditions can be weakened, as was shown in Section 2 of Chapter 3.) An illustration of the failure of S to always provide a correct ranking of commodity bundles can be found in Just *et al.* (1982, Ch. 5).

Turning next to the CV and EV measures, these measures rank bundles correctly, provided one considers only two commodity bundles, the initial and final ones (corresponding to different prices and/or incomes). Matters are different in the more general case where there are two or more final bundles.

In order to illustrate these claims, it is useful to restate the CV and EV measures of Chapter 3 in the following way:

$$\left. \begin{array}{l} CV = e(\mathbf{p}^1, U^1) - e(\mathbf{p}^1, U^0) \\ EV = e(\mathbf{p}^0, U^1) - e(\mathbf{p}^0, U^0) \end{array} \right\} \quad (4.1)$$

where the definitions given below equation (3.13) have been used to eliminate y^0 and y^1 from the measures, and a superscript 1(0) refers to final (initial) values. Since the expenditure function, by assumption, is increasing in utility, it follows that $U^1 \geq U^0$ implies that CV as well as EV have non-negative signs. This means that both measures rank any two commodity bundles in the same order as the underlying utility function. Note that this result holds also if all prices and income are changed since $\mathbf{p}$ in (4.1) refers to a vector of prices, not to a single price, and $y^1 \gtreqless y^0$.

By introducing a third price vector $\mathbf{p}^2$ corresponding to utility level U^2, it is straightforward to show that the EV measure ranks any three (any number of) bundles correctly. The EV measure uses $\mathbf{p}^0$ as base or reference prices in comparing the bundles, implying that bundles are ranked according to the utility they give to the consumer[3]. Thus, the EV measure will have the convenient properties of the compensation function introduced in Section 6 of Chapter 2. Recall that for fixed base prices, $\mathbf{p}^0$ say, the compensation function ranks commodity bundles in the same order as the underlying utility function.

The CV measure, on the other hand, evaluates changes at *final* prices. In the case of three bundles, we have to compare (4.1) and

$$CV_1 = e(\mathbf{p}^2, U^2) - e(\mathbf{p}^2, U^0) \qquad (4.2)$$

Suppose that $U^1 = U^2$ so that the two final bundles refer to the same level of utility. Then, in order to correctly evaluate the change, the two CV measures in (4.1) and (4.2) must coincide. However, since the measures are based on two different (base) price vectors, we may end up with two different compensating variations for the unique change in utility. Hence, the CV measures may wrongly tell us that one change is preferred to the other. It has been shown (see Chipman and Moore, 1980; Hause, 1975) that only homothetic (with income fixed) and quasi-linear (with $p_n = 1$) utility functions ensure that the CV measure correctly ranks any number of commodity bundles or projects. The reader is also referred to the appendix to Chapter 6.

This result has led some economists, notably McKenzie (1983), McKenzie and Pearce (1982), and Morey (1984), to argue that the EV measure is the dollar measure of utility change. For the sake of completeness, however, the following should be noted. If there are two or more initial commodity bundles but only one final bundle, then it is straightforward to show that the bundles are ranked in the same order by both the CV measure and the consumer. This is not necessarily true for the EV measure. Hence, as pointed out by Ng (1979 p. 100), neither measure can be regarded as strictly superior to the other.

We now turn to the question of whether money measures of utility changes can be used to figure out *how much* a consumer prefers a project A over a project B. For example, if $EV_A = \$100$ and $EV_B = \$50$, does it follow that the consumer likes A twice as much as B?

In an *ordinal* world, we only require that our money measure ranks commodity bundles correctly, i.e. in the same order as that chosen by the consumer. This is equivalent to requiring that 'the money measure associated with a shift in the price–income vector has a positive sign if and only if the level of satisfaction increases'. In a restricted sense, there exist such money measures of utility change. For example, the EV measure has been shown to rank bundles correctly provided we restrict ourselves to a single initial commodity bundle or set of reference prices. We have also established conditions which ensure that the ordinary consumer surplus measure S and the CV measure respectively, rank bundles correctly.

In general, however, it is not true that $\triangle U = \lambda EV$ say, since λ is not constant with respect to changes in prices and/or income. It is important here to note that the path independency of the CV and EV measures is due to the symmetry of the cross-substitution effects and *not* to a constancy of the 'marginal utility of income'. Hence, one faces the above 'conversion' problem regardless of which money measure is used.

We have established conditions which ensure that the marginal utility of income (money) λ is independent of a subset of prices and/or income. The requirement is that the utility function is either homothetic or quasi-linear. For these classes of utility functions, it may seem meaningful to say that a certain project is twice as good as some other project. However, the marginal utility of income is *not* left unaffected by a monotone increasing transformation of the utility function. Let us consider the indirect utility function $V(\mathbf{p}, y)$. In an ordinal world, $G = f(V(\mathbf{p}, y))$, where $\partial f/\partial V > 0$, will serve equally well since the ordering is preserved. Taking the partial derivatives of V and G respectively with respect to the ith price yields

$$\left. \begin{aligned} \frac{\partial V}{\partial p_i} &= -\lambda x_i \\ \frac{\partial G}{\partial p_i} &= \frac{\partial f}{\partial V}\frac{\partial V}{\partial p_i} = -\frac{\partial f}{\partial V}\lambda x_i \end{aligned} \quad \text{for all} \quad i \right\} \quad (4.3)$$

This shows that we cannot establish a linear relationship between the marginal money measure x_i and the change as measured by a utility index (and matters are not simpler in the discrete change case). Only the sign of the change in utility, i.e. the ranking of bundles, makes sense in an ordinal world. The transformation in (4.3) obviously preserves the signs of both the money measure and the utility change since $\partial f/\partial V > 0$. In point of fact, the money measure, but not the size of the 'utility change', is left unaffected by the considered transformation.[4]

To sum up, in an ordinal world we 'only' require that the money measure is a monotone increasing transformation (a sign-preserving transformation) of the utility function. The cardinal magnitude of differences, such as $\text{EV}_A = \$100$ while $\text{EV}_B = \$50$, reveal nothing about the intensity of preferences. Because an ordinalist's preferences do not have intensities, one can only infer that project A is preferred to project B.

We now turn to the question: What about a cardinal world? In such a world, the utility function $U(\mathbf{x})$ is unique except for an affine transformation $F(\mathbf{x}) = a + bU(\mathbf{x})$, where a and b are constants ($b > 0$). If λ is constant over the entire path considered, it now makes sense to say that the consumer likes A twice as much as B. If λ is not a constant, we can infer no more from our money measures than in an ordinal world. They tell us no more than that the consumer thinks project A is better than project B. Moreover, the conditions that are necessary for a money measure to yield a correct ranking are as restrictive in a cardinal as in an ordinal world (for further details, see Morey, 1984).

In closing, we turn to quite a different question, often raised by students, namely whether a consumer surplus measure can be infinitely large. With regard to a price fall, the compensating variation is bounded by y^0, while the equivalent variation may be infinite. In the case of price increases, the opposite result holds. A sufficient condition for a non-inferior good, say x_1, to have a finite uncompensated consumer's surplus is that the good is what Willig (1978) calls non-essential. The assumption of non-essentiality is both necessary and sufficient in order for the compensated surplus measures to always be finite. Non-essentiality of x_1 means that for any bundle $\mathbf{x} = x_1, \ldots, x_n$ where $x_1 > 0$ there exists a bundle $x_1' = 0, x_2', \ldots, x_n'$ such that $U(\mathbf{x}) = U(\mathbf{x}')$, i.e. any bundle including x_1 can be matched by a bundle excluding x_1. Geometrically, this is equivalent to all indifference surfaces intersecting the $x_1 = 0$ hyperplane. Unbounded measures may cause some problems in empirical investigations, e.g. when estimating the willingness to pay (EV) for having a natural resource preserved. We will return to this issue below; see also the appendix to Chapter 6.

2 Aggregation over individuals

Thus far, the chapter has dealt with the single consumer case. The aggregate demand for a commodity at any given price–income vector is the sum of the quantities demanded by the individual consumers. Thus, we must investigate under what conditions aggregate consumer surpluses, i.e. areas under ordinary and compensated market demand curves respectively, can be used to measure the gain or loss to the group as a whole.

Consider first the ordinary consumer surplus case. Areas to the left of ordinary market demands can be given a welfare interpretation if the (constant) *social* marginal utility of income is identical for all individuals. In order to show this, we introduce a Bergsonian welfare function of an H-household society. This function is written as

$$W = W(U^1(\mathbf{x}^1), \ldots, U^H(\mathbf{x}^H)) \tag{4.4}$$

This function, which relates the welfare of society or perhaps of a 'social planner' to the utility levels of the individuals, is usually assumed to have the following properties: (1) an increase in the utility level of any individual while all other individuals utility levels are kept constant increases social welfare; (2) if the utility of one individual is reduced, the utility of at least one other individual must then be increased for social welfare to be unchanged; and (3) the welfare weight of an individual depends on his/her utility level.

In order for a social welfare function to become a useful concept, full comparability of utility is often assumed. This means that the utility levels are expressed in units that can meaningfully be compared across individuals. It is thus not very useful to talk about a welfare function being defined over ordinal utilities. For example, consider the utilitarian welfare function which adds utilities, $W = \Sigma_h U^h$. If U^H is a utility index for the Hth consumer, any positive monotonic transformation, $f(U^H)$ say, of it is also a utility index. Nevertheless, the sum of utilities and hence the properties of the welfare function are changed by the transformation. Even an affine transformation, $a^H + b^H U^H$, applied to one of the utility functions, changes the properties of the welfare function. For this reason, one generally only allows transformations where both a and b are identical for all households (see Arrow, 1951; Bergson, 1938; Deaton and Muellbauer, 1983, Ch. 9; Just *et al.*, 1982, Ch. 3; Ng, 1982; Samuelson, 1947, Ch. 8, for discussion of the properties of social welfare functions).

We shall now use the social welfare function to examine the conditions under which an aggregate consumer surplus measure has any welfare significance. Assume that the welfare function is continuously differentiable. Thus differentiation of (4.4) and substitution of the indirect utility functions (3.2) yields

$$dW = \sum_{h=1}^{H} \frac{\partial W}{\partial V^h} \, dV^h = \Sigma \frac{\partial W}{\partial V^h} \lambda^h [-\mathbf{x}^h d\mathbf{p} + dy^h] \tag{4.5}$$

where $\partial W / \partial V^h > 0$ for all h gives the welfare weight of household h according to the 'social planner'.

According to the marginal welfare change measure (4.5), each individual is weighted by the product of the marginal welfare weight given to him/her and his/her marginal utility of income. If we want to consider discrete changes in prices and incomes, (4.5) must be integrated between initial and final price–income vectors.

Let us assume that the product of the welfare weight and the marginal utility of income is constant and equal across all individuals (implying that the welfare distribution is optimal as is demonstrated in the appendix to this chapter). The sum of changes in consumer surpluses, i.e. areas to the left of market demands, is then proportional to the change in social welfare; since $\partial W / \partial V \cdot \lambda$ is a constant, it can be factored out from the right-hand side of (4.5), if the expression is integrated between initial and final price vectors. This assumption, however, has the probably unreasonable implication that the welfare weight of a high-income household exceeds the welfare weight of a low-income group. This would be the case if λ is a strictly decreasing function of income.

Even if we consider the case in which all individuals have the same constant welfare weight and λ^h is constant for all individuals, one problem remains. In order that the sum of the changes in the consumers' surpluses be proportional to the change in social welfare, λ^h must not only be a constant but also identical for all individuals.

If the product of the welfare weight and the marginal utility of income varies across individuals, the sum of the consumer's surpluses and the change in social welfare need not then have the same sign. In order to be able to put a sign on the effect of a project on aggregate welfare, we must figure out the welfare weight given to each affected individual as well as his/her marginal utility of income. Of course, in addition we must calculate the change in each individual's consumer surplus. In the case of non-marginal changes, we also face the problem that neither $\partial W/\partial V^h$ nor λ^h needs to be constant.

The concepts of compensating and equivalent variation appear to be less restrictive in the above sense. Suppose the sum of changes in consumer surpluses evaluated to the left of compensated demands is positive in a multi-household society. Accordingly, the amount of money necessary to hold losers on their intitial or pre-project utility levels is less than the amount of money that can be extracted from the gainers of the project without leaving them worse off than without the project (the sum of CVs is positive). Furthermore the amount of money the gainers must be given to be persuaded to forgo the project exceeds the amount of money the losers are willing to pay to avoid the project (the sum of EVs is positive).

The sum of the consumers' surpluses represents what is left over after losers have been compensated. The project passes the Pareto test, i.e. no one is made worse off and the net surplus can be distributed so as to increase welfare of, for example, all individuals. It can be seen from (4.5) that if $dU^h = dV^h \geq 0$ for all h and $dV^h > 0$ for at least one h, then social welfare unambiguously increases. The argument assumes, however, that compensation is paid. If this is not the case some individuals may gain from the project while others lose. Hence one faces the same problem as when adding ordinary consumer surpluses over individuals. Accordingly, a social welfare function must be used to examine whether the weighted sum of gains and losses is positive or negative.

In Section 1 it was shown that the individual CV and EV measures usually differed in magnitude. Hence their aggregate counterparts may also differ. This means that one may end up in a situation where the costs of a project, such as the loss of producer's surplus, fall somewhere in between consumers aggregate CV and aggregate EV (both assumed to be positive so that consumers gain from the project). In such a case, no conclusive decision can be made regarding the desirability of the project.

Hence, according to one criterion, the project is desirable while the other criterion tells us that the project is not desirable.

In particular, this may be a serious problem in environmental economics. In order to illustrate this point let us assume that a decision is under way to close a national park and convert the land to other uses, such as mining or forestry. Accordingly, the visitors are questioned regarding their willingness to pay for having the park preserved. The maximum amount of money, the EV, that any user is willing to pay for this must be limited by his/her budget. Thus, this particular measure must be finite. On the other hand, the sum that must be given to a visitor to make him/her as well off without as with the park, the CV, may be infinitely large. If the cost of preserving the park falls somewhere in between the CV and the EV, no simple decision criterion is available.

A final remark is in order. The discussion in this section has not explicitly been based on the compensation criteria developed by Hicks (1939), Kaldor (1939), and Scitovsky (1941) (see Just *et al.*, 1982, Ch. 3 for definitions). However, the reader familiar with compensation criteria recognizes the close relationship between compensating and equivalent variations on the one hand and compensation criteria on the other hand. In fact, it has recently been demonstrated that if $\Sigma CV^h > 0$, then gainers can more than compensate losers (see Just *et al.*, 1982, Appendix D). The Just *et al.* (1982) result, if correct, resolves what has been known as the Boadway paradox in the literature. Boadway (1974) argued, in a general equilibrium context, that a positive aggregate compensating or equivalent variation does not indicate that gainers can more than compensate losers. The reader interested in this controversy is referred to Boadway (1974), Boadway and Bruce (1984), Just *et al.* (1982), Mishan (1976), and Smith and Stephen (1975).

3 *Estimation of consumer surplus*

It remains to briefly indicate what approaches can be used to estimate consumer surpluses in real world situations. The basic problem is that the Hicksian demand curves are unobservable. At best, Marshallian demand curves can be estimated directly. Several different approaches of the estimation of the compensating and equivalent variations have been suggested in the literature.

One of these approaches assumes that ordinary demand functions have been estimated. Then, if an expenditure function exists it must satisfy the following system of partial differential equations:

$$\frac{\partial e(\mathbf{p}, \bar{U})}{\partial p_i} = \tilde{x}_i(\mathbf{p}, \bar{U}) = x_i(\mathbf{p}, e(\mathbf{p}, \bar{U})) \quad \text{for all } i \qquad (4.6)$$

where $\bar{U}$ is the specified utility level, say initial or final. It must also satisfy the initial condition

$$e(\bar{p}, \bar{U}) = \bar{p}x(\bar{p}, \bar{y}) = \bar{p}\bar{x} = \bar{y} \qquad (4.7)$$

In principle, this system can be solved to obtain the expenditure function which in turn can be used to construct compensated demand functions (see Hurwics and Uzawa, 1971; Varian, 1978). Hausman (1981) and Bowden (1984) have used this approach to show that in some cases, it is a fairly straightforward matter to derive compensated demand curves from observed market demand curves. An example can be found in the appendix to this chapter.

A second approach assumes that a utility function, either direct or indirect, has been specified. This function can be used to derive a functional form for the ordinary demand functions. Once these are estimated, the estimated parameters are substituted into the utility function.

Advocates of this second approach do not need CV and EV measures since the direct or indirect utility function can be used to rank projects. Even advocates of the first approach may find money measures unnecessary. This is the case at least in relation to the solution of the integrability problem. The underlying utility function can then be derived and used in ranking projects. However, to date, only particular solutions have been worked out even in the minimally realistic case of price variation in two goods. For this reason it is useful to have some reasonably simple method which can be used to estimate CV and EV measures from market data.

It should be recalled that the Hicksian demand curves, contrary to the Marshallian curves, are unobservable. On the other hand, money measures based on Hicksian curves rank commodity bundles correctly (under the conditions stated in Section 1). This is not in general true for measures based on the Marshallian demand concept.

In order to illustrate the latter, it is useful to consider Harberger's (1971) approximate consumer surplus measure. This measure, in the form presented by Harberger, is

$$\frac{\Delta U}{\lambda + 0.5 \, \Delta\lambda} = \Sigma p_i \Delta x_i + 0.5 \, \Sigma \Delta p_i \Delta x_i + \frac{0.25 \, \Delta\lambda\Sigma\Delta p_i\Delta x_i}{\lambda + 0.5 \, \Delta\lambda} \qquad (4.8)$$

Harberger argues that the third term on the right can be ignored, because it is a third-order term. Since $\lambda + 0.5 \, \Delta\lambda$ is positive, the sum of the two right-hand side terms, calculated from market data, and ΔU will have the same sign.

However, it was shown in Chapter 2 that λ, contrary to the demand functions, is not invariant under a monotone increasing transformation of the utility function. By a suitable choice of the transformation, the third term in (4.8) becomes as small or as large as we wish to make it. For this reason, there is no simple relationship between areas under ordinary demand curves and the sign of the underlying utility change in (4.8). (See McKenzie, 1983, Ch. 6 for a detailed discussion of the properties of the Harberger measure; see also Zabalza, 1982.)

Let us now turn to methods which can be used to estimate CV and EV measures from market data. (A comprehensive survey of the literature on estimating a theoretically plausible demand system is given by Blackorby *et al.*, 1978, Ch. 8.) One such approximation procedure uses the familiar Slutsky equation. If we have an econometric estimate of the ordinary demand function $x_i(\mathbf{p}, y)$, we know the own-price derivative $\partial x_i/\partial p_i$ as well as the income derivative $\partial x_i/\partial y$. Since the substitution effect can be calculated from this information (see below), it is possible to obtain an estimate of the slope of the compensated demand. Thus, by estimating (possibly a system of) Marshallian demands, one obtains all the information needed to estimate CV and EV measures of price changes. This is the case at least if we are able to estimate ordinary demand functions for the individual consumer.

Unfortunately, matters are more complicated if only market (aggregate) data are available. In general, we cannot deduce the properties of the consumer's demand functions from market data. However, one can figure out the conditions under which the aggregate compensated demand function can be computed from an econometric estimate of the Marshallian market demand function. The procedure is exact if each consumer has the same marginal propensity to consume the good, i.e. if $\partial x_i^h/\partial y^h = \gamma^h$ is the same for everyone, and each household's share of aggregate income is fixed and constant with respect to changes in prices and incomes. Suppose then, that we have a point estimate of the slope of the aggregate uncompensated demand curve. Moreover, assume that the Slutsky decomposition can be made:

$$\partial \bar{X}_i/\partial p_i = \alpha_i = \beta_i + \gamma X_i \tag{4.9}$$

where $\beta_i = \partial X_i/\partial p_i$, and capital letters denote aggregates, i.e. $\Sigma_h \bar{x}_i^h$ etc. According to (4.9) the aggregate substitution effect of a change in the own price is equal to the total effect less the aggregate income effect of the price change. A second-order Taylor series expansion of the sum of the expenditure functions, with all prices except p_i fixed, and using (4.9) yields

$$\Sigma_h \triangle e^h \approx \Sigma_h \frac{\partial e^h}{\partial p_i} \triangle p_i + 0.5 \, \Sigma_h \frac{\partial^2 e^h}{\partial p_i^2} \triangle p_i \triangle p_i$$

$$= X_i \triangle p_i + 0.5\alpha_i \triangle p_i \triangle p_i$$

$$= X_i \triangle p_i + 0.5(\beta_i + \gamma X_i) \triangle p_i \triangle p_i \tag{4.10}$$

where all derivatives are evaluated at initial values of prices and expenditures. Equation (4.10) states that a Slutsky decomposition can be used to calculate aggregate CV or EV measures of a discrete price change from aggregate market data, provided that the aforementioned aggregation conditions hold. This approach is an example of the so-called aggregation theory, which deals with the conditions that are necessary for market demands to correspond to a utility function and its solution.

In general, the conditions necessary for exact aggregation are quite restrictive. For example, we require that the indirect utility functions are quasi-homothetic,[5] i.e. of the Gorman polar form, and given by

$$V^h(\mathbf{p}, y^h) = \frac{y^h - a^h(\mathbf{p})}{b(\mathbf{p})} \quad \text{for all } h \tag{4.11}$$

where, although y and a are indexed by h, $b(\mathbf{p})$ is not. To see why, use Roy's identity to obtain the ordinary demand functions

$$x_i^h = \frac{\partial a^h}{\partial p_i} + (y^h - a^h) \frac{\partial b / \partial p_i}{b} \quad \text{for all } i \tag{4.12}$$

A check shows that the income effect is itself independent of income, $\partial x_i^h / \partial y^h = (\partial b / \partial p_i)/b$, and hence is the same for each consumer. Provided individuals maximize utility (and preferences are such as to satisfy the aggregation condition), average demands $X_i/H = \bar{x}_i = \bar{a}_i(\mathbf{p}) + \gamma_i \bar{y}$, where a bar denotes an average, will automatically be consistent with utility maximization. Moreover, since the income effect is independent of income, the aggregate substitution effect needed in (4.10) is easily calculated.

If aggregation is to hold for global changes in prices but with a fixed distribution of income, then all individuals must have homothetic utility functions. If aggregation holds for all income distributions, then individuals must have identical homothetic utility functions. These are very stringent requirements, and they are generally violated by aggregate demand data.

Another approach, developed by Willig (1973; 1976), aims at determining error bounds when ordinary consumer surpluses are used as a proxy for the compensating or equivalent variations. Varian (1978, pp. 212–13) derives the following approximation of the Willig formulae:

$$\frac{CV - S_i}{S_i} \approx -\frac{S_i \eta}{2y^0} \tag{4.13}$$

where S_i is the ordinary consumer surplus, CV is the compensating variation, η is the income elasticity, and y^0 is initial income (expenditure). This expression gives the relative error when S_i is used instead of

CV. The error is likely to be small in practice as demonstrated by Willig (1973; 1976) and Just *et al.* (1982). The Willig approach can be generalized to the multiple price change case (see Just *et al.*, 1982, pp. 375–86 for details).

This approach may seem simple to apply in real world situations. However, it is important to note that (4.13) is derived for a single consumer. In a multi-household economy, the approach requires information about each and every consumer's income and income elasticity. One can then determine from market data upper and lower bounds for the sum of compensating and equivalent variations. If there are large variations in income and/or income elasticity of demand between consumers, the aggregate error may become quite large (see Just *et al.*, 1982, Appendix B for details; see also McKenzie, 1983; Stahl, 1984; Vartia, 1983, for discussion of the Willig approach).

A similar procedure has been suggested by Seade (1978). The procedure is designed to be relevant for systems exhibiting linear Engel curves, i.e. for utility functions of the Gorman polar form. It is possible to show (see McKenzie, 1983) that Seade's approximation of the EV measure can be written as

$$\mathrm{EV} \approx -\frac{(\exp(\eta S_i/y)-1)y}{\eta} \tag{4.14}$$

Thus, if we have estimates of the ordinary consumer surplus change, income, and the income elasticity, we can calculate an approximation to the EV measure.

In common with the Willig method in (4.13), Seade's approximation procedure in (4.14) is likely to generate accurate approximations when only one price varies. However, once again, the measure is derived for a single consumer. In a multi-household economy, the approach requires information about each and every consumer's income and income elasticity.

It should also be recalled that the Seade approach assumes a particular form of utility function. Once the ordinary demand functions are estimated, the estimated parameters can be substituted into the utility function. This function can be used to rank any changes in prices and income. Thus, given that a particular form of the utility function is postulated, it may seem a bit unnecessary to worry about the properties of different money measures.

A technique for determining the equivalent variation has been developed by McKenzie (1983) and McKenzie and Pearce (1982). They write the EV measure in terms of a Taylor series expansion. This approach only requires information on the demand functions in a neighbourhood of the initial price–income configuration $\mathbf{p}^0$, y^0. On the other hand, it seems as if the McKenzie–Pearce approach, as was the case with the Willig approach, requires information on each individual's demand equations. If so, the approach is less useful in empirical investigations where, in general, only market demand equations can be estimated.

Finally, it is important to emphasize that the sum of the consumers' surpluses does not necessarily have the same sign as the change in welfare according to some social welfare function. This was discussed at some length in the previous section. In some cases, we may be able to derive the weights from the implicit trade-offs underlying actual decisions or from some other source. Otherwise, a disaggregation which identifies those who gain and those who lose from a particular project may be useful. At least, such a disaggregation gives the policy maker an opportunity to apply his/her own distributive weights to the material.

Appendix

Welfare maximization

In Section 2 of Chapter 4 it was claimed that the product of the welfare weight and the marginal utility of income is equal among individuals if the welfare distribution is optimal. In order to show this, we maximize the social welfare function

$$W = W(U^1(x_1^1, \ldots, x_n^1), \ldots, U^H(x_1^H, \ldots, x_n^H)) \tag{A4.1}$$

subject to an implicit aggregate production function of the economy

$$F(x_1, \ldots, x_n) = 0 \tag{A4.2}$$

where

$$x_i = \sum_{h=1}^{H} x_i^h \quad \text{for all } i$$

Using the first-order conditions for utility maximization, the first-order conditions for maximization of (A4.1) subject to (A4.2) are

$$\frac{\partial W}{\partial U^h} \frac{\partial U^h}{\partial x_i^h} = \frac{\partial W}{\partial U^h} \lambda^h p_i = \theta \frac{\partial F}{\partial x_i} \quad \text{for all } i, h \tag{A4.3}$$

where θ is the Lagrange multiplier associated with (A4.2).

Rearranging (A4.3), it can be seen that

$$\frac{\partial W}{\partial U^a} \lambda^a = \frac{\partial W}{\partial U^b} \lambda^b \tag{A4.4}$$

for any two households a, b. Thus, an interior solution (assuming the second-order conditions are satisfied) requires that the product of the welfare weight and the marginal utility of income is equal among households.

The integrability problem

The following example is adapted from Hausman (1981). Consider the non-stochastic demand function

$$x = \beta p + \lambda y + \delta \mathbf{z} \tag{A4.5}$$

where both p and y are deflated by the price of the other good, and $\mathbf{z}$ is a vector of socioeconomic characteristics.

Let us assume that we remain on a given indifference curve. As the price changes we will use the equation $V(p(t), y(t)) = \bar{U}$. Hence, in order to stay on the indifference curve we have along a path of price change

$$\frac{\partial V}{\partial p}\frac{dp}{dt} + \frac{\partial V}{\partial y}\frac{dy}{dt} = 0 \tag{A4.6}$$

From (A4.6) and Roy's identity, we obtain

$$\frac{dy(p)}{dp} = \beta p + \gamma y + \delta \mathbf{z} \tag{A4.7}$$

This ordinary differential equation can be solved to yield

$$y(p) = Ce^{\gamma p} - \frac{(\beta p + (\beta/\gamma) + \delta \mathbf{z})}{\gamma} \tag{A4.8}$$

where C is the constant of integration. Set $C = \bar{U}$. Solving (A4.8), we then find the indirect utility function

$$V(p, y) = C = e^{-\gamma p}\left[y + \frac{\beta p + (\beta/\gamma) + \delta \mathbf{z}}{\gamma}\right] \tag{A4.9}$$

If we have estimated the Marshallian demand function (A4.5), the parameter estimates can be substituted into (A4.9). The partial derivative of (A4.9) with respect to p can then be used to calculate the impact on welfare associated with a change in the price of x. Thus, it is not necessary to calculate CV or EV measures in this case; but the expenditure function follows simply from (A4.9) by interchanging the utility level with the income variable.

According to the second approach discussed in Section 3 of this chapter, the procedure is reversed. First, specify a utility function, for example of the form in (A4.9). Second, derive the demand equation(s), (A4.5) say.

CHAPTER 5

Consumer surplus measures in quantity-constrained regimes

In many situations individuals could be expected to face quantity constraints. Governments, for example, sometimes impose price ceilings or floors which result in excess demand or supply in markets for goods and factors. In other circumstances quotas are imposed. This is sometimes the case when drugs or chemicals are considered harmful and consumption is therefore restricted; possibly a total ban is imposed.

Quantity constraints are also of considerable importance in the analysis of recreation activities. For example, U.S. waterfowl hunters face three different quantity constraints or institutional limits. These are the maximum number of waterfowl that may be bagged in one day, the maximum number of days during which waterfowl may be shot, and the maximum number of birds a hunter may have in his possession (Hammack and Brown, 1974, p. 18). Similarly, the carrying capacity of a natural area for recreational activities may be limited so that the number of visitors must be restricted. In order to be useful in such situations, the consumer surplus measures, derived in the previous chapters, need to be modified.

The seminal work on utility maximization subject to quantity constraints is that of Tobin and Houthakker (1950/1). They examined a situation where constraints are just on the verge of binding at the examined point. More recently, the Tobin–Houthakker results have been generalized to situations where the rationing constraints are not optimal (see Howard, 1977; Mackay and Whitney, 1980; Neary and Roberts, 1980). There are also a few attempts to derive consumer's surpluses in quantity-constrained regimes (see, for example, Cornes and Albon, 1981; Just et al., 1982; Randall and Stoll, 1980).

The major purpose of this chapter is to derive consumer surplus measures to be used in quantity-constrained situations. It is organized as follows: Section 1 presents the model of a consumer maximizing utility

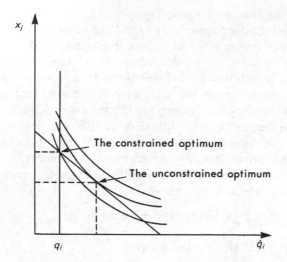

Figure 5.1 Utility maximization subject to both a budget constraint and a quantity constraint

subject to both a budget constraint and quantity constraints on the consumption of some goods. Section 2 derives a consumer surplus measure which is obtained as an area under an ordinary or uncompensated marginal willingness to pay curve and examines path independency conditions for such a measure. This measure and its relation to an area below an ordinary demand curve is illustrated by means of an example in Section 3. Section 4 derives concepts of compensating and equivalent variation (surplus) in quantity-constrained situations. Finally, Section 5 offers an interpretation of the results in terms of market clearing prices.

1 *Quantity-constrained utility maximization*

Consider a household which faces quantity constraints on its consumption of goods $\hat{q}_1, \ldots, \hat{q}_m$, but is unconstrained in its consumption of goods $x_1, \ldots, x_n$. The household's well-behaved utility function is written as[1]

$$U = U(\mathbf{x}, \hat{\mathbf{q}}) \tag{5.1}$$

The budget constraint is given by

$$\mathbf{px} + \mathbf{P}\hat{\mathbf{q}} - y = 0 \tag{5.2}$$

where $\mathbf{P} \gg 0$ is the vector of prices of rationed goods. Moreover, the household faces the quantity constraints

$$\mathbf{q} = \hat{\mathbf{q}} \tag{5.3}$$

where $\mathbf{q} \geqslant 0$ is a vector of imposed quantities. Only the under-consumption case, illustrated in Figure 5.1, in which the household is compelled to consume less of $\hat{\mathbf{q}}$ than it would choose if unconstrained, is considered. However, a 'feasible' $\mathbf{x}$ cannot always be found; for example, if $U = \hat{q}_1 - 1/x_1$, then utility is bounded above by q_1 (Neary and Roberts, 1980, p. 30). However, in this chapter it is assumed that a feasible $\mathbf{x}$ always exists. Moreover, as is indicated by the assumption regarding the properties of the direct utility function, attention is restricted to functions, which are appropriately differentiable or smooth (on a set Ω_{Iq} of strictly positive prices, quantity constraints and incomes).

The quantity-constrained indirect utility function associated with this maximization problem is written as

$$V(\mathbf{p}, y - \mathbf{Pq}, \mathbf{q}) = \max_{\mathbf{x}} \ \{U(\mathbf{x}, \mathbf{q}) | \mathbf{px} + \mathbf{Pq} - y = 0\}$$

$$= U(\mathbf{x}(\mathbf{p}, y - \mathbf{Pq}, \mathbf{q}), \mathbf{q}) \tag{5.4}$$

This function has the following properties, as is demonstrated in the appendix to this chapter

$$\frac{\partial V}{\partial \mathbf{p}} = -\lambda \mathbf{x}(\mathbf{p}, y - \mathbf{Pq}, \mathbf{q})$$

$$\frac{\partial V}{\partial y} = \lambda(\mathbf{p}, y - \mathbf{Pq}, \mathbf{q})$$

$$\left. \begin{array}{c} \\ \\ \\ \end{array} \right\} \tag{5.5}$$

$$\frac{\partial V}{\partial \mathbf{P}} = -\lambda \mathbf{q}$$

$$\frac{\partial V}{\partial \mathbf{q}} = \frac{\partial U(\mathbf{x}(\cdot), \mathbf{q})}{\partial \mathbf{q}} - \lambda \mathbf{P}$$

The first line of (5.5) gives the ordinary or uncompensated demand functions for unrationed goods (multiplied by the marginal utility of income, λ, which in general depends on the same factors as demand for unrationed goods, as is seen from the second line). These demand functions have the following properties. As in the unrationed case considered in Chapter 2, a change in the price of an unrationed good has both a substitution effect and an income effect. A reduction in a quantity constraint also causes two distinct impacts. Firstly, it has an income effect, i.e. the household reduces its expenditures on (normal) unrationed goods in order to be able to consume more rationed goods. Secondly, the marginal utilities of unrationed goods are affected by a reduction in rationing. This impact is captured by the last argument in the demand functions. An increased price of rationed goods causes an income effect, but not a substitution effect. This is because the household is unwilling to reduce its consumption of a rationed good even if its price increases, provided the rationing is binding. This property is revealed by the third line of (5.5).

The final line of (5.5) gives the effect of a reduction in the severity of rationing on the household's utility level. The effect of a marginal change in q_i is equal to the difference between the marginal valuation of q_i and the market price of q_i (converted to units of utility through multiplication by the marginal utility of income). Clearly, this difference is positive as long as the household is compelled to consume less of q_i than it would if unconstrained; only at an unconstrained interior optimum, is an equality obtained, i.e. $\partial U/\partial \mathbf{q} = \lambda \mathbf{P}$. The reader interested in detailed examinations of the properties of the behaviour functions under rationing is referred to Benassy (1982), Cuddington *et al.* (1984) and Neary and Roberts (1980).

2 *Consumer's surplus under rationing*

Consider now a change in the vector $\mathbf{q}$ from $\mathbf{q}^0$ to $\mathbf{q}^1$, assuming that the constraints are binding over the entire path, and holding all prices and income fixed. The associated change in utility can be written as

$$\triangle U = V(\mathbf{p}, y - \mathbf{Pq}^1, \mathbf{q}^1) - V(\mathbf{p}, y - \mathbf{Pq}^0, \mathbf{q}^0)$$

$$= \int_c V_{\mathbf{q}}(\mathbf{p}, y - \mathbf{Pq}, \mathbf{q})d\mathbf{q} = \int_c [U_{\mathbf{q}}(\mathbf{x}(\mathbf{p}, y - \mathbf{Pq}, \mathbf{q}), \mathbf{q}) - \lambda \mathbf{P}]d\mathbf{q} \quad (5.6)$$

where a subscript $\mathbf{q}$ denotes a partial derivative with respect to $\mathbf{q}$, and c (in Ω_{Iq}) is some path between initial and final $\mathbf{q}$-vectors. Inspection of the arguments of $U_{\mathbf{q}}$ in the final expression shows that this derivative includes the effect of changed optimal demands for unrationed goods as $\mathbf{q}$ is changed. The integrand in (5.6) is an exact differential of the indirect utility function (5.4) with respect to $\mathbf{q}$, implying that (5.6) is path independent. Recall that the last equality of (5.6) is obtained from the final line of (5.5).

The change in utility as $\mathbf{q}$ is changed from $\mathbf{q}^0$ to $\mathbf{q}^1$ is evaluated by the sum of the changes in the areas under marginal valuation 'curves' for rationed goods less the change in expenditures on such goods; the latter terms are converted to units of utility through multiplication by λ.

A money measure is obtained by eliminating λ from the final expression in (5.6). This money measure is proportional to $\triangle U$ if the marginal utility of income is constant with respect to changes in the rations for goods. A sufficient condition for this to be the case is that λ only depends on the price of an unconstrained good, say x_n, which is taken as a *numéraire* (see the appendix to this chapter). This is Samuelson's second interpretation of the constancy of the marginal utility of income (money) discussed in Chapter 3. More importantly, this assumption ensures that

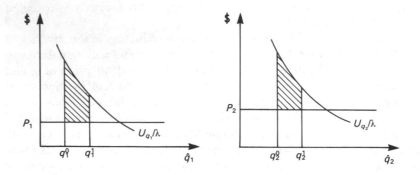

Figure 5.2 Change in 'consumer surplus' caused by a change in $\mathbf{q}$ from q_1^0, q_2^0 to q_1^1, q_2^1 (when only two goods are rationed) where

$$U_{q_1} = U_{q_1}(\mathbf{x}^a, q_1, q_2^0) \qquad\qquad U_{q_2} = U_{q_2}(\mathbf{x}^b, q_1^1, q_2)$$

$$\mathbf{x}^a = \mathbf{x}(\mathbf{p}, y - P_1 q_1 - P_2 q_2^0, q_1, q_2^0) \qquad \mathbf{x}^b = \mathbf{x}(\mathbf{p}, y - P_1 q_1^1 - P_2 q_2, q_1^1, q_2)$$

the money measure is path independent. If $\lambda = \lambda(p_n)$, the money measure of utility change becomes

$$\frac{\triangle U}{\lambda(p_n)} = S_{\mathbf{q}} = \int_c [\frac{U_{\mathbf{q}}}{\lambda(p_n)} - \mathbf{P}]d\mathbf{q} \qquad\qquad (5.7)$$

which states: Use the change in the difference between the marginal willingness to pay for a rationed good and the market price of the good to evaluate a change in a quantity constraint. If several constraints are altered, the order in which rations are changed makes no difference, but the area under the marginal willingness to pay curve for a particular good must be evaluated subject to all previously considered changes in rations, as is illustrated in Figure 5.2. On the other hand, if the utility function is such that the money measure is path dependent, then one can find a path of integration such that $S_{\mathbf{q}} < 0$ even if $\triangle U > 0$ (compare Chapter 4). The reader interested in detailed path independency conditions is referred to the appendix to this chapter.

It is important to note that, in this chapter, prices remain fixed while rations are changed. This means that there is no 'windfall' gain (loss) from the original amount of expenditure on the good (i.e. following a changed price, i.e. $\triangle \mathbf{P} \cdot \mathbf{q}^0$). For this reason, one must be careful in interpreting the gain from a reduction in a quantity constraint in terms of an area under a demand curve. Empirical applications would be greatly simplified if one could use areas under ordinary demand curves to calculate changes in consumer's surplus under rationing. This is because market demand curves can often be estimated (identified) even under conditions of rationing (see, for example, White and Ziemer, 1983). The relationship between the money measure (5.7) and areas under ordinary demand curves is illustrated by means of an example in the subsequent section.

3 *An example*

In this section the transformed Cobb–Douglas model of Section 4 in Chapter 3 is used to illustrate the derivation of a quantity-constrained consumer surplus measure. In particular, we illustrate its relationship to an area under an ordinary demand curve. Suppose the household is rationed in the market for the first good. The household then maximizes

$$U = \alpha \ln q_1 + (1-\alpha)\ln x_2 \qquad (5.8)$$

subject to the usual budget constraint. Straightforward calculations yield the indirect utility function

$$V(p_2, y - P_1 q_1, q_1) = \alpha \ln q_1 + (1-\alpha)\ln(y - P_1 q_1) - (1-\alpha)\ln p_2 \qquad (5.9)$$

Taking partial derivatives of (5.9), it is easily demonstrated that the properties of these derivatives resemble those of the derivatives in (5.5).

Next, the ordinary unrationed demand function $x_1 = \alpha y/p_1$, from Section 4 of Chapter 3, is examined to ascertain whether it can be used to obtain a money measure of utility change. In order to perform this investigation, invert the demand function for x_1 to obtain the demand price, and take the difference between the marginal willingness to pay $(\partial U/\partial q_1)/\lambda$, obtained by differentiating (5.8) and (5.9) with respect to q_1 and y respectively, and the demand price $p_1 = \alpha y/x_1$ for $q_1 = x_1$ to obtain

$$\left.\begin{aligned} \frac{(\partial U/\partial q_1)}{\lambda} - p_1 &= \frac{\alpha(y - P_1 q_1)}{(1-\alpha)q_1} - \frac{\alpha y}{x_1} \\[2mm] &= \frac{\alpha}{(1-\alpha)q_1}(p_1 q_1 - P_1 q_1) \end{aligned}\right\} \qquad (5.10)$$

This expression has a non-negative sign since $P_1 \leqslant p_1$ by assumption. It should be recalled that P_1 is fixed below the 'market-clearing' level.

This result shows that the ordinary demand curve is not, in general, suitable for use in calculating a money measure of a changed ration level. The problem is caused by an 'income effect'. The marginal willingness to pay is derived from the assumption that the household pays P_1 per (additional) unit of the commodity. On the other hand, the use of the ordinary demand curve assumes that the household pays $p_1 \geqslant P_1$ for marginal units of the commodity. Hence the household must adjust (reduce) its consumption of other commodities over and above what is required if the price remains fixed at P_1. It can easily be checked that a utility function of the form $U = U(x_1, \ldots, x_{n-1}, \mathbf{q}) + x_n$ where x_n is the *numéraire* commodity, avoids this problem since demands are independent of income (see Section 4 of Chapter 3).

4 *Compensating and equivalent variations (surpluses) in quantity-constrained situations*

The investigation performed in the previous sections demonstrates that ordinary demand curves are of limited use under conditions of rationing. This section examines whether measures based on compensated demand functions are applicable. In addition to the concepts of compensating and equivalent variation, which were discussed at some length in the previous chapters, Hicks (1943) introduced so-called compensating and equivalent surplus measures. The latter measures refer to situations where the consumer is constrained to consume at the new (old) prices, the same quantity he would buy in absence of compensation. Obviously, these surplus concepts are of interest in quantity-constrained situations. However, the case dealt with in this chapter is more general since the consumer is constrained in some markets and unconstrained in others. For this reason, the compensated measures to be derived in this section will be denoted (quantity-constrained) compensated and equivalent variations.

In order to derive concepts of quantity-constrained compensating and equivalent variation, it is useful to specify the quantity-constrained expenditure function. This function, which by assumption is appropriately differentiable, denotes the minimum level of expenditure for any given prices, values of the quantity constraints, and level of utility

$$e(\mathbf{p}, \mathbf{P}, \mathbf{q}, \bar{U}) = \min_{\mathbf{x}} \{\mathbf{px} + \mathbf{Pq} | U(\mathbf{x}, \mathbf{q}) \geqslant \bar{U}\}$$

$$= \mathbf{p\tilde{x}}(\mathbf{p}, \mathbf{q}, \bar{U}) + \mathbf{Pq} \tag{5.11}$$

Taking partial derivatives of (5.11) one obtains

$$\frac{\partial e}{\partial \mathbf{p}} = \tilde{\mathbf{x}}(\mathbf{p}, \mathbf{q}, \bar{U})$$

$$\frac{\partial e}{\partial \mathbf{P}} = \mathbf{q} \qquad \qquad \left.\right\} \tag{5.12}$$

$$\frac{\partial e}{\partial \mathbf{q}} = \mathbf{P} + \mathbf{p}\frac{\partial \tilde{\mathbf{x}}}{\partial \mathbf{q}} = \mathbf{P} - \frac{U_q(\tilde{\mathbf{x}}, \mathbf{q})}{\lambda}$$

In Chapter 2 it was shown that a change in a price has a substitution but not an income effect, on compensated demands. This is still true for changes in prices of unrationed goods. However, since **q** is fixed, a change in a P_i has no substitution effect, implying that the compensated demands for unrationed goods are left unchanged. This is also seen from the second line of (5.12). A change in a q_i, on the other hand, affects compensated unrationed demands in a complicated way, at least in the case of multiple quantity constraints. The reader is referred to Mackay and Whitney (1980) and Neary and Roberts (1980) for further details.

In order to interpret the effect of a change in a q_i on the level of expenditure, it should be noted that the right-hand side expression in the bottom line of (5.12) is obtained in the following way: Differentiate the utility function with utility held constant and insert the first-order conditions for cost minimization. This operation yields the expression in question, as is shown in the appendix to this chapter. Thus, $\partial e/\partial q_i$ in (5.12) is equal to the price of the rationed good less the compensated marginal willingness to pay for the good. Note that both $U_\mathbf{q}$ and λ are evaluated given the specified level of utility. It has been demonstrated, by for example, Mackay and Whitney (1980), that the Lagrange multiplier λ of the quantity-constrained maximized utility problem equals the inverse of the Lagrange multiplier, say μ, of the quantity-constrained cost minimized problem, provided λ and μ refer to the same level of utility (commodity bundle). This result is indeed confirmed by (5.12), where $1/\lambda = \mu$ appears in the right-hand side of the expression.

Using the bottom line of (5.12), the compensating variation associated with a change in quantity constraints from $\mathbf{q}^0$ to $\mathbf{q}^1$ can be written as

$$CV_\mathbf{q} = e(\mathbf{p}, \mathbf{P}, \mathbf{q}^0, U^0) - e(\mathbf{p}, \mathbf{P}, \mathbf{q}^1, U^0)$$

$$= \int_c \left[\frac{U_\mathbf{q}(\tilde{\mathbf{x}}, \mathbf{q})}{\lambda} - \mathbf{P} \right] d\mathbf{q} \tag{5.13}$$

where prices and income are fixed, for simplicity, and utility is being held constant at the initial level.

If the household's utility is fixed at the final level, the equivalent variation associated with a move from $\mathbf{q}^0$ to $\mathbf{q}^1$ is defined as

$$EV_\mathbf{q} = e(\mathbf{p}, \mathbf{P}, \mathbf{q}^0, U^1) - e(\mathbf{p}, \mathbf{P}, \mathbf{q}^1, U^1)$$

$$= \int_c \left[\frac{U_\mathbf{q}(\tilde{\mathbf{x}}, \mathbf{q})}{\lambda} - \mathbf{P} \right] d\mathbf{q} \tag{5.14}$$

where the unconstrained compensated demand functions $\tilde{\mathbf{x}}$ and the marginal utility of income λ now are evaluated given $U = U^1$.

By construction, the integrands of (5.13) and (5.14) are exact differen-

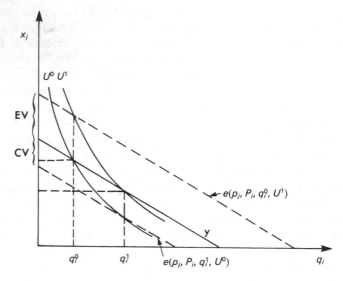

Figure 5.3 The compensating variation and the equivalent variation associated with a change in q_i from q_i^0 to q_i^1 where

$$y = e(p_j, P_i, q_i^0, U^0) = e(p_j, P_i, q_i^1, U^1)$$

tials of the constrained expenditure function with respect to $\mathbf{q}$. Hence, both money measures (5.13) and (5.14) are path independent, i.e. the order in which rations are changed makes no difference. This is shown in the appendix to this chapter. The CV measure gives the maximum (minimum) sum of money that must be taken from (given to) the household while leaving it just as well off as before the change in rations $\mathbf{q}$. The equivalent variation gives the minimum (maximum) sum of money that must be given to (taken from) the household to make it as well off as it would be with an increase (reduction) in $\mathbf{q}$. Using indifference curves, these measures can be illustrated as in Figure 5.3. Alternatively, both measures can be calculated as the change in the area under a compensated marginal willingness to pay curve for, say, good q_i between q_i^0 and q_i^1 less the change in expediture on the good. If several rations are changed, the curve for good q_i is evaluated subject to all previously considered changes in quantity constraints in other markets (see Figure 5.2). The aggregate or total $CV_\mathbf{q}$ and $EV_\mathbf{q}$ measures are obtained by adding the measures for the markets where rations are changed.

5 *Some further results*

It would be useful if the shadow prices U_q/λ could be related to hypothetical market prices such that an unconstrained consumer would choose, at these prices, the same commodity bundle as he chooses at prevailing market prices. In fact, such a virtual price approach has been developed by Neary and Roberts (1980); however, the first to use virtual prices was probably Rothbarth (1940/1), who used them in an analysis of the measurement of real income under rationing. The Neary–Roberts approach is more general than the approach used by Tobin and Houthakker (1950/1) since the quantity constraints can be fixed at arbitrary levels. The Tobin–Houthakker approach, on the other hand, assumes what Samuelson (1947) calls auxiliary constraints, i.e. constraints that are just on the verge of binding at the examined point.

The problem boils down to a question of specification of a virtual price vector $\hat{\mathbf{p}}$, $\hat{\mathbf{P}}$ which generates the demands $\mathbf{x}$, $\mathbf{q}$. It can be shown that $\hat{\mathbf{p}} = \mathbf{p}$, while $\hat{\mathbf{P}} \neq \mathbf{P}$ in general. Following Neary and Roberts (1980), the constrained expenditure function (5.11) is written as

$$e(\mathbf{p}, \mathbf{P}, \mathbf{q}, \bar{U}) = \mathbf{p}\bar{\mathbf{x}}(\mathbf{p}, \mathbf{q}, \bar{U}) + \mathbf{Pq}$$
$$= \mathbf{p}\bar{\mathbf{x}}(\mathbf{p}, \hat{\mathbf{P}}, \bar{U}) + \mathbf{P}\bar{\mathbf{q}}(\mathbf{p}, \hat{\mathbf{P}}, \bar{U})$$
$$= \hat{e}(\mathbf{p}, \hat{\mathbf{P}}, \bar{U}) + (\mathbf{P}-\hat{\mathbf{P}})\mathbf{q} \qquad (5.15)$$

where $\mathbf{q} = \bar{\mathbf{q}}(\mathbf{p}, \hat{\mathbf{P}}, \bar{U}) = \partial\hat{e}/\partial\hat{\mathbf{P}}$, i.e. $\hat{\mathbf{P}}$ is such that the *quantity-unconstrained* compensated demands at prices $\hat{\mathbf{P}}$, $\mathbf{p}$ are equal to the quantity constraints $\mathbf{q}$, and $\hat{e}(.,.,.)$ gives the minimum expediture for the specified utility level, given virtual prices $\mathbf{p}$, $\hat{\mathbf{P}}$. In terms of Figure 5.1, the slope and position of the budget line are changed in such a way that the budget line becomes tangent to the indifference curve at the constrained optimum.

Taking the partial derivative of (5.15) with respect to $\mathbf{q}$ yields

$$\frac{\partial e(\mathbf{p}, \mathbf{P}, \mathbf{q}, \bar{U})}{\partial \mathbf{q}} = \frac{\partial \hat{e}}{\partial \hat{\mathbf{P}}} \frac{\partial \hat{\mathbf{P}}}{\partial \mathbf{q}} - \mathbf{q}\frac{\partial \hat{\mathbf{P}}}{\partial \mathbf{q}} + (\mathbf{P}-\hat{\mathbf{P}}) = \mathbf{P}-\hat{\mathbf{P}} \qquad (5.16)$$

where $\partial\hat{e}/\partial\hat{\mathbf{P}} = \hat{\mathbf{q}}(\mathbf{p}, \hat{\mathbf{P}}, \bar{U}) = \mathbf{q}$. A comparison of equations (5.16) and (5.12) confirms what one would expect, namely that $\hat{\mathbf{P}} = U_q/\lambda$. The virtual price of any rationed good is thus equal to the compensated marginal willingness to pay for that good. This means that the gain to the consumer of a marginal reduction in a quantity constraint, say q_i, is equal to the vertical distance, measured at the imposed quantity, between the compensated demand function $\bar{q}_i(\mathbf{p}, \hat{\mathbf{P}}, \bar{U})$ and the ruling market price. This is an important result since it states that areas under the usual

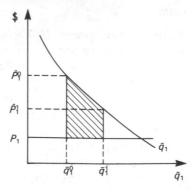

Figure 5.4 Calculating the CV or EV measures of a change in a rationed good. q_1, using the quantity-unconstrained compensated demand function where $\tilde{q}_1 = \tilde{q}_1(\mathbf{p}^0, \hat{P}_1, \bar{U})$

compensated demand curves have a distinct meaning even under conditions of rationing. In other words, the compensated demand functions derived in Chapter 3 can be used to calculate the CV and EV measures associated with a change in a quantity constraint.[2] The reader should note, however, that one must calculate an area under, not to the left of, the compensated demand curve when a ration is changed, as is shown in Figure 5.4.

The following holds for the unconstrained ordinary demand functions for $\mathbf{x}$ and $\hat{\mathbf{q}}$, respectively

$$\mathbf{x} = \mathbf{x}(\mathbf{p}, y\text{-}\mathbf{Pq}, \mathbf{q}) = \mathbf{x}(\mathbf{p}, \hat{\mathbf{P}}, \hat{y}) \tag{5.17'}$$

$$\hat{\mathbf{q}} = \hat{\mathbf{q}}(\mathbf{p}, \hat{\mathbf{P}}, \hat{y}) = \mathbf{q} \tag{5.17''}$$

where $\hat{y} = \hat{e}(\mathbf{p}, \hat{\mathbf{P}}, \bar{U}) = y + (\hat{\mathbf{P}} - \mathbf{P})\mathbf{q}$, i.e. the income which, at most, enables the consumer to reach utility level $\bar{U}$, given virtual prices $\mathbf{p}, \hat{\mathbf{P}}$. Unfortunately, (5.17'') does not imply that ordinary demand curves, if observed or estimated, can be used to calculate error bounds on the loss to the consumer of quantity constraints. The problem is that $\hat{y} > y$ as long as $\hat{\mathbf{P}} > \mathbf{P}$. This means that (5.17'') defines demand functions given that income continuously adjusts to 'clear' markets. Ordinary demand curves, on the other hand, are derived by varying the price of the good in question, holding income (and all other prices) constant. Hence, for normal goods, a 'demand' curve derived from (5.17'') falls outside the ordinary fixed income demand curve as long as $\hat{\mathbf{P}} > \mathbf{P}$ since, then, $\hat{y} > y$. Only for $\hat{\mathbf{P}} = \mathbf{P}$, $\hat{y} = y$ and the curves then coincide, unless we invoke the assumption of a constant marginal utility of income, i.e. $\lambda = \lambda(p_n)$. In the latter case, uncompensated and compensated demand functions coincide and the differences between different measures vanish. This is because the demand functions are then constant with respect to changes in income (utility).

These findings complicate applications of the Willig approach, presented in Chapter 4, for determining error bounds when the area under an ordinary demand curve is used as a proxy for compensating and equivalent variations. However, Just *et al.* (1982) and Randall and Stoll (1980) have adapted the Willig technique to situations in which quantities, rather than prices, are changed. The reader interested in details is referred to equation (7.9) in Chapter 7.

Two further results should be mentioned. Firstly, both the CV and the EV measures rank any two vectors of quantity constraints in the same order as the underlying utility function. In fact, the EV measure, but not necessarily the CV measure, can be used to compare any number of projects involving quantity constraints.[3] In order to illustrate, suppose the current price–quantity constraint–income vector is denoted by **A**, and two projects or changes involving different vectors of quantity constraints are considered. Denote these by **B** and **C**. Then, if **C** is preferred to **B** and **B** is preferred to **A**, according to the consumer's well-behaved utility function, it holds that $EV_C > EV_B > 0$ while $0 < CV_C \gtreqless CV_B > 0$. Secondly, in the single ration change case, the relationship between the sizes of the three money measures considered resembles the one derived for the quantity-unconstrained measures in Chapter 4, i.e. $CV \leq S \leq EV$ for a good whose 'demand price' is a non-decreasing function of income ($\partial(V_q/\lambda)/\partial y \geq 0$). Unfortunately, no such simple relationship is generally available in the multiple ration change case.

With regard to the application of the models, it is important to note that there exists a large and growing body of literature on disequilibrium econometrics. Using such econometric techniques, the market demand curve can be identified and estimated even in situations in which effective excess supply or demand prevail (see Bowden, 1978; also Richard E. Quandt's 'Bibliography of rationing and disequilibrium models'). Once the demand curve has been estimated, it can be used to calculate changes in aggregate consumers surpluses; however, one must keep in mind the 'income adjustment' problem discussed above. Moreover, the underlying rationing scheme is of critical importance for the interpretation in terms of welfare effects. For example, one would expect different outcomes depending on whether we have an equal ration for each household or an all-or-nothing rationing rule. To my knowledge, however, no general theory of rationing schemes and their implications for applied welfare economics is available.

Appendix

The effective demand functions

In this appendix, the effective demand functions are derived. Firstly, equation (5.3) is substituted into equations (5.1) and (5.2). The maximization of (5.1) subject to (5.2) then yields the following first-order conditions for an interior solution

$$\left. \begin{aligned} \frac{\partial U(\mathbf{x}, \mathbf{q})}{\partial \mathbf{x}} - \lambda \mathbf{p} &= 0 \\[2mm] \mathbf{px} + \mathbf{Pq} - y &= 0 \end{aligned} \right\} \qquad (\text{A5.1})$$

where λ is the Lagrange multiplier of the budget constraint.

Next, (A5.1) is totally differentiated to obtain

$$\left. \begin{aligned} U_{xx}d\mathbf{x} - d\lambda \mathbf{p} &= \lambda d\mathbf{p} - U_{xq}d\mathbf{q} \\[2mm] \mathbf{p}d\mathbf{x} + 0 &= dy - \mathbf{P}d\mathbf{q} - d\mathbf{Pq} - d\mathbf{px} \end{aligned} \right\} \qquad (\text{A5.2})$$

where U_{xx} is an $n \times n$ matrix with elements $\partial^2 U/\partial x_i \partial x_j$, and U_{xq} is a $1 \times n$ vector with elements

$$U_{x,q} = \sum_{k=1}^{m} \partial^2 U/\partial x_i \partial q_k$$

Applying Cramer's rule to (A5.2) yields

$$dx_i = \frac{\lambda \sum\limits_{j=1}^{n} D_{ji}dp_j - \sum\limits_{j=1}^{n} D_{ji}U_{x,q}d\mathbf{q} + D_{n+1i}(dy - \mathbf{P}d\mathbf{q} - d\mathbf{Pq} - d\mathbf{px})}{D}$$

$$d\lambda = \frac{\lambda \sum\limits_{j=1}^{n} D_{j(n+1)}dp_j - \sum\limits_{j=1}^{n} U_{x,q}d\mathbf{q} + D_{(n+1)(n+1)}(dy - \mathbf{P}d\mathbf{q} - d\mathbf{Pq} - d\mathbf{px})}{D}$$

$$(\text{A5.3})$$

where D is the determinant of (A5.2) and D_{ij} is the cofactor of the ith row and jth column. In more compact form, the demand functions and λ can be written as

$$\left. \begin{aligned} \mathbf{x} &= \mathbf{x}(\mathbf{p}, y - \mathbf{Pq}, \mathbf{q}) \\[2mm] \lambda &= \lambda(\mathbf{p}, y - \mathbf{Pq}, \mathbf{q}) \end{aligned} \right\} \qquad (\text{A5.4})$$

In particular, note from (A5.3) that a change in a price of a rationed good only has an income effect on demand for unrationed goods and the marginal utility of income. A change in a ration level, on the other hand, is also seen to affect the marginal utilities of unrationed goods and hence demands. A sufficient condition for the removal of this latter effect is that the utility function is weakly separable in the sense that

$$U(\mathbf{x}, \hat{\mathbf{q}}) = u(\mathbf{x}) + v(\hat{\mathbf{q}}) \tag{A5.5}$$

since in this case the terms $U_{x,q}$ in (A5.3) disappear. For details see Cuddington *et al.* (1984, Appendix A).

If the utility function is of the form

$$U(\mathbf{x}, \hat{\mathbf{q}}) = u(x_1, \ldots, x_{n-1}, \hat{\mathbf{q}}) + ax_n \tag{A5.6}$$

then the marginal utility of income only depends on the price of the *numéraire* good x_n; a is a constant in (A5.6). This corresponds to Samuelson's second interpretation of the constancy of the marginal utility of income or money. Note that the kind of separability assumed in (A5.5) is not sufficient to eliminate the influence of $\hat{\mathbf{q}}$ on the marginal utility of income; $\hat{\mathbf{q}}$ still affects λ through the budget constraint.

Finally, substitution of (A5.4) into the utility function gives the quantity-constrained indirect utility function

$$U(\mathbf{x}(\mathbf{p}, y - \mathbf{Pq}, \mathbf{q}), \mathbf{q}) = V(\mathbf{p}, y - \mathbf{Pq}, \mathbf{q}) \tag{A5.7}$$

Differentiation of the left-hand expression of (A5.7) with respect to, say, p_i yields

$$\frac{\partial U}{\partial p_i} = \sum_{j=1}^{n} \frac{\partial U}{\partial x_j} \frac{\partial x_j}{\partial p_i}$$

$$= \sum_{j=1}^{n} \lambda p_j \frac{\partial x_j}{\partial p_i} \tag{A5.8}$$

where the final expression is obtained from the first-order conditions (A5.1). Differentiation of the budget constraint in (A5.1) with respect to p_i yields

$$x_i + \sum_{j=1}^{n} p_j \frac{\partial x_j}{\partial p_i} = 0 \tag{A5.9}$$

Substituting this expression into (A5.8) we obtain

$$\frac{\partial U}{\partial p_i} = -\lambda x_i(\mathbf{p}, y - \mathbf{Pq}, \mathbf{q}) = \frac{\partial V(\mathbf{p}, y - \mathbf{Pq}, \mathbf{q})}{\partial p_i} \tag{A5.10}$$

a result that confirms the first line of equations (5.5) in the text. The remaining partial derivatives of the quantity-constrained indirect utility function can then be simply derived.

Finally, we show how to derive $\partial e / \partial \mathbf{q} = \mathbf{P} - U_q / \lambda$ in equations (5.12).

Suppose that the utility level is held constant; $U = \bar{U} = \bar{V}$. Then, inserting the expenditure function into the indirect utility function yields

$$\bar{V} = V(\mathbf{p}, e(\mathbf{p}, \mathbf{P}, \mathbf{q}, \bar{U}) - \mathbf{Pq}, \mathbf{q}) \qquad (A5.11)$$

This expression gives the minimum expenditure or income necessary to reach the fixed utility level $\bar{U} = \bar{V}$ for any given prices and levels of quantity constraints. Equivalently, the maximal utility from an income equal to $e(\cdot)$ is $\bar{V}$. Differentiating (A5.11) with respect to $\mathbf{q}$, using the fact that utility remains constant, yields

$$\frac{\partial \bar{V}}{\partial \mathbf{q}} = 0 = \frac{\partial V}{\partial e}\frac{\partial e}{\partial \mathbf{q}} + \frac{\partial V}{\partial \mathbf{q}}$$

$$= \lambda(\mathbf{P} + \mathbf{p}\frac{\partial \tilde{\mathbf{x}}}{\partial \mathbf{q}}) + (U_\mathbf{q} - \lambda\mathbf{P})$$

$$= \lambda\mathbf{p}\frac{\partial \tilde{\mathbf{x}}}{\partial \mathbf{q}} + U_\mathbf{q} \qquad (A5.12)$$

Inserting the final expression into the last line of (5.12) we obtain

$$\frac{\partial e}{\partial \mathbf{q}} = \mathbf{P} - \frac{U_\mathbf{q}(\tilde{\mathbf{x}}, \mathbf{q})}{\lambda} \qquad (A5.13)$$

This is the right-hand expression in the bottom line of equation (5.12).

Path independency conditions

Let us consider the welfare change measure

$$\int_c [U_\mathbf{q}(\mathbf{x}(\mathbf{p}, y - \mathbf{Pq}, \mathbf{q}), \mathbf{q}) - \lambda\mathbf{P}]d\mathbf{q} \qquad (A5.14)$$

This measure satisfies the path independency conditions

$$U_{q_i q_j} - \lambda_{q_j}P_i = U_{q_j q_i} - \lambda_{q_i}P_j \quad \text{for all } i, j \qquad (A5.15)$$

where $U_{q_i q_j} = \partial U_q/\partial q_j = \partial^2 U/\partial q_i \partial q_j$ and $\lambda_{q_i} = \partial\lambda/\partial q_i$. These symmetry conditions can be obtained by differentiating each $\partial V/\partial q_i$ in (5.5) with respect to q_j.

The money measure

$$S_\mathbf{q} = \int_c \left[\frac{U_\mathbf{q}(\mathbf{x}(\mathbf{p}, y - \mathbf{Pq}, \mathbf{q}), \mathbf{q})}{\lambda} - \mathbf{P}\right]d\mathbf{q} \qquad (A5.16)$$

is path independent if

$$U_{q_i q_j} - \frac{\lambda_{q_j}U_{q_i}}{\lambda} = U_{q_j q_i} - \frac{\lambda_{q_i}U_{q_j}}{\lambda} \quad \text{for all } i, j \qquad (A5.17)$$

There is no reason to believe that these conditions hold in the general constrained case.

The corresponding path independency conditions for the compensated money measures hold by construction. This is because the cross-quantity derivatives of the expenditure function (5.11) in the main text are symmetric (from Young's theorem discussed in Chapter 2). Hence

$$\frac{\partial^2 e}{\partial q_i \partial q_j} = \frac{\tilde{U}_{q_i q_j} \cdot \tilde{\lambda} - \tilde{U}_{q_i} \partial \tilde{\lambda}/\partial q_j}{\tilde{\lambda}^2}$$

$$= \frac{\partial^2 e}{\partial q_j \partial q_i} \quad \text{for all } i, j \tag{A5.18}$$

where a tilde denotes a compensated function.

These are also the conditions for path independency of the measures (5.13) and (5.14).

CHAPTER 6

Public goods and externalities in consumption

In the growing body of literature on the economics of the environment, the concepts of public goods and externalities are important. There are at least two basic characteristics that distinguish pure public goods from private goods. Firstly, the same unit of a public good can be consumed by many. Secondly, once a public good is provided for some individuals, it is impossible or at least very costly to exclude others from benefiting from it. A private good, on the other hand, once consumed by one individual cannot be consumed by others. Moreover, the buyer of the good is free to exclude other individuals from consuming it.

Discussions of externalities are often concerned with the case where one party affects the consumption or production possibilities of another. However, most important external effects affect a large number of individuals. For example, a dam may flood and destroy a valuable wilderness area now used for hiking, fishing, hunting, and bird watching, and hence affect many (groups of) individuals. Another example is pollution of the air and water. These examples also show that there is a close correspondence between public goods ('bads') and externalities. In fact, it is reasonable to view a public good or 'bad' as a special kind of externality in consumption.[1]

The first part of this chapter, Sections 1–4, derives consumer surplus measures for public goods. The reinterpretation of these measures in terms of 'traditional' external effects is a straightforward matter. Accordingly we proceed in a different manner in Section 5. In many situations, it is reasonable to believe that, for example, pollution affects the *quality* of private goods, say the life of cars, and public goods, such as air quality. Similarly, the 'carrying capacity' of a natural area for recreation activity may be limited so that increased use of the area erodes the utility derived from the recreation experience. Section 5 derives measures which capture both the effects of such changes in quality attributes and permit

72

an assessment in terms of market prices. In Chapter 7 other proposed methods which can be used to measure the willingness to pay for public goods/bads, are reported.

1 *A utility maximizing household consuming private and public goods*

Consider a household which consumes n private goods $x_1, \ldots, x_n$ and k public goods $z_1, \ldots, z_k$. The household's utility function

$$U = U(\mathbf{x}, \mathbf{z}) \tag{6.1}$$

is assumed to be well-behaved. The budget constraint is

$$\mathbf{px} - y = 0 \tag{6.2}$$

where $\mathbf{p} \gg 0$, and $y > 0$ is the fixed income of the household net of any lump sum taxes to finance the government's production of public goods. Hence, households do not have to pay directly for the consumption of public goods. In particular, in a multi-household economy there need not be any correspondence between the individual household's consumption of public goods and its contribution to the government's tax revenues.

The household maximizes its utility function (6.1) subject to the budget constraint (6.2). The first-order conditions for an interior solution are

$$\left. \begin{array}{l} \dfrac{\partial U(\mathbf{x}, \mathbf{z})}{\partial \mathbf{x}} - \lambda \mathbf{p} = 0 \\[2ex] \mathbf{px} - y = 0 \end{array} \right\} \tag{6.3}$$

where λ is the Lagrange multiplier of the budget constraint.

Solving the equations in (6.3) yields ordinary demand functions (and λ) as functions of prices $\mathbf{p}$, income y and the provision of public goods $\mathbf{z}$. Substitution of these functions into (6.1) gives the indirect utility function which is defined as

$$V(\mathbf{p}, y, \mathbf{z}) = \max_{\mathbf{x}} \, \{U(\mathbf{x}, \mathbf{z}) | \mathbf{px} - y = 0\}$$

$$= U(\mathbf{x}(\mathbf{p}, y, \mathbf{z}), \mathbf{z}) \tag{6.4}$$

As usual, all functions considered are assumed to be appropriately differentiable (on a set Ω_{Iz} of strictly positive prices, vectors $\mathbf{z}$ and incomes).

The demand functions for private goods in (6.4) have the usual properties described in Chapter 2 with respect to changes in prices and income. The level of provision of public goods affects the demands for private goods through the marginal utilities of such goods, i.e. $\partial^2 U/\partial x_i \partial z_j \neq 0$ in general. By differentiating (6.4) with respect to income, the reader can easily verify that the marginal utility of income, just like the demand for private goods, is a function of prices, the levels of provision of public goods, and income, in general.

The effect of a change in the provision of a public good on utility is obtained by differentiating (6.4) with respect to z_i

$$\frac{\partial V(\mathbf{p}, y, \mathbf{z})}{\partial z_i} = \lambda \mathbf{p} \frac{\partial \mathbf{x}}{\partial z_i} + \frac{\partial U}{\partial z_i} = \frac{\partial U(\mathbf{x}(\cdot), \mathbf{z})}{\partial z_i} \tag{6.5}$$

and is equal to the marginal valuation of the good in question. The optimal levels of consumption of individual private goods may also be affected by a change in z_i, but $\mathbf{p} \partial \mathbf{x}/\partial z_i$ is equal to zero when prices and income remain fixed. This is seen from the budget constraint.

2 Public goods and uncompensated money measures of utility change

A comparison of the equation in (6.5) of this chapter and the equations (5.5) in Chapter 5 reveals that the formal analysis of public goods almost parallels the analysis of rationed goods. The difference is that rationed goods were assumed to be priced in Chapter 5. Hence, there was a kind of income effect associated with changes in rations; without charging a price, this effect vanishes. If consumers have to pay a positive price, however low, for a fixed level of consumption of public goods, then the formal analysis of public goods parallels the analysis in Chapter 5. Or, to put it the other way round, if $\mathbf{P}$ is set equal to zero in Chapter 5, then the results hold also for unpriced public goods. This is the case at least at the individual level.

Nevertheless, since the analyses differ in the multi-household case, money measures will be derived. A characteristic that distinguishes public goods from private goods is non-rivalry, i.e. the same unit of a public good can be consumed by many, possibly all, individuals. Another reason for deriving money measures for public goods is the fact that most textbooks on welfare economics restrict the formal analysis to private goods. Hence, it is useful to also supply a formal treatment of public goods.

Proceeding in the same way as in the previous chapters, especially Chapter 5, we obtain the following individual utility change measure when $\mathbf{z}$ is changed from $\mathbf{z}^0$ to $\mathbf{z}^1$

$$\triangle U^h = V^h(\mathbf{p}, y^h, \mathbf{z}^1) - V^h(\mathbf{p}, y^h, \mathbf{z}^0)$$

$$= \int_c \frac{\partial V^h}{\partial \mathbf{z}} d\mathbf{z} = \int_c \frac{\partial U^h(x^h(\mathbf{p}, y, \mathbf{z}), \mathbf{z})}{\partial \mathbf{z}} d\mathbf{z} \tag{6.6}$$

where a superscript h refers to the hth household, and c is some path (in Ω_{Iz}) between initial and final $\mathbf{z}$-vectors. Summing over all H individuals yields

$$\Sigma_h \triangle U^h = \Sigma_h \int_c \frac{\partial U^h}{\partial \mathbf{z}} d\mathbf{z} \tag{6.7}$$

Accordingly, the effect of a change in the provision of public goods is equal to the sum of the individual marginal valuations of $\mathbf{z}$ between $\mathbf{z}^0$ and $\mathbf{z}^1$. If only a subset of individuals, say those living in a certain area, are affected, then (6.6) will be equal to zero for all other individuals living in the country under consideration.

Equation (6.7) must be interpreted with care; (6.7) gives the sum of the individuals valuation of the change in $\mathbf{z}$. From the discussion of aggregate welfare change measures in Section 2 of Chapter 4 it should be obvious that the change in society's welfare need not be equal to the unweighted sum of individual utility changes. A direct correspondence between the change in the society's welfare and the change reported by expression (6.7) holds only if the welfare weights are equal across all affected individuals over the entire path considered. This should be remembered when reading the remainder of this chapter.

Since, in general, utility functions are unobservable it is useful to convert (6.6) and (6.7) to money measures of utility change. This is done by dividing by λ^h, the marginal utility of income of the hth individual. A sufficient condition for λ^h to be constant with respect to changes in $\mathbf{z}$ is that the utility function is weakly separable in $\mathbf{z}$, i.e. there exists a monotone transformation such that $U = u(\mathbf{x}) + v(\mathbf{z})$. From the first-order conditions (6.3) for utility maximization it is seen that this property eliminates the influence of $\mathbf{z}$ on both demands for goods and the marginal utility of income. An alternative approach would be to assume that the utility function is quasi-linear with some private good, say the nth good, being the *numéraire* good. This assumption ensures that ordinary uncompensated measures and compensated measures coincide, since $\lambda^h = a/p_n$, where $a > 0$ is a constant, from the first-order conditions for utility maximization. As is demonstrated below, the aforementioned separability assumption does not ensure this property.

More importantly, the assumption that λ^h is constant with respect to changes in $\mathbf{z}$ for all h ensures that the money measure of utility change is path independent and can be written as

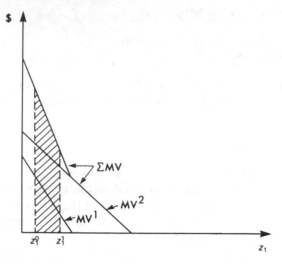

Figure 6.1 Individual and aggregate ordinary marginal willingness to pay curves for a public good; $MV^i = [\partial U^i(\mathbf{x}^i, \mathbf{z})/\partial z_1]/\lambda^i$

$$\Sigma_h \triangle U^h/\bar{\lambda}^h = S_{\mathbf{z}} = \Sigma_h \int_c \frac{\partial U^h(\mathbf{x}^h, \mathbf{z})/\partial \mathbf{z}}{\bar{\lambda}^h} d\mathbf{z} \tag{6.8}$$

where $\bar{\lambda}^h$ is a constant.

This measure yields the sum of each individual's uncompensated marginal willingness to pay for a change in the vector $\mathbf{z}$ from $\mathbf{z}^0$ to $\mathbf{z}^1$. This is illustrated in Figure 6.1 for the single public good case. For the sake of simplicity, assume that only two individuals are affected. Their marginal valuations of the public good are vertically added since the consumption of a public good by one individual does not restrict the other individual(s) consumption of the good. The shaded area in the figure gives the aggregate willingness to pay for a change from z_1^0 to z_1^1. This area is proportional to the sum of changes in utility provided λ^h is constant over the considered path for each indvidual.

3 *Compensating and equivalent variations*

In empirical investigations, households are typically asked, for example, to make financial sacrifices in return for better air quality or are offered compensation in order to induce them to accept worse air quality. For this reason the concepts of compensating variation and equivalent variation are useful. In order to derive income compensated measures, the expenditure functions are defined as

$$e^h(\mathbf{p}, \mathbf{z}, \bar{U}^h) = \min_{\mathbf{x}^h} \{\mathbf{p}\mathbf{x}^h | U^h(\mathbf{x}^h, \mathbf{z}) \geqslant \bar{U}^h\} \quad \text{for all } h$$

$$= \mathbf{p}\bar{\mathbf{x}}^h(\mathbf{p}, \mathbf{z}, \bar{U}^h) \tag{6.9}$$

The expenditure function of the hth individual gives the minimum expenditure required to reach the specified utility level, given prices $\mathbf{p}$ and the provision of public goods $\mathbf{z}$.

The compensated demand functions for private goods in (6.9) have the usual properties with respect to changes in $\mathbf{p}$ and $\bar{U}^h$. An increase in $\mathbf{z}$ affects demands for private goods through the marginal utilities of such goods, in general. Moreover, since an increase in $\mathbf{z}$ increases utility, expenditure on private goods must fall in order to maintain the individual at the specified utility level. In general, the sign of the total effect of a change in a z_i on the demand for a private good is ambiguous. It should be noted, however, that the separability assumption discussed in Section 2 ensures that the effect on the marginal utilities of private goods vanishes. Then, if private goods are normal, an increase in $\mathbf{z}$ reduces demand for such goods. This is because income must be reduced in order for the individual to remain at the specified utility level.

Differentiating (6.9) with respect to $\mathbf{z}$ yields

$$\frac{\partial e^h}{\partial \mathbf{z}} = \mathbf{p}\partial\bar{\mathbf{x}}^h/\partial \mathbf{z} = -\mu^h \frac{\partial U^h(\bar{\mathbf{x}}^h, \mathbf{z})}{\partial \mathbf{z}} \tag{6.10}$$

i.e. the negative of the sum of marginal valuations of public goods multiplied by the marginal cost μ^h of utility. Expenditure on private goods must be reduced in order to restore the prespecified level of satisfaction since an increased provision of public goods increases utility. To obtain the final expression in (6.10), the utility function (6.1) is totally differentiated, the utility level is held constant and the usual first-order conditions for expenditure minimization are inserted, to obtain

$$d\bar{U}^h = \frac{\partial U^h}{\partial \bar{\mathbf{x}}^h}d\bar{\mathbf{x}}^h + \frac{\partial U^h}{\partial \mathbf{z}}d\mathbf{z}$$

$$= \frac{1}{\mu^h}\mathbf{p}d\bar{\mathbf{x}}^h + \frac{\partial U^h}{\partial \mathbf{z}}d\mathbf{z} = 0 \tag{6.11}$$

where $\mu^h = \mu^h(\mathbf{p}, \mathbf{z}, \bar{U}^h)$ is the Lagrange multiplier of the cost minimization problem. Equation (6.11) explains the equality obtained in (6.10).

The aggregate compensating variation associated with discrete changes in the provision of public goods $\mathbf{z}$ can be defined as

$$\mathrm{CV_z} = \Sigma_h[e^h(\mathbf{p}, \mathbf{z}^0, U^{h0}) - e^h(\mathbf{p}, \mathbf{z}^1, U^{h0})]$$

$$= \Sigma_h\int_c \frac{\partial e^h}{\partial \mathbf{z}}d\mathbf{z} = \Sigma_h\int_c(\mu^h\frac{\partial U^h(\bar{\mathbf{x}}^h, \mathbf{z})}{\partial \mathbf{z}})d\mathbf{z} \tag{6.12}$$

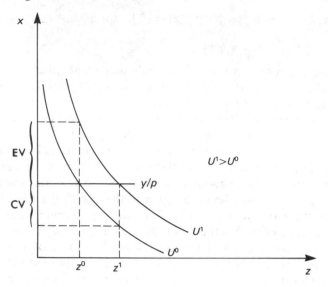

Figure 6.2 Compensated money measures associated with an increase in the provision of a public good z. Note that the equivalent variation associated with a decrease in z from z^1 to z^0 is equal to $-CV$ while the compensating variation is equal to $-EV$

where, for expositional simplicity, all prices and exogenous income are fixed. The change in $\mathbf{z}$ is now evaluated under compensated marginal willingness to pay curves. In order to interpret the CV_z measure, let us first consider the individual consumer. The compensating variation is the maximum amount of money that the individual is willing to pay to secure an increased provision of public goods. If the supply of z is reduced, then the CV_z measure gives the minimum compensation that must be given to the individual while leaving him as well off as before the reduction in $\mathbf{z}$. See Figure 6.2 for a graphical illustration of these results. In order to obtain an aggregate measure, as in (6.12), the compensating variations for all affected individuals are added together. In the case of an equivalent variation measure, each individual remains at his final, as opposed to his initial, level of satisfaction. This measure represents the sum of the minimum (maximum) sum of money that must be given to (taken from) each individual to make him as well off as he would have been following an increase (decrease) in $\mathbf{z}$.

The CV_z measure (like the EV_z measure) is path independent since the integrand in (6.12) is an exact differential of the expenditure function.[2] Hence, the order in which z_i and z_j are changed makes no difference, but

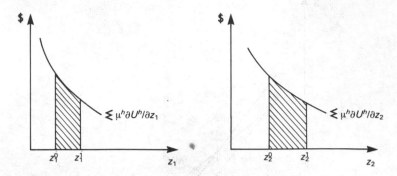

Figure 6.3 Evaluating a change in the levels of provision of two public goods, where

$\mu^h = \mu^h(\mathbf{a})$ 　　　　　　　　　　$\mu^h = \mu^h = \mu^h(\mathbf{b})$

$\partial U^h/\partial z_1 = f^h(\bar{\mathbf{x}}^h(\mathbf{a}), z_1, z_2^0)$ 　　　$\partial U^h/\partial z_2 = f^h(\bar{\mathbf{x}}^h(\mathbf{b}), z_1^1, z_2)$

$\mathbf{a} = (\mathbf{p}, z_1, z_2^0, U^0)$ 　　　　　$\mathbf{b} = (\mathbf{p}, z_1^1, z_2, U^0)$

the individual's marginal willingness to pay curve for z_i must be evaluated subject to all previously considered changes in the provision of other public goods. This is illustrated in Figure 6.3. Moreover, it is a straight-forward matter to generalize the measures to capture changes in prices and exogenous income since the path independency conditions remain valid. General measures that capture changes in prices, the provision of public goods, and quantity constraints can be found in the appendix to this chapter and in Section 1 of Chapter 11.

4 *On the properties of money measures*

In general the CV_z and EV_z measures impute different dollar values to a utility change. This is because the marginal willingness to pay for a public good depends on the utility level. Once again, however, a quasi-linear utility function ensures that $S_z = CV_z = EV_z$, i.e. that all money measures impute the same money gain to the utility change that follows from an increase in the provision of public goods. The reader should also note that the weak separability assumption discussed in Section 2 ensures that the ordinary money measure is proportional to $\triangle U$, since the marginal utility of income will be constant with respect to changes in $\mathbf{z}$. However, this is not the case for the compensated money measures of an increase in $\mathbf{z}$ since income must be reduced in order to maintain the individual at the specified utility level. Some inspection of the first-order

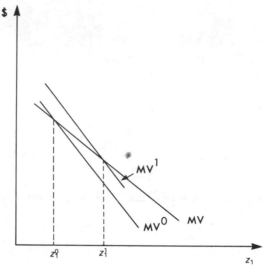

Figure 6.4 Aggregate marginal willingness to pay curves for a public good. The MV^0-curve (MV^1-curve) maintains each individual at his initial (final) utility level, while the MV-curve assumes that each individual is free to adjust his utility level

conditions (6.3) should convince the reader that λ ($= 1/\mu$) depends on income even when the utility function is weakly separable in public goods.

However, if public goods are 'normal', then $CV_z < S_z < EV_z$ in the case of a change in supply of a single public good. For a 'normal' public good, the marginal willingness to pay is an increasing function of income, i.e. $\partial(V_z/\lambda)\partial y > 0$. The result then follows by noting that the money measures refer to gradually higher utility (income) levels (see, for example, Hicks, 1946). In other words, when a public good is normal in the above sense, a marginal willingness to pay curve that refers to a higher utility level must lie above a curve that refers to a lower utility level. This is illustrated in Figure 6.4.

This has an important implication for applied research in the field. Let us assume that we have collected preference information by asking the consumers how much they are willing to pay for some change in the provision of a public good or an environmental service. If this measure is interpreted as a compensating variation and the good is normal, we know that the resulting amount of money would be smaller than if the consumers had been questioned regarding their equivalent variations (or, for that matter, ordinary willingness to pay).

These money measures are also unaffected if the utility function is subjected to a monotone increasing transformation $f(U(\mathbf{x},\mathbf{z}))$. Intuitively, indifference surfaces are unaffected by the transformation; they are simply relabelled. Therefore, the minimum cost or income necessary to reach any given indifference surface (commodity bundle) remains unchanged. This may be easily verified using (6.12). The new marginal cost of utility, μ^* say, can be seen to be equal to the initial one divided by $\partial f/\partial U$. Thus, this last derivative appears in both the numerator and the denominator of the money measure.

Nevertheless, by performing such a transform of the utility function, it can be easily verified that in terms of the example used in Chapter 4, where $EV_A^k = \$100$ and $EV_B^k = \$50$, we are unable to conclude that the consumer likes project A twice as much as project B. This is the case, at least in an ordinal world, where preferences lack intensities, i.e. only the ranking of bundles (projects) makes sense. In a cardinal world, the above relationship between A and B holds if and only if the marginal utility λ of income is constant over the entire path considered. In all other cases, the only inference that can be made from $EV_A^k = \$100$ and $EV_B^k = \$50$ is that the consumer prefers project A to project B.

It is also important to note that if we compare two (or more) final vectors of public goods, e.g. $\mathbf{z}^1$ and $\mathbf{z}^2$, the EV measure will rank these, and the initial vector $\mathbf{z}^0$, say, in the same order as the consumer. This is not necessarily true for the CV measure, as is demonstrated in the appendix to this chapter. The EV measure always selects the cheapest commodity bundle necessary to reach a particular (the final) utility level. Thus, if $\mathbf{z}^1$ is cheaper than $\mathbf{z}^2$, the former must correspond to a lower utility level. The CV measure, on the other hand, compares the cost of achieving the *initial* utility level when $\mathbf{z}$ is fixed at $\mathbf{z}^1$ and $\mathbf{z}^2$ respectively. Even if the two vectors should correspond to the same *final* utility level, the associated changes in costs need not coincide. Hence the inference from the CV measure that one vector is preferred to the other may be incorrect. Figure 6.2 can be used to give an idea of these results. For example, the CV of an increase in income from y to $y+EV$ with $\mathbf{z}=\mathbf{z}^0$ is equal to EV and exceeds the CV of an increase in $\mathbf{z}$ from $\mathbf{z}^0$ to $\mathbf{z}^1$ with income held fixed at y. The two EV measures, on the other hand, coincide and hence correctly indicate that the consumer is indifferent between the two considered changes.

From a practical point of view, these results are extremely important. If only a single z_i is changed, both the CV measure and the EV measure rank the change in the same order as the consumer would do. In fact, both measures are suitable for any *binary* comparison, i.e. for the comparison of any two vectors of public goods. However, if a study involves the comparison of more than two vectors, only the EV measure will necessarily rank the vectors correctly. In order to illustrate this point, assume that a decision to close one of two national parks is under way. The visitors are assumed to be indifferent with regard to which park is closed. Nevertheless, let us further assume that information is collected about the compensation that would have to be paid for the initial level of satisfaction to be maintained following the closure of either park. The resulting aggregate CV measures may provide an incorrect indication that visitors are more concerned about the preservation of one of the parks.[3] The two EV measures, on the other hand, will be of equal size and hence correctly indicate that the consumer is indifferent with regard to which park is closed. The reader who still needs to employ the CV measure may assume that the utility function is such that the ordinary money measure is path independent. This assumption ensures that the CV measure can be used to compare any number of z-vectors. The same kind of restriction on the utility function applies in the case of rationing.

Finally, it should also be noted that (uncompensated as well as compensated) consumer surplus measures may be infinite if the MV-curves in Figure 6.4 do not intersect the $-axis (see the appendix to this chapter for further details). It does not seem unlikely that certain environmental goods have infinite consumer surpluses in terms of the compensation required for utility to remain unchanged if the resource is destroyed. For example, advances in technology cannot augment the supply, and reduce the scarcity value, of the amenity resources of a natural environment. The value of its extractive resources on the other hand may be reduced by changes in technology and production of close substitutes (see Fisher and Peterson, 1976; also Knetsch and Sinden, 1984). Hence, the loss of a unique environment may be more irreversible than the extraction of a non-renewable resource since substitutes for the latter can be made available. This issue will be further discussed in Chapters 9 and 11.

5 *External effects, quality changes, and market data*

An external effect occurs when the utility of a consumer depends upon the consumption or production levels of other agents in the economy. As noted earlier in this chapter, Samuelsonian public goods represent a type of externality in consumption. For this reason, the consumer surplus measures derived in Sections 1–4 can be given quite broad interpretations. The measures can be used for an analysis of positive external effects and, with reversed signs, negative external effects. This is because an externality, like a public good, is usually modelled by including the externality as a separate argument in the utility functions of households.

Moreover, neither externalities nor public goods appear in the budget constraint of a household.

However, the measures derived in the previous sections are not directly observable from market data. This section, following Bradford and Hildebrandt (1977), Mäler (1971; 1974), Small and Rosen (1981), and Willig (1978), develops an approach which can be tested with market data. Suppose z_i represents the quality attributes of the private good x_i or is a public good which is complementary to x_i. Below we employ the stronger assumption that when $x_i = 0$ then the level of z_i makes no difference, i.e. $\partial U(x_1, \ldots, 0, \ldots, x_n, \mathbf{z})/\partial z_i = 0$. Next assume that x_i is non-essential. Formally, for any commodity bundle $\mathbf{x}, \mathbf{z} \geqslant 0$ there exists $\mathbf{x}', \mathbf{z}$ such that $U(\mathbf{x}, \mathbf{z}) = U(x_1', \ldots, 0, \ldots, x_n', \mathbf{z})$, i.e. any bundle including x_i can be matched by some other bundle which excludes x_i.

Willig (1978) has shown that when $x_i = 0$, then $\partial U(\cdot)/\partial z_i = 0$ if and only if, the indirect utility function (6.4) has the following property:

$$\lim_{p_i \to \infty} \frac{\partial V(p_i, \bar{\mathbf{p}}, \bar{y}, z_i^0, \bar{\mathbf{z}})}{\partial z_i} = 0 \tag{6.13}$$

for all $\bar{\mathbf{p}} \geqslant 0$ and $\bar{y} > 0$, where $\bar{\mathbf{p}}$ and $\bar{\mathbf{z}}$ are row vectors whose elements are the fixed prices of goods x_j and the fixed levels of z_j for all $j \neq i$ respectively. Moreover, z_i^0 denotes the initial level of z_i. *Condition (6.13) simply states that if the price of good x_i is so high that the good is not consumed, then its quality does not matter.*

Using these assumptions, it is possible to derive a money measure of quality changes which can be estimated from market data. Since these calculations are fairly tedious, they have been placed in the appendix to this chapter. The money measure associated with a discrete change in z_i can be written as

$$S_z = -\int_{p_i^0}^{\infty} [x_i(p_i, \bar{\mathbf{p}}, \bar{y}, z_i^0, \bar{\mathbf{z}}) - x_i(p_i, \bar{\mathbf{p}}, \bar{y}, z_i^1, \bar{\mathbf{z}})] dp_i \tag{6.14}$$

The right-hand side of (6.14) gives the change in the area to the left of the ordinary demand curve for the ith commodity as it shifts in response to a shift in the quality parameter z_i. This is illustrated in Figure 6.5. A simple example, which may help to clarify this result, can be found in the appendix to this chapter.

Hence, it is possible to infer the value that the consumer places on a change in the quality of a private good or in the supply of complementary public good by calculating the change in the consumer's surplus of a private good. Thus, it is not necessary to derive the underlying utility and expenditure functions, or to estimate complete systems of demand

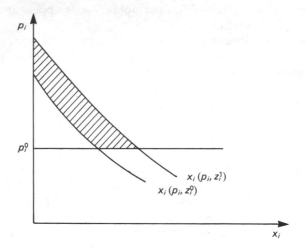

Figure 6.5 The value of a change in the quality attributes of a good (shaded area)

equations. However, as usual, this assumes that the path independency conditions apply.

Equation (6.14) applies to a single consumer, whereas most available demand data refers to the market behaviour of consumers in the aggregate. The market demand function for x_i can be used to measure the effect of a quality change provided all individuals find the good non-essential, and the path independency conditions are satisfied for all H individuals. For example, the latter conditions apply when there are no income effects on demands for goods. Given this assumption, the change in consumers surplus, measured left of the market demand curve, would be an exact measure of the sum of the individual gains.

The assumptions needed to establish this result may seem quite restrictive. None the less, in many circumstances, the availability of a method that only requires data on demand functions for private goods could turn out to be valuable. In particular, the approach does not require the econometric estimation of complete systems of demand equations. The above analysis has demonstrated that the method requires only information on the demand for the single commodity. The approach also suggests a practical methodology for the calculation of so-called hedonic price adjustments. This will be shown in Chapter 7, where different empirical methods are reviewed.

However, before turning to this review, a compensated measure of quality changes in a non-essential good is presented. It should be borne in mind that compensated measures are constructed in such a way that the path independency conditions are satisfied. In general this is not true for uncompensated measures. The compensated measure, which is derived in the appendix to this chapter, can be written as

$$\text{CV}_z = -\int_{p_i^0}^{\infty}[\bar{x}_i(p_i, \bar{\mathbf{p}}, z_i^0, \bar{\mathbf{z}}, \bar{U}) - x_i(p_i, \bar{\mathbf{p}}, z_i^1, \bar{\mathbf{z}}, \bar{U})]dp_i \tag{6.15}$$

This suggests that changes in compensated demand curves can be used to provide a direct measure of the willingness to pay for quality changes or changes in the provision of certain types of public goods or 'bads'. Adding the compensating variations (6.15) for all consumers one obtains the aggregate compensating variation. The error made when the area left of an ordinary demand curve is used instead of the CV or EV measures can be calculated from formulas developed by Willig (1976) and Randall and Stoll (1980).

In closing, it should also be noted that the analysis of quality attributes is easily generalized in diverse directions. For example, each private and public good could be assumed to have certain quality characteristics. These attributes may be affected by, for example, pollution. Cicchetti and Smith (1976) and Stahl (1983c) have developed such a model within the framework of Lancaster's (1966) theory of consumer choice in which the household's utility function is written as $U = U(\mathbf{ax}, \mathbf{bz})$, where $\mathbf{a}$ and $\mathbf{b}$ are vectors of characteristics, i.e. $\mathbf{ax}$ and $\mathbf{bz}$ give the quality-adjusted levels of consumption of private and public goods. The quality attributes are exogenous from the point of view of the household. If the quality of a commodity decreases for one reason or the other, then one unit of the commodity (x_i or z_j) yields less utility than before the deterioriation in quality. The demand functions for private goods are obtained by maximizing the utility function subject to the household's budget constraint (6.2). From a purely formal point of view, the analysis of this model almost parallels the analysis in the previous sections of this chapter. For this reason the interested reader is referred to Stahl (1983c) for a detailed investigation of the properties of a similar model.

Hori (1975) developed a household production model incorporating public goods as inputs to the household production function. The model is used to suggest an approach to the determination of individual demand for public goods from information derived from private goods markets. In order to illustrate the spirit of household production function models, consider the following utility function:

$$U = U(\mathbf{x}, f(\mathbf{X}, \mathbf{z})) \tag{6.16}$$

where $\mathbf{x}$ is a vector of private goods consumed, and $Z = f(\mathbf{X}, \mathbf{z})$ is a good or a service produced by the household using private and public goods as inputs. For example, Z could be a trip to a recreation area which is 'produced' using a car (X) and roads (z) as inputs. The household maximizes (6.16) subject to the budget constraint $y = px + PX$, and the given supply of public goods.

If the production function f(   ) is known, the marginal willingness to pay for z can easily be calculated once the demand functions $X = X(p, y, z)$ are estimated. In general, however, the functional form of the household production function is unknown. Nevertheless, Mäler (1981) has shown that, by making assumptions about certain broad characteristics of the production function, such as whether an input is essential or not or whether two inputs are substitutes or complements, it is possible to calculate the marginal willingness to pay for z from market data. The analysis, which assumes that just two inputs (a private good and a public good) are used to produce Z, largely parallels the above analysis of quality changes and is not performed here. The interested reader is referred to Hori (1975) and Mäler (1981).

In the models discussed so far, the quality attributes, like the prices and income, are exogenous to the consumer, i.e. the analysis focuses on objective measures of quality. Recently, however, Hanemann (1984c) has assumed subjective perceptions of quality, and used Shannon's entropy statistic as a means of measuring the degree of consensus in ordinal ratings of recreation site quality. The advantage of this approach is that differences in choices may be explained by differences in consumer's perception of quality, as well as in their underlying preferences (see Hanemann, 1984c, for details).

Appendix

Some comments on the properties of the EV and CV measures

In order to demonstrate that the EV measure ranks any number of commodity bundles correctly (provided there is a single reference vector), it is sufficient to consider the following example:

$$
\left.
\begin{aligned}
EV^1 &= e(p^0, P^0, q^0, z^0, U^1) - e(p^0, P^0, q^0, z^0, U^0) \\
EV^2 &= e(p^0, P^0, q^0, z^0, U^2) - e(p^0, P^0, q^0, z^0, U^0)
\end{aligned}
\right\} \quad (A6.1)
$$

where p and P are vectors of prices, q is a vector of rations, z is a vector of public goods, and a superscript refers to a particular level of prices, etc. Since the expenditure function is strictly increasing in utility, it follows that $U^2 \geqslant U^1 \geqslant U^0$, then $EV^2 \geqslant EV^1 \geqslant 0$, i.e. the EV measure ranks the different bundles in the same order as the underlying utility function.

Consider next the corresponding CV measures:

$$CV^1 = e(\mathbf{p}^1, \mathbf{P}^1, \mathbf{q}^1, \mathbf{z}^1, U^1) - e(\mathbf{p}^1, \mathbf{P}^1, \mathbf{q}^1, \mathbf{z}^1, U^0)$$

$$CV^2 = e(\mathbf{p}^2, \mathbf{P}^2, \mathbf{q}^2, \mathbf{z}^2, U^2) - e(\mathbf{p}^2, \mathbf{P}^2, \mathbf{q}^2, \mathbf{z}^2, U^0) \qquad \left.\right\} \quad \text{(A6.2)}$$

Thus, $U^2 \geqslant U^1 \geqslant U^0$ implies that both measures in (A6.2) have non-negative signs. However, it is far from self-evident that $CV^2 \geqslant CV^1$ since the measures are based on different values of $\mathbf{p}$, $\mathbf{q}$ and $\mathbf{z}$. In fact it is fairly easy to demonstrate that the CV measure may fail to rank the changes correctly. For example, using the simple utility function $U = (x_1 z_1 + 1)(x_2 + 1) + (z_1 z_2)^{1/2}$, the reader can easily check that the CV measure fails to correctly rank the three $\mathbf{z}$-vectors $\mathbf{z}^0 = (1,1)$, $\mathbf{z}^1 = (2,1)$ and $\mathbf{z}^2 = (1,994.7)$ for $p_1 = p_2 = 1$, $U^0 = 10$, $U^1 = U^2 \approx 67.5$, and no quantity constraints. This example is sufficient to prove the claim that the CV measure need not rank any three or more bundles correctly.

A utility function that is separable in $\mathbf{z}$ produces a CV measure that provides a correct ranking of any number of $\mathbf{z}$-vectors. This is easily verified using

$$V(\cdot) = f(\mathbf{p}, y) + v(\mathbf{z})$$

$$e(\cdot) = \mathbf{p}\bar{\mathbf{x}}(\mathbf{p}, \bar{U} - v(\mathbf{z}))$$

Moreover, the CV measure associated with the (quasi-linear) utility function

$$V(\cdot) = g(\mathbf{p}, \mathbf{q}, \mathbf{z}) - \mathbf{Pq} + y$$

with $p_n = 1$, is easily shown to rank $\mathbf{p}, \mathbf{P}, \mathbf{q}, y, \mathbf{z}$-vectors correctly.

Using (A6.1) and (A6.2) it can be shown fairly simply that the CV measure, although not necessarily the EV measure, ranks any number of bundles correctly when there are several *initial* bundles but one final bundle. This exercise is left to the reader.

Finally, let us use, for example, the first line of (A6.2) to obtain a money measure that generalizes those derived in Chapters 3, 5 and 6:

$$CV^1 = \int_c [-\bar{\mathbf{x}} d\mathbf{p} + (\mu U_\mathbf{q} - \mathbf{P}^0) d\mathbf{q} - \mathbf{q}^1 d\mathbf{P} + \mu U_\mathbf{z} d\mathbf{z}] \qquad \text{(A6.2')}$$

where c is some path between initial and final $\mathbf{p}$, $\mathbf{q}$, $\mathbf{P}$, $\mathbf{z}$ vectors, $U_\mathbf{k} = \partial U(\bar{\mathbf{x}}, \mathbf{q}, \mathbf{z})/\partial \mathbf{k}$, with $\mathbf{k} = \mathbf{q}, \mathbf{z}$ and $\bar{\mathbf{x}} = \bar{\mathbf{x}}(\mathbf{p}, y - \mathbf{Pq}, \mathbf{q}, \mathbf{z})$. As usual a particular change is evaluated subject to all previously considered changes in prices, rations and the provision of public goods.

Quality changes

In order to derive an observable measure of quality changes, we need the properties of the indirect utility function $V = V(p, \bar{\mathbf{p}}, \bar{y}, z^0, \bar{\mathbf{z}})$, where z^0 denotes the initial level of z_i, and $p = p_i$. For convenient reference, these properties are repeated in a slightly different form here, suppressing the constants $\bar{p}$, $\bar{y}$ and $\bar{z}$ in order to simplify notation

$$
\left.
\begin{aligned}
\frac{\partial V(p, z^0)/\partial p}{\lambda} &= \frac{V_p}{\lambda} = -x(p, z^0) \\[6pt]
\frac{\partial V(p, z^0)}{\partial y} &= V_y = \lambda(p, z^0) \\[6pt]
\frac{\partial V(p, z^0)/\partial z}{\lambda} &= \frac{V_z}{\lambda} = \frac{U_z}{\lambda}
\end{aligned}
\right\} \tag{A6.3}
$$

First, using the middle expression of the final line in (A6.3) and letting p take values p^0 and p^f respectively, where p^0 is the actual market price of x_i for which $x_i^0 > 0$, and p^f $[p^f \in (p^0, \infty)]$ denotes a price which is so high that x_i is not consumed 'at all', we obtain

$$
\begin{aligned}
\frac{V_z(p^f, z^0)}{\lambda(p^f, z^0)} - \frac{V_z(p^0, z^0)}{\lambda(p^0, z^0)} &= \int_{p^0}^{p^f} \frac{\partial (V_z/\lambda)}{\partial p}\, dp \\[6pt]
&= \int_{p^0}^{p^f} \frac{V_{zp}\lambda - V_z\lambda_p}{\lambda^2}\, dp \\[6pt]
&= -\frac{V_z(p^0, z^0)}{\lambda(p^0, z^0)} \tag{A6.4}
\end{aligned}
$$

where subscripts z and p denote partial derivatives. The final expression follows from the fact that $V_z = 0$ while λ still is positive and finite when $p \geqslant p^f$ (see Willig, 1978).

Next, the first line in (A6.3) is differentiated with respect to z and both sides integrated between $p = p^0$ and $p = p^f$ to obtain

$$
\begin{aligned}
\int_{p^0}^{p^f} \frac{\partial (V_p/\lambda)}{\partial z}\, dp &= \int_{p^0}^{p^f} \frac{V_{pz}\lambda - V_p\lambda_z}{\lambda^2}\, dp \\[6pt]
&= -\int_{p^0}^{p^f} x_z(p, z^0)\, dp \tag{A6.5}
\end{aligned}
$$

Comparing the final equalities in (A6.4) and (A6.5), it can be seen that

$$
\frac{V_z(p^0, z^0)}{\lambda} = \int_{p^0}^{p^f} x_z(p, z^0)\, dp \tag{A6.6}
$$

if $V_z\lambda_p = V_p\lambda_z$. which, by invoking (A6.3), can be shown to be the path independency condition. Then (A6.6) gives the change in the area to the left of the ordinary demand curve as it shifts in response to a marginal shift in the quality paramenter z. Integration between z_i^0 and z_i^1 yields the measure discussed in the main text. See also equation (A6.10).

The assumptions made regarding the properties of the utility function, i.e. good x_i is non-essential and $\partial U/\partial z_i = 0$ whenever $x_i = 0$, imply that the expenditure function has the following properties:

$$\left.\begin{array}{l} \lim_{p_i \to \infty} e(p_i, z_i^0, \bar{U}) = L < \infty \\[2em] \lim_{p_i \to \infty} \dfrac{\partial e(p_i, z_i^0, \bar{U})}{\partial z_i} = 0 \end{array}\right\} \qquad (A6.7)$$

where all prices and levels of quality attributes except p_i and z_i^0 have been omitted since they remain fixed throughout the analysis. The equations in (A6.7) state that if the price of a non-essential good approaches infinity then expenditure reaches and remains at a finite level L. Moreover, this level is constant with respect to changes in the quality of x_i, because none of the good is consumed.

The (compensating variation) change in the consumer's surplus when p_i is increased from $p_i = p_i^0$ to $p_i \to \infty$, *ceteris paribus*, can be written as

$$CV_p = e(p_i^0, z_i^0, U^0) - e(\infty, z_i^0, U^0)$$
$$= -\int_c \tilde{x}_i(p_i, z_i^0, U^0)dp_i \qquad (A6.8)$$

This measure gives the area to the left of the compensated demand curve for x_i between its intersection with the price axis and the price p_i^0. The fact that the integrand is zero for sufficiently high price levels causes no difficulty in integrating (A6.8).

Differentiating (A6.8) with respect to z_i, using the second property given in (A6.7), we obtain

$$\frac{\partial e(p_i^0, z_i^0, U^0)}{\partial z_i} = -\int_c \frac{\partial \tilde{x}_i}{\partial z_i} dp_i \qquad (A6.9)$$

This result enables us to evaluate marginal quality changes in terms of changes in the consumer's surplus. Integration of (A6.9) between z_i^0 and z_i^1 yields

$$CV_{z_i} = -\int_{p_i^0}^{\infty} \int_{z_i^0}^{z_i^1} [\partial \tilde{x}_i(p_i, \bar{p}, z_i, \bar{z}, \bar{U})/\partial z_i]dz_i dp_i$$
$$= -\int_{p_i^0}^{\infty} [\tilde{x}_i(p_i, \bar{p}, z_i^0, \bar{z}, \bar{U}) - \tilde{x}_i(p_i, \bar{p}, z_i^1, \bar{z}, \bar{U})]dp_i \qquad (A6.10)$$

where previously omitted constants have been inserted. This is the compensated money measure of a change in the quality of a private good discussed in the main text.

An example may be useful. Let us assume that the indirect utility function is

$$V = \ell n \, z_1 - \ell n \, p_1 - \ell n \, p_2 + y + \frac{p_1}{z_1} \qquad (A6.11)$$

Taking partial derivatives yields

$$\frac{\partial V}{\partial p_1} = -\lambda x_1 = -\frac{1}{p_1} + \frac{1}{z_1}$$

$$\left.\begin{array}{l} \\ \\ \end{array}\right\} \qquad (A6.12)$$

$$\frac{\partial V}{\partial z_1} = \frac{1}{z_1} - \frac{p_1}{z_1^2}$$

The money measure (A6.6) can be written as

$$\int_c \frac{\partial x_1}{\partial z_1} dp_1 = \int_c \frac{1}{z_1^2} dp_1$$

$$= \frac{z_1}{z_1^2} - \frac{p_1^0}{z_1^2} = \frac{\partial V}{\partial z_1} \qquad (A6.13)$$

where $c = (p_1^f, p_1^0)'$, and $p_1^f = z_1$ since $x_1 = 0$ if $p_1 \geqslant z_1$ as can be seen from the first line of (A6.12).

Finally, it should be mentioned that the indirect utility function (A6.11) corresponds to a direct utility function of the form $U = \ell n(z_1 x_1 + 1) + \ell n \, x_2 + x_3$.

'Kinks', 'jump discontinuities', and 'improper integrals'

In Section 5 of this chapter as well as in Chapter 8 we consider demand functions for non-essential commodites that have the property that $x_i > 0$ for $p_i < p_i^f$ and $x_i = 0$ for $p_i \geqslant p_i^f (p_i^f < \infty)$. The integration over the resulting 'kink' (or point of discontinuity of the unconditional demand function for on-site time in Chapter 8) does not present any difficulties. A function which is continuous in a closed interval, i.e. an interval that contains its end points, is integrable. The same is more generally true of bounded functions that are defined and continuous (in closed or open intervals) with the possible exception of a finite number of points.

Consider the integral

$$\int_{p_i^0}^{p_i^*} x_i(p_i, \bar{\mathbf{p}}, y) dp_i = \int_{p_i^0}^{p_i^f} x_i(p_i, \bar{\mathbf{p}}, y) dp_i + \int_{p_i^f}^{p_i^*} x_i(p_i, \bar{\mathbf{p}}, y) dp_i \qquad (A6.14)$$

and assume that $x_i \in C$ on $p_i^0 \leqslant p_i \leqslant p_i^f$ and on $p_i^f \leqslant p_i \leqslant p_i^*$ but $x_i(p_i^f +, \bar{\mathbf{p}}, y) \neq x_i(p_i^f -, \bar{\mathbf{p}}, y)$, i.e. the function approaches values from the right (+) and left (−) that differ. Thus, there is a discontinuity or finite jump in the integrand at the considered point. Nevertheless, the integral (A6.14) exists as is shown in, for example, Widder (1961, Ch. 5). This result is useful when we integrate the unconditional demand function for on-site time in Chapter 8. The demand functions considered in Section 5 of this chapter, are (kinked but) continuous on $p_i^0 \leqslant p_i \leqslant p_i^*$. This is also true of the conditional demand functions in Chapter 8. Thus, the integration of these functions does not present any difficulties. (Of course, the value of the integral (A6.14) is equal to the value of the first term on the right since

$$\int_{p_i^f}^{p_i} 0 \, dp_i = 0$$

recall that we have assumed that $x_i = 0$ for $p_i \geqslant p_i^f$.)

Suppose next that x_i is positive, continuous, and bounded in the (finite) right half-open interval $[p_i^0, p_i^f)$ but is not necessarily defined or continuous at the end point p_i^f. As a matter of fact, we can assign to x_i any value, e.g. $x_i = 0$, at the end point and still obtain a proper integral, i.e. the first integral on the right-hand side of (A6.14) (see, for example, Courant and John, 1965, Ch. 3, for a proof). Thus, it means no real loss of generality to restrict attention to an open set Ω_I of strictly positive prices and incomes that generates interior solutions, i.e. $\mathbf{x} \gg 0$, as in Chapters 2–5.

In order to illustrate these results we consider the demand function $x_i = (2/p_i) - 1$ defined on $\Omega_p = \{p_i | 0 < p_i < 2\}$. Suppose the interval of integration is $[1, 2]$. We find that

$$\int_1^2 [\frac{2}{p_i} - 1] dp_i = \lim_{\epsilon \to 0} \int_1^{2-\epsilon} [\frac{2}{p_i} - 1] dp_i$$

$$= \lim_{e \to 0} [2\ell n(2-\epsilon) - (2-\epsilon) + 1]$$

$$= 2\ell n \, 2 - 1 \qquad\qquad (A6.15)$$

Alternatively, since x_i is continuous and bounded in $[1, 2]$ we can assign to x_i any value, e.g. $x_i = 0$, at the right-hand side end point and obtain $\int_1^2 [\quad] dp_i$ directly as a proper integral. If, instead, $\Omega_p = \{p_i | 0 < p_i \leqslant 1.5\}$ and $x_i = 0$ for $p_i \geqslant 1.5$, we obtain a kind of jump discontinuity. The corresponding interval of integration in (A6.15) is $[1, 1.5]$ since $x_i = 0$ for $p_i \geqslant 1.5$. These results illustrate the extensions of the concept of integral discussed above.

Finally, we briefly illustrate two other extensions of the concept of integral. First of all, the integrand in (A6.15) may become unbounded for $p_i \to 0$. If some price approaches zero, the consumer might want an infinite amount of the corresponding good. This explains the fact that it is generally assumed that $p_i > 0$ for all i. Although geometrical intuition suggests that an integral of a function with an infinite discontinuity at the point $p_i = 0$ diverges, such improper integrals may converge, i.e. exist (see, for example, Silverman, 1969, Ch. 13; Widder, 1961, Ch. 9).

Another kind of improper integral involves an infinite interval of integration. For example, the integral

$$- \int_1^A \frac{1}{p_i^n} dp_i = -\frac{A^{1-n}-1}{1-n} \tag{A6.16}$$

converges if $n > 1$ since

$$\lim_{A \to \infty} A^{1-n} = 0$$

For the case $n = 1$ the integral fails to exist since $\ln A$ tends to infinity as A does. The same result is obtained when $n < 1$. Note that the integrand in (A6.16) can be interpreted as a demand curve that does not intersect the price axis. If the considered commodity is non-essential, then $n > 1$. The Cobb–Douglas demand functions in Section 4 of Chapter 3, on the other hand, correspond to the case $n = 1$.

CHAPTER 7

How to overcome the problem of preference revelation; practical methodologies

Several different practical methods, which can be used to measure the willingness to pay for public goods (bads), have been suggested in the literature. This chapter presents the most frequently used methods (survey techniques, hedonic approaches, and travel costs methods). Each of these methods has its own serious weaknesses. However, apart from a few exceptions, no comprehensive discussion of these problems will be undertaken here. Instead the reader is referred to the references given below which provide an extensive discussion of the shortcomings associated with the different methods. In addition Fisher and Peterson (1976) and Freeman (1979a) present informative reviews of the environment in economics. Comparisons of methods for valuing environmental commodities can be found in Brookshire et al. (1981), Johnson et al. (1983), Knetsch and Davis (1966), Mäler (1974), Shapiro and Smith (1981), and Schulze et al. (1981).

1 Survey data

Direct demand-revealing methods for public goods have been suggested and also used by several authors.[1] Roughly speaking these approaches collect preference information by asking the consumers how much they are willing to pay for some change in the provision of a public good or an environmental service, or about the minimum compensation consumers require if the change is not carried out. For example, the following questions may be asked of the respondent

(CV) Suppose the provision of z is increased from z^0 to z^1. What is the most you would be willing to pay for this increase?

(EV) Suppose that the government refrains from increasing the provision of z. What is the minimum compensation you would need in order to be as well off as after an increase in z?

See Figure 6.2 in Chapter 6 for a graphical illustration of these concepts.

The most well-known problem associated with such methods is 'the free rider problem'. This is as follows: if consumers have to pay on the basis of their stated willingness to pay, they may try to conceal their true willingness to pay in order to qualify for a lower price. On the other hand, if consumers believe that the price (or the tax) charged is unaffected by their response, they may have an incentive to overstate their willingness to pay in order to secure a large supply of the public good.

However, Peter Bohm, in a series of articles, has argued that the free rider problem can be handled in quite a simple way. The following example is adapted from Bohm (1979). Suppose two large samples of the population are confronted with the task of revealing their true willingness to pay for a public good project, such as improved environmental quality. If the project were to be carried out, people in the first sample would pay an amount related to their stated willingness to pay. People in the second sample pay nothing or possibly a symbolic sum of money. If the average willingness to pay coincides for the samples, the hypothesis that there are incentives to misrepresent the willingness to pay, so-called strategic bias, is not supported.

If the average willingness to pay differs between the samples the results can be used to locate an interval in which the true willingness to pay must fall. This is the case at least if people in the first sample, i.e. those paying, have incentives to understate their true willingness to pay while the opposite holds for people in the second sample, i.e. those not paying.

Because of the hypothetical nature of the survey technique, several other potential biases may also occur. The following example is adapted from Schulze *et al.* (1981) who compare six different studies that all use the same survey technique, the contingent bidding survey approach. This technique is characterized by the fact that the valuation is contingent on the specific hypothetical change identified through photographs, brochures, or other means and was first empirically applied by Randall *et al.* (1974). One of the studies, reported in Rowe *et al.* (1980) and assessed in Schulze *et al.* (1981), was the so-called Farmington Experiment, which attempted to establish the economic value of visibility over long distances for Farmington residents and recreators at Navajo Reservoir (where visibility was threatened by power plant emissions).

The interviewee was shown a set of pictures depicting visibility ranges. The pictures were of views in different directions from one location (the San Juan Mountains and Shiprock). A sequence of questions on maximum willingness to pay and minimum compensation were then asked.

For strategic bias investigation, the survey instrument was structured so that the individual was told he would have to pay the average bid, not his own. It is difficult for individuals to bid strategically to achieve a specific outcome in such a case. For instance all previous and future bids must be known. The results also suggested that individuals do not act strategically in order to bias the outcome.

With regard to so-called information bias, it was suggested to the individual that his or her bid was not sufficient to keep power plant emissions at present levels for sustained high quality ambient air. One-third revised their bids when confronted with the possibility that their bids were insufficient. This result indicates that new information may affect bidding behaviour.

Furthermore, so-called instrument bias was addressed in this study. It was observed that the higher the starting bid suggested by the interviewer, the higher the maximum willingness to pay. Also individuals were willing to pay more when confronted with a payroll tax than with an increase in entrance fees.

These (and other) results reported by Schulze *et al.* (1981) indicate that one must be very careful with both the instrument used for payment and the amount and quality of information given to the interviewee at initiation of the interview. Nevertheless, the Farmington Experiment demonstrated reasonable consistency with other similar studies. Moreover, the detailed comparisons of studies in Schulze *et al.* (1981) and in Cummings *et al.* (1986) suggest that the survey technique yields values that are well within one order of magnitude in accuracy. After this brief sketch of the survey technique, we now turn to a more detailed presentation of a study, concerned with air pollution in Norway, based on this technique.

2 *A study based on the bidding technique*

Industry located in the Grenland area south west of Oslo, the capital of Norway, is a heavy polluter of the air. Although the emissions have been reduced during recent years, pollution is still causing problems, in particular through reduced visibility (haze). Therefore, the Norwegian Environmental Protection Agency is interested to 'know' whether further reductions of emissions are called for. For this reason, Hylland and Strand (1983) were asked to estimate the benefits and costs of such reductions in order to arrive at the societal gain or loss of improved air quality in the Grenland area. As a measure of the benefits, Hylland and Strand used the CV measure, not the EV measure, since their aim was to see if the total willingness to pay of the Norwegian population was sufficiently high to cover the costs of reducing/eliminating air pollution in the Grenland area.

In order to estimate the benefits of an improved air quality, two samples of persons were investigated. First of all, a sample of the population in the Grenland area was interviewed using the contingent bidding survey approach. Secondly, a sample of the Norwegian population (except those living in the Grenland area) was asked a number of questions regarding their valuation of improved air quality in the Grenland area. There are at least two reasons for including the whole population in the study. Some of those who are living in other parts of the country may, at some future date, visit Grenland, and, hence impute a value to an improved air quality in Grenland. Even those who do not expect to visit Grenland may impute a value to the existence of good air quality in the area. A reason for this attitude may be that they are concerned about the well-being of others. In particular, they may be willing to reduce their standard of living if this contributes to an improved and more healthy environment for future generations.

The sample of Norwegians

The main question asked to a sample of Norwegians was the following one.

> Q1 The Grenland district, i.e. the area around Skien and Porsgrunn, is the industrial area in Norway that has been worst affected by air pollution. A reduction in air pollution to the levels prevailing in other Norwegian towns would require a once-and-for-all expenditure of 1,000 million NEK. Let us assume that this expenditure is financed by means of a one year special surcharge levied on the incomes of all Norwegians. This tax surcharge would be equivalent to approximately 0.6 per cent of annual income, i.e. a person who earns 100,000 NEK would pay 600 NEK while a person who earns 50,000 NEK would pay a tax surcharge of 300 NEK.
> Do you support this measure to reduce air pollution if it is financed in this manner?

This question, and a number of questions concerning age, sex, income, home town, and so on, were answered by around 1,000 Norwegians as a part of a nationwide Gallup poll carried out monthly. About 56 per cent of the answers were yes responses. Obviously, the answers cannot be used to calculate the distribution of the maximum willingness to pay (the CV) for improved air quality. We only know that some people are willing to pay a once and for all amount corresponding to 0.6 per cent or more of

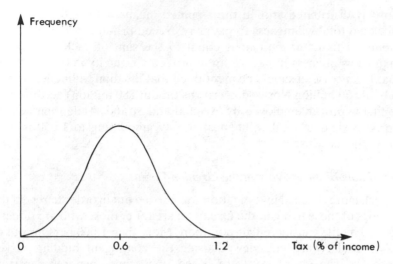

Figure 7.1 The normal distribution

their current yearly income, while others are not willing to pay this much. (The reason for not asking further questions was probably limited financial resources. The authors wanted to concentrate on a detailed investigation of the attitudes of those living in the polluted area.)

In order to arrive at a rough estimate of the aggregate willingness to pay, Hylland and Strand used two different methods. According to the first approach, they simply added 0.6 per cent of the annual income of each person who voted 'yes'. The total willingness to pay of the population is obtained by multiplying the resulting amount of money by the raising factor total population/sample size. The second approach employs Bowen's (1943) median voter theorem. This theorem states that the median voter can be replaced by the average voter provided, in this case, willingness to pay is symmetrically distributed among the population, as in Figure 7.1. Since around 50 per cent voted yes and 50 per cent voted no to question Q1 stated above, Hylland and Strand obtained the total willingness to pay by multiplying 0.6 per cent of the average annual income by the number of people (voters) in the population. Hence, according to this approach, total willingness to pay among the population for improved air quality in the Grenland area is 0.6 per cent of national income.

However, total willingness to pay is underestimated, since more than 50 per cent (56 per cent) voted yes and Bowen's approach also ignores that there may also be those who are prepared to pay more than 1.2 per cent of their income. This applies at least if the population is close to normally distributed around the assumed mean value. Otherwise, the calculated total willingness to pay may exceed or fall short of the 'true' amount. This latter amount is equal to the sum of each individual's maximal willingness to pay for an improved air quality in the Grenland area. In any case, it should be mentioned that the total willingness to pay is about 630 million Norwegian crowns (about $80 million) according to the first approach employed by Hylland and Strand, while their second approach yields a total willingness to pay amounting to 1,050 million Norwegian crowns.

The sample of those living in the Grenland area

A much more detailed investigation was carried out in order to reveal the attitudes of those living in the Grenland area, i.e. those who are directly affected by the considered air pollution. More than 1,000 persons out of 68,000 adults were interviewed using the contingent bidding survey approach. The interviews were based upon three pictures depicting visibility ranges. Picture A shows the selected area, a day with heavy haze; about every tenth day is that hazy. Picture B depicts the same area on an average day, while the range of visibility in Picture C is so good that only every fifth day is that clear.

The interviewees were divided into three subsamples of equal size. One subsample, S1, was shown pictures A and C, a second subsample, S2, was shown pictures B and C, and the third subsample, S3, was shown, or asked to compare, pictures A and B and then B and C. There are at least two reasons for this approach. First of all, the approach allows the calculation of the 'marginal' willingness to pay for an improved air quality over a certain range, i.e. for an improvement from A to B and for the further improvement to C. Second, the approach opens up a possibility to check if the answers are 'path independent'. Reasonably, one should obtain approximately the same willingness to pay for a change from A to C regardless of whether we go directly from A to C or from A to B to C.

In order to make the interviewees familiar with the considered hypothetical changes in the environment, they were asked to estimate the number of days per year which are as hazy as pictures A and B, respectively. Then the following question was asked.

Q2 It is impossible to eradicate all of the fog since part of it is caused by natural conditions. However a reduction in the discharge of industrial waste would undoubtedly lead to much cleaner air.
    A reduction in the discharge of industrial waste may be financed by the company itself, the local population, society in general or

by all three categories on a joint basis. In order to establish whether a further reduction in air pollution is desirable, it is essential to examine the effect of cleaner air on the welfare of the local population. One measure of this improvement in welfare is the maximum amount that an individual is willing to pay in order to receive a given improvement in visibility, provided that the local population and local companies are themselves required to meet a substantial share of the costs involved. In this study, we are interested in finding out how *individuals* themselves evaluate the advantages of cleaner air. Let us assume that it is possible to halve the number of days of type (A) and instead have a level of visibility approximating to type (B). It is further assumed that a proportion of the expenditure on the reduction of air pollution is financed jointly by means of a general income tax on all income-earners in the district. It is not easy to determine in advance the actual level of expenditure required by these improvement measures.

Would they themselves be prepared to pay ( ) per cent of their income towards such a project in the coming years if all of the other income-earners in the area were also prepared to do the same thing? It should be noted that a 1 per cent tax for an individual who earns 100,000 NEK per annum is equivalent to 1,000 NEK per annum or 2.70 NEK per day. Similarly a 5 per cent tax is equivalent to 5,000 NEK per annum or 13.70 NEK per day.

This question was the first one in a series of questions. The highest tax increase accepted by the respondent was considered to be his bid (CV). In order to be able to address the instrument bias issue, different parts of the sample were confronted with different starting bids and/or sequences of bids, e.g. the bid was raised from 1 per cent to 3 per cent to 5 per cent or, say, directly from 3 per cent to 5 per cent. The choice of starting bids was based on results obtained when testing the survey instrument on a small sample.

Subsamples S1 and S2 answered question Q2 while subsample S3 in addition was asked the following question.

Q3 Let us assume that further measures are taken to reduce air pollution. As a result the number of days where visibility corresponds to type A were reduced by half. The new improved situation is depicted by photograph C. Such measures would be more expensive than those first envisaged. Would they be prepared to pay additional taxation of ( ) per cent in order to obtain this additional reduction in air pollution?

Table 7.1 *Willingness to pay as per cent of annual income for an improved air quality in the Grenland area*

Tax (%)	Sequence of pictures (subsample)				
	AB (S3)	BC (S2)	AC (S1)	BC|AB (S3)	AB+BC (S3)
0	59	60	59	77	58
0.5–6	41	40	41	23	40
7–8	0	0	0	0	2
Average tax (%)	1.0	0.9	0.9	0.3	1.3
No. of observations	334	336	334	334	334

The results are summed up in Table 7.1. It is noteworthy that around 60 per cent of the respondents are not willing to pay at all for an improved air quality in the area. None in the sample was willing to pay more than 8 per cent of his annual income. The average willingness to pay for a change from A to C is 0.9 per cent for subsample S1 and 1.3 per cent for subsample S3. In relation to these results three points can be made.

Firstly, the willingness to pay of subsample S2 for an improvement from B to C exceeds the corresponding willingness to pay of subsample S3. A possible reason is that the latter sample already has 'paid' for an improvement from A to B. That is, the change from B to C is evaluated conditional on the change from A to B. This should reduce the willingness to pay, a hypothesis that is confirmed by the results presented in Table 7.1. This can also be seen by noting that for subsample S2, Hylland and Strand in fact calculate the following individual compensating variation measure:

$$CV(BC) = e(\mathbf{p}, z^B, U^B) - e(\mathbf{p}, z^C, U^B) \tag{7.1}$$

where a superscript B (C) denotes the initial (final) level of pollution z. The corresponding measure for subsample S3 reads as follows:

$$CV(BC|AB) = e(\mathbf{p}, z^B, U^A) - e(\mathbf{p}, z^C, U^A) \tag{7.2}$$

If air quality is a 'normal' public good, then the CV in (7.1) exceeds the one in (7.2) since utility level B is higher than utility level A; compare Figure 6.4 in Chapter 6. As a comparison of columns 2 and 4 in Table 7.1 reveals, this is also the result obtained by Hylland and Strand.

Secondly, one would expect the compensating variation of a shift from A to C to be independent of the particular path chosen. Table 7.1 shows that this is not the case in the Hylland–Strand study. Those who were asked to compare A and C are on average willing to pay 0.9 per cent, while those who were confronted with a shift from A to B and then from B to C are prepared to pay 1.3 per cent for an improvement from A to C. Unfortunately, there seems to be no simple or straightforward interpretation of this bias. The reader may suspect that the bias is due to the fact that the CV measure fails to correctly rank certain changes, as was discussed in Chapter 6. Fortunately, this is not the source of the bias. This can be checked by defining CV measures for the changes from A to B and from A to C, respectively, and invoking equations (7.1) and (7.2). Possibly, however, some individuals may not have fully understood the conditional assumption invoked in question Q3 and therefore overestimate their willingness to pay for the improvement from B to C.

Thirdly, as mentioned earlier, the instrument bias issue was addressed by Hylland and Strand. It turns out that the final bids are influenced by the magnitude of the starting bids. For example, given a starting bid of 1 per cent, the average willingness to pay is 0.6 per cent. Those who were confronted with a starting bid of 3 or 5 per cent, on the other hand, are prepared to pay more than 1 per cent. The starting point bias problem can be avoided by allowing the individual to specify a maximum willingness to pay, instead of giving one of two responses, yes or no, to a sequence of bids. Alternatively, the respondent is confronted with a single bid which he has to accept or reject; but different subsamples are offered (asked to pay) different amounts of money. In fact, Hylland and Strand also use a variation of this latter closed-ended approach, as is illustrated below. The problem, however, is that there is some empirical evidence which indicates that the open-ended method provides significantly lower estimates of average willingness to pay than the closed-ended approach. See Seller *et al.* (1985) for a discussion of this issue, and Boyle *et al.* (1985) for a detailed examination of the starting point bias issue.

Next, let us turn to the aggregation issue. Hylland and Strand use two methods to obtain the total annual willingness to pay for clean air. If the estimates obtained for the various subsamples are consistent estimates of the corresponding population values, the total willingness to pay is easily calculated by multiplying the estimates by the appropriate raising factors. Using this approach, Hylland and Strand find that the adult population in the Grenland area is willing to pay 35–50 million Norwegian crowns a year for the change from air quality level A to air quality level C.

Hylland and Strand suggest another way to arrive at an aggregate willingness to pay. In particular, they want to get rid of the starting point bias problem. Therefore, they exploit the fact that not all respondents were confronted with the same starting bid when answering question Q2. Three different starting bid levels, 1, 3, and 5 per cent, were used. Hylland and Strand begin by estimating the proportion of yes answers on

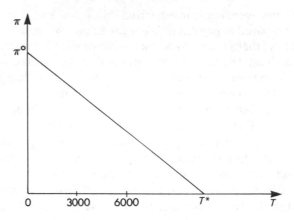

Figure 7.2 The frequency of yes answers on the starting bid as a function of the magnitude of the starting bid

the starting bid as a linear function of the tax corresponding to the starting bid and various other independent variables. For example, the following equation was obtained:

$$\pi = 25 + 0.01y - 4.3T \qquad (7.3)$$
$$ (18.2) \quad\ \ (29.1)$$

where π is the proportion (%) yes answers on the starting bid, y is household income, T is the tax corresponding to the starting bid (in thousands of Norwegian crowns), and F-statistics are shown in parentheses. For any given y, the relationship is the one depicted in Figure 7.2. Integrating between zero and T^* yields a measure of the expected willingness to pay, i.e. area $0-\pi^0-T^*$. Intuitively, each tax amount is multiplied by the probability that the respondent accepts that he should pay this particular amount of money to secure clean air. Summing (integrating) the resulting weighted amounts, one obtains the expected willingness to pay. Finally, multiplying by the number (in hundreds) of adults in the area yields an estimate of the total willingness to pay for clean air in the area. See Sections 6 and 7 of Chapter 8 for further discussion of this kind of approach to the estimation of consumer surplus measures.

Hylland and Strand argue that there can hardly be any starting point bias if only the frequency of yes answers on the starting bid is used. What the magnitude of the starting bid can affect is the size of the final bid accepted. Nevertheless, there is the problem that there are no observations far to the right in Figure 7.2. Recall that there are only three different starting bids. For this reason, and to obtain 'conservative' estimates, Hylland and Strand (arbitrarily) assume that the willingness to pay is zero for taxes exceeding 6,000 and 3,000 crowns respectively. This reduces the total willingness to pay from about 100 million crowns to 95 and 60 million crowns respectively. Still, however, these figures are much above the one, i.e. 35–50 million crowns, obtained when using the traditional aggregation procedure. Hylland and Strand suggest that the latter procedure is the most appropriate one if there is no starting point bias. On the other hand, in the presence of such bias the approach illustrated in Figure 7.2 may be the appropriate one. This applies at least where it can be assumed that the respondents do not systematically misrepresent their preferences when accepting or rejecting the starting bid.

The total willingness to pay

In order to arrive at an estimate of the total benefits of clean air in the Grenland area, it is necessary to specify a time horizon. Recall that question Q2 requires the respondent to pay the accepted bid during an unspecified number of years. Unfortunately, there is no accepted theoretic foundation or even rule of thumb for the choice of time horizon. Moreover, in general, future benefits and costs must be discounted since a consumer must normally receive a positive minimum compensation before he will postpone a dollar's worth of consumption in a period. Hylland and Strand use a time horizon of 20 years and calculate present values given discount rates of 5 per cent, 10 per cent, and 15 per cent. In this way, they find that 400 million crowns is a reasonable lower bound for the present value of the willingness to pay of the adult population in the Grenland area. Adding to this amount, the 600 million crowns that those living in other parts of the country may be willing to pay, the total benefits of clean air (a change from situation A to situation C) amounts to at least 1 billion crowns. Provided the unknown cost of cleaning the air falls short of this amount of money, the suggested improvement is worthwhile for society. At least this would be the case provided that we can simply add individual benefits and costs, regardless of the distribution of income/welfare between individuals.

In any case, the results reported here illustrate that it is far from a trivial matter to construct a survey instrument. Even though surveys, and the contingent valuation approach in particular, are widely applied, questions obviously remain about the appropriate method of asking the central valuation question.

3 *Hedonic prices*

There has been a growing interest in using property values as a source of information on the benefits of controlling environmental disamenities. The idea is that differences in environmental quality variables are reflected in housing sale prices. The most popular approach is probably the hedonic price technique developed by Griliches (1971) and Rosen (1974). This is a method that is used to estimate the implicit prices of the characteristics which differentiate closely related products. Closely following Freeman (1979a; 1979b), suppose any unit h of housing can be completely described by j locational, K neighbourhood and m environmental characteristics. Then the price of this housing unit is a function of these characteristics:

$$P_h = f_h(S_{h1}, \ldots, S_{hj}, N_{h1}, \ldots, N_{hK}, Z_{h1}, \ldots, Z_{hm}) \quad \text{for all } h \qquad (7.4)$$

where S denotes locational, N neighbourhood and Z environmental characteristics. This is the hedonic or implicit price function.

In fact, this function is a locus of household equilibrium marginal willingnesses to pay. In order to illustrate this, let us write the utility maximization problem of a representative household in the following way:

$$\max_{a} U(\mathbf{x}, \mathbf{S}, \mathbf{N}, \mathbf{Z})$$

$$\text{s.t. } y = \mathbf{px} + h(\mathbf{S}, \mathbf{N}, \mathbf{Z}) \qquad (7.5)$$

where $\mathbf{a} = (\mathbf{x}, \mathbf{S}, \mathbf{N}, \mathbf{Z})$, all variables are assumed to be continuous, and $c = h(\ )$ is rent or periodic cost of housing corresponding to P_h in equation (7.4). This simple form of modelling the problem is sufficient for our limited purposes, although the model is not necessarily in each respect the one underlying equation (7.4).

By examining the first-order conditions associated with an interior solution to this utility maximization problem, it can be easily verified that the marginal implicit prices (e.g. $\partial h / \partial Z_m$), associated with the housing bundle actually chosen must be equal to the correpsonding marginal willingness to pay ($\partial U / \partial Z_m \lambda$) for those characteristics. Inserting the optimal levels of $\mathbf{S}$, $\mathbf{N}$ and $\mathbf{Z}$ into the rent function yields the rent paid by the utility maximizing household. This explains that equation (7.4) is interpreted as a locus of household equilibrium marginal willingnesses to pay.

Suppose that a (non-linear) version of (7.4) has been estimated for housing in an area. The coefficient(s) for the partial derivative with respect to environmental characteristic Z_m

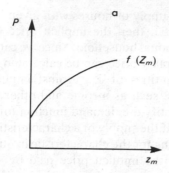

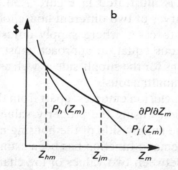

Figure 7.3 (a) the partial relationship between P_h and Z_m; (b) the marginal implicit price of Z_m and the inverse demand curves for two households

$$\frac{\partial P}{\partial Z_m} = f_z(Z_m) \tag{7.6}$$

where constant characteristics have been suppressed, indicates the increase in (equilibrium) expenditure on housing that is required to obtain a house with one more unit of Z_m (see Figure 7.3). As can be seen from Figure 7.3b, each household chooses a location where its marginal willingness to pay for Z_m is equated with the marginal implicit price of Z_m.

The question is if (7.6) can be interpreted as an inverse demand function for Z_m. The answer is positive if all households have identical utility functions and incomes. These assumptions ensure that all individuals have identical demand functions, implying that all observations in Figure 7.3b must lie on the same (inverse) demand curve.

If individuals are not alike, the supply side of the housing market must

be considered. If the supply of houses with given bundles of characteristics is perfectly elastic, then the implicit price of a characteristic is
exogenous to the individual household. Since we can observe Z_m for each
household and the implicit price can be calculated from (7.6), a regression of observed quantities of Z_m against implicit prices and other
independent variables, such as income and other socioeconomic characteristics, should identify the demand function for Z_m.

On the other hand, if the supply of a characteristic is fixed, individuals
can be viewed as bidding for the characteristic in question. Then, we can
use (7.6) to calculate the implicit price paid by each household, and
regress this variable on observed quantities of Z_m and various socioeconomic variables. As a result, the inverse demand curves for different
households do not generally coincide, implying that (7.6) cannot be
interpreted as an inverse demand curve unless households are identical in
every respect. This is illustrated in Figure 7.3b, where the marginal
willingness to pay curves of two different households are drawn.

In the intermediate case, where supply adjusts, but not infinitely
rapidly, a simultaneous equation approach must be used. Hence, we
must specify equations for the supply side as well as for the demand side,
and estimate these simultaneously.

Thus no simple conclusion emerges, apart from the possibly trivial one
that in empirical studies using the property value approach, one must
carefully examine the supply side of the housing market. Nevertheless,
once the (inverse) demand function has been estimated, the area under
the demand curve between two values of the characteristic determines
the change in uncompensated consumer surplus caused by a changed
quantity of the characteristic. Adding across households yields the
aggregate change in consumer surplus. However, the (lack of) proportionality between this measure and the underlying utility changes is the
usual one described in the previous chapters.

4 *A property value study*

In order to illustrate how property values can be used to derive
willingness to pay measures for environmental quality, this section
summarizes a study by Brookshire *et al.* (1981) that analysed the housing
market within a sample plan of communities of the South Coast Air
Basin in Southern California. Specifically, Brookshire *et al.* considered
whether households actually pay for cleaner air through higher property
values for homes in clean air communities.

The data base contains information on 719 owner-occupied single-
family residences in 14 communities sold in the January 1977–March

Table 7.2 *Variables used in analysis of housing market*

Variable	Definition (assumed effect on housing sale price)	Units	Econometric equation
Dependent			
Sale Price	Sale price of owner occupied single family residences.	($1,000)	
Independent-Housing			
Sale Date	Month in which the home was sold (positive, indicator of inflation).	January 1977=1 March 1978=15	0.018 (10.1)
Age	Age of home (negative, indicator of obsolesence and quality of structure).	Years	−0.003 (−3.5)
Bathrooms	Number of bathrooms (positive, indicator of quality).	Number	0.148 (9.3)
Living Area	Living area (positive, indicator of the quantity of home).	Square feet	0.000 (14.0)
Pool	Zero–one variable which indicates the presence of a pool (positive, indicator of quality).	Zero=no pool One=pool	0.090 (4.2)
Fireplaces	Number of fireplaces (positive, indicator of quality).	Number	−0.104 (7.8)
Independent-Neighborhood			
Distance to Beach	Distance to the nearest beach (negative, indicator or relative proximity to main recreational activity).	Miles	−0.014 (−9.1)
School Quality	School quality as measured by student percentile scores on the California Assessment Test-12th grade math. (positive).	Percentile ×100	0.001 (2.0)
Ethnic	Ethnic composition – percent white in census tract(s) which contain sample community (positive).	Percent ×100	0.008 (1.3)
Population Density	Population density in surrounding census tract (negative, indicator of crowding).	People per square mile	−0.000 (−7.8)
Housing Density	Housing density in surrounding Census tract (negative, indicator of crowding).	Houses per square mile	
Distance to Employment	Weighted distances to eight employment centers in the South Coast Air Basin (negative indicator of proximity to employment).	Miles/Employment Density	−0.270 (−11.7)
NO_2	Nitrogen dioxide concentrations.	Parts per hundred million (pphm)	−0.001 (−2.7)
TSP	Concentrations of total suspended particulates.	Micrograms per cubic meter ($\mu g/m^3$)	—
Independent-Community			
Public Safety Expenditures	Expenditures on public safety per capita (positive, indicator of attempt to stop criminal activity).	$/People	0.000 (5.1)
Crime	Local crime rates (negative, indicator of peoples' perception of danger).	Crime/People	−2.280 (−2.4)
Tax	Community tax rate (negative, measurers cost of local public services.	$/$1,000 of home value	−0.031 (−1.8)

Source: Brookshire *et al.* (1981) pp. 157–8, 164.

1978 time period. Table 7.2 contains a detailed description of the data employed in the study (and a regression equation to be discussed below). Needless to say, housing data of such quality are rarely available for studies of this nature. Usually only aggregated data, i.e. census tract averages, are available. The Brookshire *et al.* study therefore gives an idea of what can be but is not usually achieved using housing market data.

The study encompasses two separate but related approaches. The first approach involves a comparison of average housing values in pairs of communities, standardizing only for house size. Provided the variation between pairs of houses is minimal with respect to all characteristics other than air quality, any sale price differential will reflect individual willingness to pay for clean air. The second approach, which is reported here, uses a multistep econometric procedure, originally developed by Harrison and Rubinfeld (1978), which allows air pollution abatement to be valued differently by households.

The first step in this approach is to estimate a hedonic housing value equation of the kind stated in (7.4). It turned out that non-linear functional forms perform somewhat better than the linear form, at least if measured by R^2. One of the estimated equations, with the logarithm of home sale price as dependent variable and based on 719 observations, is shown in the final column of Table 7.2. All coefficients have the expected signs, and all, except ethnic composition, are statistically significant at the 5 per cent level; *t*-statistics are shown in parentheses in the table. Note that Brookshire *et al.* include the squared pollution term (and the logarithm of taxes). It was found that this formulation performed (insignificantly) better than either the first-order or cubic terms.

It is important to note that this regression equation is a locus of equilibrium values. By inserting, the actual values of the various independent variables for any home in the sample, one should derive, at least in theory, the actual sale price of that home. Thus, the considered regression equation cannot be used to directly identify the individual's valuation of changes in air pollution. Recall the discussion in Section 3.

The second step is to calculate the marginal willingness to pay for improved air quality of the average household in each community. Taking the partial derivative of the regression equation in Table 7.2 with respect to the air pollution variable, i.e. the concentration of nitrogen dioxide, yields the (negative of) marginal willingness to pay for a change in NO_2. Since the formulation in Table 7.2 assumes a non-linear relationship, i.e. is of the form

$$\ell n\, P = a + bZ^2 + \dots \tag{7.7}$$

where Z is the nitrogen dioxide concentration, the magnitude of $\partial P/\partial Z$ ($=2bPZ$) depends on the level of all independent variables. Thus, the marginal willingness to pay for improved air quality varies between communities. Brookshire *et al.* calculate community specific values by assigning to the variables their community mean values.

The third step is to regress the marginal willingness to pay variable on community average income and pollution levels. This procedure should make it possible to identify an inverse demand function. Thus, Brookshire *et al.* treat the supply of houses with given bundles of characteristics as fixed. Recall the discussion in Section 3. Linear as well as log-log forms were estimated. The linear formulation, based upon the 14 community observations, yields the following result:

$$\text{MWP} = -1601 + 0.05y + 162.7Z \quad R^2 = 0.86 \tag{7.8}$$
$$\quad\quad\quad\quad (8.3) \quad\quad (3.8)$$

where MWP is marginal willingness to pay in dollars, y is community income, and t-statistics are shown in parentheses. Varying Z with income fixed identifies an inverse demand curve for improved air quality.

The final step is to integrate (7.8) between initial and final pollution levels, assigning the income variable its mean value, to obtain

$$\int \text{MWP} dZ = (-1601 + 0.05\bar{y})\triangle Z + \frac{162.7(Z_1^2 - Z_0^2)}{2} \tag{7.8'}$$

where a subscript refers to a particular pollution level, $\triangle Z = Z_1 - Z_0$, and $\bar{y}$ is average community income. Brookshire *et al.* find that an improvement in air quality from poor to fair is valued at \$5,800 per home.[2] The value which corresponds to the fair-good change is \$4200. The total benefits for the total number of affected homes are around \$10 billion. In annual terms, total benefits amount to \$0.95 billion, which corresponds to \$510 per home. These figures are much lower than those obtained by a comparison of average housing values in a pair of communities, standardizing only for house size. In other words, the latter approach probably attributes to the environmental variable a willingness to pay, which in part is due to other variables than air quality.

Equation (7.8') is an uncompensated money measure of utility change. In order to get an idea of the magnitude of the relative error when an uncompensated measure is used instead of CV or EV, Willig's formula, as defined in equation (4.13) of Chapter 4, can be used. Since air quality is a public good, the income elasticity η in Willig's formula should be replaced by the price flexibility of income, which, using (7.8) is defined as $\epsilon = (\partial \text{MWP}/\partial y)(y/\text{MWP})$ when the consumer has y units of money to spend on other goods. Since the price flexibility seems to be rather close to one, assuming that the (unreported) average household income is $35,000, to a first approximation the error is less than 1 per cent ($-510/2 \times 35,000$). For convenient reference, we state, without proof, the following more exact error bound formula:

$$A \geqslant [(1+(1-\epsilon_U)\frac{S}{y^0})^{1/(1-\epsilon_U)} - 1 - \frac{S}{y^0}]\frac{y^0}{|S|} \tag{7.9}$$

where $A = (CV - S)/|S|$, $|S|$ is the absolute value of the ordinary money measure, and ϵ_U is the calculated upper bound on ϵ. Replacing ϵ_U by the lower bound ϵ_L reverses the inequality (7.9), i.e. yields an upper bound, instead of a lower bound, of the percentage error in using S to approximate CV. By reversing the signs of the terms $(1-\epsilon)$ and S/y a formula is obtained for the percentage error in estimating EV. See Cornwall (1984, pp. 634–5) for a derivation of (7.9) and a correction of an error in Randall and Stoll (1980). These formulas can be used for public goods as well as rationed private goods.

In interpreting the results reported by Brookshire *et al.* it should also be noted that they ignore the effect of real property and income taxation on property values. The sign of the net effect of ignoring taxation in calculating benefits is generally ambiguous, as is shown in Freeman (1979a). Nevertheless, a properly conducted study should account for the effects of taxation.

Brookshire *et al.* estimate separate equations for the nitrogen dioxide and total suspended particulate variables. The reason for not including both pollutants in one and the same regression equation is collinearity in the data set. Multicollinearity among attributes is, beside specification errors, one of the most serious problems in the estimation of implicit prices. Multicollinearity, while not resulting in biased estimates, can be the source of wrongly signed coefficients. It should also be mentioned that Halvorsen and Pollakowski (1981) have developed a general 'quadratic Box–Cox functional form' for hedonic price equations which incorporates, as special cases, the functional forms that are normally used in empirical hedonic analyses (linear, log-linear, semi-log, etc; see the informative table in Freeman (1979a, pp. 156–60) for the key features of a number of air pollution–property value studies). However, although a study may make proper use of the Box and Cox (1964) technique to estimate hedonic regressions, it is not unusual that the ordinary least squares procedure is used in order to find the maximum likelihood estimates of the regression coefficients. For example, this seems to be the case in the study by Brookshire *et al.* (1981). However, they do not report the actual method of estimation or indeed the general approach that has been adopted. Spitzer (1982) has shown that OLS estimates of coefficient variances are biased downwards, thereby yielding t-statistics for individual parameters which have an upward bias in absolute terms. Since importance is usually attached to the significance of individual site characteristics, the estimation of accurate t-statistics for indivdiual parameters is crucial. (See Blackley *et al.* (1984) for details and some empirical evidence of the magnitude of the bias of OLS variances.)

In addition, Brown and Rosen (1982) have stressed that one will fail to identify the structural demand functions, i.e. (7.8), unless prior, possibly arbitrary, restrictions on functional form are imposed or marginal prices are estimated from equations fitted separately for spatially distinct markets. For example, the reader can easily verify that if (7.7) is replaced by the price function $P = a + bZ^2$, then estimation of (7.8) would be meaningless. Brookshire *et al.* (1981) avoid estimating an identity by choosing such a functional form that the marginal price function for Z, obtained from (7.7), cannot be expressed as some exact combination of the arguments of (7.8).

In sum, this section has demonstrated that households' aggregate benefits from a public good, in this case clean air, can be measured indirectly from market data. In the cases where property values are available, the property value approach is of great importance because it is much less expensive than the survey method (but see Mäler (1977) for a critical assessment of the property value method). The main drawback of the property value method is the fact that property values are of no relevance when dealing with many types of public goods, i.e. national parks, endangered species, nationwide acid rains, and so on. Moreover, a comparison of money measures of utility change calculated from property values and those measures obtained by other methods still requires to be carried out. This important issue is addressed in the next section.

5 *A comparison of survey and hedonic approaches*

In a recent study Brookshire *et al.* (1982) report on an experiment designed to validate the survey approach by direct comparison to the hedonic property value study presented in the previous section. The Los Angeles metropolitan area was chosen for the experiment because of the well-defined air pollution problem and because of the existence of detailed property value data.

Brookshire *et al.* (1982) start from a simple theoretical model in order to obtain testable hypotheses regarding the sign of the difference between the marginal willingness to pay from survey responses and the rent differential associated with air quality improvement from hedonic analysis of property value data.

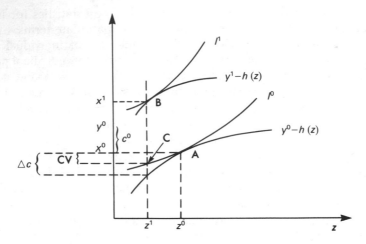

Figure 7.4 The relationship between the rent differential $\triangle c$ and the marginal willingness to pay CV for improved air quality
Source: Brookshire *et al.* (1982, p. 168)

Consider a household which acts as if it maximizes utility

$$U = U(x, z) \tag{7.10}$$

subject to the budget constraint

$$y - px - h(z) = 0 \tag{7.11}$$

where x is a composite good, z is the level of air pollution, and $c = h(z)$ is rent or periodic cost of housing. It is assumed that $\partial U/\partial x > 0$, while $\partial U/\partial z$, $\partial h/\partial z < 0$. This latter assumption means that lower rents will be paid for homes in more polluted areas.

Figure 7.4 illustrates, graphically, the solution of this maximization problem. Given income y^0, the household would maximize utility at point A along indifference curve I^0, choosing to locate at pollution level z^0, consume x^0, and pay rent c^0. If income increases to y^1 the household would relocate, choosing point B on indifference curve I^1, at a lower pollution level z^1 with higher consumption x^1.

The household in equilibrium at point A in the figure was asked how much x it would forgo to experience z^1 rather than z^0 while maintaining the same utility level. Since the household is indifferent between points A and C it would be willing to pay CV dollars to achieve the considered reduction in air pollution.

The hedonic rent gradients $h(z)$ themselves only provide point estimates of the marginal rates of substitution between pollution and other goods for individuals with possibly differing preferences and income. However, the change in rent $\triangle c$ between locations with air quality levels z^0 and z^1 in Figure 7.4, must for any household located at point A be no less than the bid CV. This can be checked by using the second-order conditions for utility maximization. Note that the rent gradient $h(z)$ need not be strictly concave or convex, but must lie below the relevant indifference curve.

Brookshire *et al.* (1982) go on to show that the above result, i.e. $\triangle c \geqslant CV$, holds even in the case of multiple housing attributes, e.g. attributes such as the square footage of the home, number of bathrooms, fireplaces, and neighbourhood characteristics (compare equation (7.5) in Section 3). Thus, their first hypothesis for testing the validity of the survey technique is: for each household in a community, $\triangle c \geqslant CV$. In turn this implies that the average rent differential across households $\triangle \bar{c}$, must be at least as large as the average willingness to pay $\bar{CV}$ for an improvement in air quality. The second hypothesis formulated by Brookshire *et al.* (1982) is that, given the political history of air pollution control in the State of California, mean bids in each community are non-negative, i.e. $\bar{CV} \geqslant 0$, although, to a European, this seems to be quite a superfluous hypothesis.

An hedonic rent gradient was estimated in accordance with the approach summarized in Section 4. Housing sale price is assumed to be a function of housing structure variables, neighbourhood variables, accessibility variables, and air quality as measured by total suspended particulates or nitrogen dioxide. Implicit or hedonic prices for each attribute are then determined by examining housing prices and attribute levels. Recall Table 7.2 in Section 4 of this chapter.

The survey approach followed the works summarized in Sections 1 and 2 of this chapter. The hypothetical market was defined and described both in technical and institutional detail. Air quality was described by the survey instrument to the respondent in terms of easily perceived levels of provision such as visual range through photographs and maps depicting good, fair, and poor air quality levels over the region. The respondent was asked to react to alternative price levels posited for different air quality levels. Payment mechanisms were either of the lump-sum variety, or well-specified schemes such as tax increments or utility bill additions.

Brookshire *et al.* (1982) tested the two specified hypothesis, i.e. $\triangle \bar{c} \geqslant \bar{CV}$ and $\bar{CV} \geqslant 0$, using the *t*-statistic. The hypotheses tests indicate that the empirical analysis is entirely consistent with the theoretical structure given by equations (7.10) and (7.11). However, the results, like those reported by Bishop and Heberlein (1979), indicate that survey estimates of willingness to pay might be biased downward by about 50 per cent. Nevertheless, in situations where market data for hedonic analysis is difficult to acquire, the survey approach is preferable to no information at all on which to base the decision-making process. In particular this is the case when the (underestimated) benefits exceed the costs.

6 *Utility functions and demand equations*

Another approach sometimes used in order to estimate the valuation of public goods/bads is to assume that the utility functions take a particular form and estimate complete demand systems. Recently, McMillan (1979) has used the translog utility function to establish a system of demand equations for housing characteristics.[3] In a sense, however, McMillan's approach consists of two steps. Households first decide on how much they will allocate to housing and then they decide on the combination of housing characteristics they want to acquire. Hedonic prices are used to create a system of budget share equations for housing characteristics so that the demand for environmental characteristics can be estimated within the housing budget constraint.

Assuming a Cobb–Douglas utility function within each considered income group, Polinsky and Rubinfeld (1975) estimate willingness to pay for changes in air quality. However, as noted in Chapter 4, once a particular form of utility function is assumed, the change in utility can be calculated directly, i.e. it seems superfluous to estimate money measures which in general are not proportional to the change in utility.

In order to illustrate this point, and also some of the methods discussed in Chapter 6, a recent study by Shapiro and Smith (1981) is described. They applied a slightly different method than that of Bradford–Hildebrandt–Mäler–Willig, described in Section 5 of Chapter 6, to data characterizing 28 counties in the southern half of California and obtained implicit prices for four 'environmental' goods: rainfall, temperature, public expenditures, and pollution.

The specification of the indirect utility function used by Shapiro and Smith (1981) is similar to the translog function, except that variables are not taken in their log form

$$V\left(\frac{\mathbf{p}}{y}, \mathbf{z}\right) = -\sum_i \alpha_i \hat{p}_i - \sum_i \sum_j \beta_{ij} \hat{p}_i \hat{p}_j - \sum_i \sum_k \gamma_{ik} \hat{p}_i z_k \qquad (7.12)$$

where $\hat{p}_i = p_i/y$, and z_k denotes an environmental quality variable ($k = 1, \ldots, m$). Using (7.12), assuming $\beta_{ij} = \beta_{ji} = 0$ for all i and j, which makes preferences homothetic in the market commodities, one can easily derive expenditure share equations

$$\frac{p_i x_i}{y} = (\alpha_i p_i + \sum_k p_i \gamma_{ik} z_k)/(\sum_j \alpha_j p_j + \sum_j \sum_k \gamma_{jk} p_j z_k) \tag{7.13}$$

Estimation of this expenditure share system (or the demand equations) yield parameter values that may be used to calculate the implicit prices of environmental quality variables

$$\frac{(\partial V/\partial z_k)}{V_y} = \sum_i \gamma_{ik} p_i / \sum_j (\alpha_j p_j + \sum_k \gamma_{jk} p_j z_k) \tag{7.14}$$

Hence, the calculation of the implicit prices depends only upon the parameters that are able to be estimated using the expenditure share system (7.13). The estimation of the prices of environmental goods was carried out in two stages using maximum likelihood techniques. Firstly, parameter estimates were obtained from $(n-1 \text{ of})$ the market share equations (7.13). Secondly, these estimates were used to estimate the prices of environmental goods using equations (7.14). Obviously, however, the parameter estimates can also be used to estimate the indirect utility function, and hence, can be used to calculate the change in utility of changes in prices, income and environmental goods.

In spite of the use of extremely aggregated data, e.g. only three classes of private goods, were employed to estimate the implicit prices, Shapiro and Smith found several indications that the analysis might be on the right track (see Shapiro and Smith, 1981, pp. 116–19). Moreover, the technique has the advantage of being able to be carried out with less expense than any other except the traditional hedonic price technique.

7 *The travel cost method*

The services of a recreation site are usually provided at a low price. Although this is efficient in the absence of congestion, it makes estimation of demand functions difficult. However, every user pays a price measured by his travel costs. Suppose the estimated relationship between visit rates x and travel cost p is given by $x = x(p)$. Then the change in consumers' surplus resulting from, say, a polluted stream which is cleaned up to permit its use for sport fishing is

$$S = -\sum_j n_j \int_{p_j^0}^{p_j^1} x(p) dp \tag{7.15}$$

where n_j is the population in zone j, p_j^0 is the travel cost for fishing trips from zone j to streams situated farther away, and p_j^1 is the new travel cost. This method, proposed by Hotelling in a letter in 1947, was first

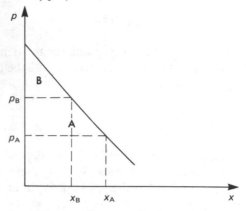

Figure 7.5 Illustration of the travel cost method

used by Clawson (1959). For a recent application of the method to the problem of valuing a day's fishing, the reader is referred to Vaughan and Russell (1982).

The basic idea of the approach is illustrated in Figure 7.5. Suppose, for simplicity, that there is a single stream that can be reached by individuals living in the considered area. The number of trips originating from zone A, expressed as a percentage of the total population living in the zone, is x_A. The average travel cost for these fishing trips is $\$p_A$. From zone B, which is situated farther away from the stream than zone A, x_B trips per capita are recorded. The average travel cost amounts to $\$p_B$. Given a number of such observations, a distance decay equation for fishing trips, like the one in Figure 7.5, can be estimated with travel costs and, say, socioeconomic characteristics as independent variables. A fisherman from zone A earns a consumer surplus equal to area A+B per trip. Multiplying by the number of trips from the zone yields the total consumers' surplus accruing to zone A. Similarly, multiplying area B in the figure by the number of visits from zone B gives the consumers surplus assigned to zone B. Summing all zones, one obtains a measure of total consumer surplus. Figure 7.5 can also be used to derive a demand curve for fishing. First, by assumption, the actual number of fishing trips is known. Second, introduce an admission fee and assume that fishermen respond to an increased fee in the same way as they, according to Figure 7.5, respond to an increased travel cost. That is, if the fee increases from zero to $\$(p_B - p_A)$ per fisherman, the proportion of the zone A population travelling to the stream falls from x_A to x_B, and so on. Summing all zones, a point on the demand curve is derived. Other points on the curve are found by further variations in the entry fee.

It should also be observed that the quality change measure (6.14) in the previous chapter is useful here. This is the case at least if fishing trips are a non-essential commodity. In this situation, we simply interpret x_i in equation (6.14) of Chapter 6 as the number of fishing trips to the stream under consideration, p_i as the travel cost, and z_i as a measure of the degree of pollution of the stream. We are thus equipped with a willingness to pay measure of quality changes which can, at least in principle, be calculated on the basis of market (travel costs) data. The reader is also referred to Bowes and Loomis (1980) who use the expenditure function to show that an increase in travel costs is equivalent to an increase in entry prices provided fishing trips are a non-essential commodity.

The remainder of this section is devoted to a presentation of a recent application of the simple or pure travel cost method. In March 1983 it was suggested that a Nature Reserve, protected from forest harvesting, be created in the Vålå Valley (the V Valley for short) in Northern Sweden. A conflict arose between the Swedish Forest Service, on the one hand, and tourism, nature conservation, and reindeer husbandry interests, on the other. In particular, the Swedish Nature Conservation Movement, supported by quite a few researchers within the field, argued that reforestation is impossible in mountainous areas such as the V Valley. In such areas, cutting may cause more or less irreversible damage to the environment. For this reason, the Swedish Environment Protection Agency initiated a social cost–benefit analysis of the two considered development scenarios. This section briefly presents one particular part of the study, namely a travel cost approach to the estimation of the environmental values involved (see Bojö, 1985, for a full presentation of the results).

The V Valley is an attractive area for tourism, in particular for skiing activities. A total of 282 households were interviewed while visiting the Valley during February to April in 1985. Separate surveys were directed at the local population and local commercial interests, but these will not be reported here.

The sample of respondents was not chosen randomly from the population of visitors since such an approach turned out to be impossible to use from a practical point of view. Instead, the selection of respondents was governed by the possibility of contact with adult visitors. The survey was carried out during the second part of each week selected for the study. Most visitors stay one full week, thus they are quite familiar with the area by the end of the week. The survey instrument, directed at the visitors, consists of six parts: a written introduction presenting the study; a map of the county showing the Nature Reserve; a questionnaire to be filled in by the respondent; a large map of the Nature Reserve, where forests and potential cutting areas are marked in clear colours; a commentary to the map, explaining how the proposed cutting activities will affect different parts of the reserve; and a personal interview to locate the willingness to pay for a preservation of the area.

Since our concern is with the travel cost method, we will focus on the questionnaire filled in by the respondents. The questionnaire covered, for example, the following subjects: home area, means of travel, travel costs, length of stay, main activities during the stay, valuation of the trip to the area as well as the area itself, alternative recreation sites, and disposable household income. Using this information, estimates were made of the following function:

$$H_i = f(p_i, y_i, s_i, D_i) \tag{7.16}$$

where H_i is the number of visitors from zone i, expressed as a proportion of the total number of inhabitants in that zone, p_i is travel costs per household from the origin zone to the V Valley and return, y_i is average disposable household income in zone i, s_i is an index of alternative recreation sites, and D_i is a dummy variable referring to transportation mode. Each of these variables will be briefly discussed in turn.

The numbers H_i were calculated in several steps. Firstly, the respondents were stratified according to home county. Secondly, it was assumed that the distribution of the sample of visitors by home county does not significantly deviate from the corresponding distribution of the total population of visitors during a typical year. Given information on the total number of visitors, it is then a relatively simple matter to calculate the number of visitors from county i as a proportion of the population in that county.

The V Valley can be reached by car, train, bus, and aeroplane. As only a couple of the respondents had come by bus or aeroplane, they had to be excluded from the study since the results would have been too unreliable if these visitors had been included. Furthermore, sportsmen and business men whose trips were not paid by themselves were excluded (although these may earn a 'rent' during their stay). Multiple site visitors were also excluded due to the joint cost problem, i.e. the problem to allocate the travel costs between the different sites.

In order to calculate the travel costs of those visitors travelling by car or train, two different methods were used. The respondents were asked to estimate the money cost of the trip. If travelling by car, the travel costs were considered to approximate to the costs of petrol. Repairs and maintenance costs were not included since the respondent was expected to have difficulties in estimating the magnitude of such costs. This complication is also noted by Seller *et al.* (1985). The second method of calculation of the travel costs is to use stereotyped rules, e.g. $0.1 per mile for those travelling by car, and economy class fare, times family size, for those travelling by train.

In addition, there is an opportunity cost for the time spent on a trip to the recreation site. As a first approximation, the after tax wage rate can be used to calculate this opportunity cost. This is because the travel time reduces working time and/or leisure time. At the margin, the latter 'crowded-out' activities are valued at the after tax wage rate by the individual, neglecting any distortions such as unemployment or fixed numbers of working hours. However, this approach assumes that the trip *per se* does not affect utility. Depending on the circumstances, one can imagine that a household derives positive or negative satisfaction from the trip to a recreation site. In the former (latter) case, the sum of money costs of the trip plus travel time costs evaluated at the after tax wage rate overestimates (underestimates) the true or full travel cost. However, there seems to be little empirical evidence in this respect. Available studies of work travel time, as summarized, for example, in Cesario (1976), indicate that the shadow price of such travel time is much lower than the wage rate. Needless to say, there is no strong case for believing that households consider travels to work and trips to recreation sites as equivalent 'commodities'.

In any case, neglecting the non-monetary parts of the travel costs can lead to biased estimates. In particular, if the non-monetary cost or net opportunity cost of the time spent in travel is strictly positive, then a failure to account for this cost will cause the aggregate consumer surplus to be underestimated, *ceteris paribus*. In terms of Figure 7.5, the estimated curve will be located inside and be less steep than the 'true' one, except possibly for those living very close to the recreation site, since the underestimation of costs increases in relation to distance from the visitor's zone of origin.

For similar reasons, a failure to correctly account for the opportunity cost of time on site may cause a bias. This is so at least if on-site time varies systematically with the distance to the recreation site. On the other hand, if on-site time is a constant, it does not matter whether an opportunity cost is included or not.

In the study summarized in this section, no travel time costs were included. This, of course, probably implies an underestimation of the costs. It should be noted, however, that almost 80 per cent of the respondents found the trip to the V Valley to be a positive experience. This indicates that the underestimation of total travel costs is somewhat less serious than appears to be the case at first sight. Regarding on-site time, no evidence was found that it varies with the zone of origin of the visitor.

In part, differences between zones in visit frequences may be due to differences in income. For this reason, the analysis includes an income variable. The income variable does not relate to the visitor but to the home county of the visitor. The income concept used is disposable household income.

The analysis must also take account of the fact that there may be several recreation sites which are substitutes for one another. For example, the variation in the relative number of visitors from different zones of origin may in part be due to a difference in the availability of similar recreation sites close to the zone of origin. For this reason, Bojö (1985) constructed a kind of substitute availability index. This index is defined as

$$s_i = \sum_{j=1}^{n} \frac{p_i W_j}{p_j} \tag{7.17}$$

where p_i is the travel cost per household from the origin zone to the V Valley and return, p_j is the corresponding travel cost to the jth substitute site, and W_j is a measure of the degree of substitutability between sites i and j.

Since (7.17) reduces to a constant (W_j) for a site situated close to the V Valley, all sites in that county were excluded from the analysis. Three groups of domestic substitute sites, situated far away in three different parts of the country, remain. According to the views expressed in the questionnaire, one of these three groups of sites was the main alternative for about 55 per cent of the respondents. Less than 15 per cent suggested a foreign site, e.g. the Alps, so this substitute was excluded by Bojö; the basic problem being that it turned out to be impossible to construct a reliable index for such sites.

Four functional forms for (7.16), linear, quadratic, semi-logarithmic, and logarithmic, were chosen for examination. In general, the results were far from encouraging. The following linear distance decay function yields the most reasonable result:

$$H_i = 4.1 - 1.4 p_i - 43.4 y_i - 5.7 s_i + 518.5 D_i \quad R^2 = 0.43 \tag{7.18}$$

where $D_i = 1$ if the household travels by train, and $D_i = 0$ otherwise. All coefficients, except the income variable, are significant at the 5 per cent level. Thus, equation (7.18) confirms what one would expect, namely that an increase in travel costs reduces the proportion of visitors from a particular zone.[4] Moreover, the supply of similar sites in other parts of Sweden affects H_i in the expected way. Disposable household income, on the other hand, has no significant influence on the relative number of visitors from a particular zone.

Bojö (1985) does not indicate which estimation procedure is used. However, note that estimating (7.18) by OLS may result in heteroscedasticity. As is demonstrated by Bowes and Loomis (1980), one should expect that the larger the origin's population, the smaller the variance of the visits per capita variable H_i. To show this, Bowes and Loomis define the variance of H_i as σ^2/N_i, where σ^2 is the variance of the individual visitation rate, assumed to be constant between zones, and N_i is zone population. One possible way of eliminating this heteroscedasticity problem is by estimating (7.18) by generalized least squares (GLS). See Johnston (1984, Ch. 8) for a detailed investigation of the properties of the OLS and GLS estimators in the presence of heteroscedastic disturbances in cross section studies. Unfortunately, there is also the problem that the variance σ^2 need not be independent of the distance to the site. Therefore, no simple solution to the heteroscedasticity problem in travel cost models seems to be available. For further discussion of this issue, the reader is referred to Bowes and Loomis (1980; 1982), Christensen and Price (1982), and Vaughan *et al.* (1982).

Taking the partial derivative of (7.18) with respect to p_i, a linear curve, like the one depicted in Figure 7.5, is obtained for any given (average) values of the remaining independent variables in (7.18). Proceeding along the lines discussed in relation to Figure 7.5, the aggregate consumer surplus is easily calculated. Adding somewhat speculative figures for excluded groups of visitors (those travelling by bus or aeroplane, sportsmen not paying for their stay themselves, etc.) Bojö arrives at a total consumer surplus amounting to around 1 million Swedish crowns (about $0.13 million). It has been argued that converting the examined area to forestry use causes irreversible damage to the environment. Thus, it is reasonable to argue that a closure of the recreation site causes a yearly loss of 1 million Swedish crowns forever, assuming, of course, that the sum does not vary over time. Using a discount rate of 5 per cent, Bojö arrives at a present value of about 25 million crowns.

Finally, it should be mentioned that the travel cost method produces approximately the same consumer surplus estimate as the contingent valuation method; Bojö (1985) used an open-ended bidding game approach similar to the one presented in Section 2 above. Seller *et al.* (1985) report similar results. They, however, argue that one should expect the travel cost method to produce higher benefits than a contingent valuation method, at least in the case of small income effects; recall that the former approach gives an uncompensated measure while the latter gives a compensated measure. Even in the case of zero income effects a difference would be expected to occur since the travel cost method gives a measure of the valuation of the total recreation experience, while the contingent valuation method usually provides an estimate of a particular attribute or characteristic, e.g. skiing. However, enquiring about the amount that the respondent would pay in order to prevent an area from being 'destroyed', as Bojö did, one would rather expect the reverse outcome. In particular, this is because the respondent may attribute to the resource an existence value, a value that is not captured by the travel cost method. Further work in comparison of the methods is needed before ultimate conclusions can be drawn regarding their relative reliability.

8 *Some further notes on the travel cost method and similar approaches*

A variant of the travel cost approach was applied by Pearse (1968) to big-game hunting in Canada. Hunters were stratified on the basis of income. The person with the highest costs within a stratum was considered a marginal user who had received no net benefits. All others within the same stratum were assumed to have obtained net benefits equal to the difference between their costs and those of the specified marginal user. In this way a consumer surplus measure was obtained for each stratum (see Pearse, 1968, for details).

Recently, Burt and Brewer (1971) and Cicchetti *et al.* (1976) have used an extended variation of the travel cost method to estimate the increment to consumer surplus resulting from the introduction of a new ski site. The approach taken by these authors is in a sense more general than the single equations approach presented in the previous section. Basically, these authors estimate a (linear) system of demand equations for existing sites:

$$\mathbf{x} = \mathbf{a} + \mathbf{b}\mathbf{p} \tag{7.19}$$

where $\mathbf{x}$ is an $m \times 1$ vector of visitation rates for each of m existing sites, $\mathbf{p}$ is an $m \times 1$ vector of travel costs to each of the sites, $\mathbf{a}$ is an $m \times 1$ vector of coefficients, and $\mathbf{b}$ is an $m \times m$ vector of coefficients.

Once this system is estimated, the authors select the site which is supposed to be the closest substitute for the new still undeveloped, recreation site. The benefits, i.e. reductions in travel costs, resulting from the introduction of this new site are measured in the following way. First evaluate (7.19) for the given travel costs for all existing sites. Then, evaluate (7.19) with the travel costs measured for the substitute site replaced by those to the new site.

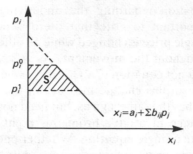

Figure 7.6 Consumers surplus gain due to a fall in travel costs from p_i^0 to p_i^1

The consumer surplus measure, corresponding to (7.15), for this single price reduction from, say p_i^0 to p_i^1, is written as

$$S = -\int_{p_i^0}^{p_i^1} x_i dp_i$$

$$= p_i^0(a_i + \sum_{j \neq i} b_{ij}p_j + \frac{b_{ii}\,p_i^0}{2}) - p_i^1(a_i + \sum_{j \neq i} b_{ij}p_j + \frac{b_{ii}p_i^1}{2}) \qquad (7.20)$$

This measure, which is illustrated in Figure 7.6, indicates the change in consumer surplus due to reduced travel costs if a new recreation site is introduced. This is the case at least if the demand function for the substitute site i coincides with the demand function for the hypothetical new site. Note that this measure is, in a sense, more general than the one in (7.15) since demand now depends not only on the own price but also on the levels of other prices (travel costs). In any case, Burt and Brewer (1971) and Cicchetti *et al.* (1976) do not use the measure (7.20). Instead they use the whole system (7.19) to obtain the line integral

$$S = (\mathbf{a'p}^0 + \frac{\mathbf{p}^{0'}\mathbf{bp}^0}{2}) - (\mathbf{a'p}^1 + \frac{\mathbf{p}^{1'}\mathbf{bp}^1}{2}) \qquad (7.21)$$

where, in the single price change case, only p_i differs between the price vectors $\mathbf{p}^0$ and $\mathbf{p}^1$, and primes denote transposed vectors.

It should be emphasized that both approaches yield the same 'answer' in the single price change case if the cross-price terms $\partial x_i/\partial p_j = b_{ij}$ are symmetrical, i.e. $b_{ij} = b_{ji}$. That is, in this case (7.21) reduces to (7.20), as is easily demonstrated by expanding (7.21). Hof and King (1982), who clarified these issues, also pose the question of what happens if cross-price terms are not symmetrical. In Chapter 3 it was demonstrated that symmetry of the cross-price effects is a prerequisite for path independency in the multi-price change case. In cases where this condition is not met, areas to the left of ordinary demand curves, i.e. the measure (7.21), provide no information regarding the underlying change in utility. However, it is important to note that there is no path dependency problem if just a single price is changed while all other prices and income are held fixed throughout the movement. As was shown in Chapter 3, equation (7.20), but not equation (7.21), except when $b_{ij} = b_{ji}$, yields the ordinary consumer surplus change measure in the single price change case. This measure has the same sign as, but need not be proportional to, the underlying change in utility. From this point of view then, it is sufficient to estimate a single equation. Whether one actually decides to estimate a single equation or a whole system of equations is a question of data collection costs and data quality, on the one hand, and econometric considerations, on the other.

The approaches discussed thus far aim at valuing a specific site. Even if site-specific bundles of characteristics are included so as to characterize each site, as in Burt and Brewer (1971), Cicchetti *et al.* (1976), Morey (1981), and Smith and Desvousges (1985), it is sites, not the separate characteristics of those sites which are valued. In contrast, Brown and Mendelsohn (1984) use a hedonic travel cost method in order to value specific characteristics. As Brown and Mendelsohn (1984, p. 427) put it, the travel cost method can measure the value of the Colorado River, the hedonic travel cost method can value scenic quality, fish density, crowdedness, etc. Basically, the hedonic travel cost method resembles the property value method, but with property values replaced by travel costs. For this reason, there will be no further discussion of the hedonic travel cost method.

Another possible approach is the household production function technique outlined in Chapter 6. This method values the outputs of households rather than an input, e.g. a recreation site. A recent application to congestion and participation in outdoor recreation is given by Deyak and Smith (1978). The method, however, is associated with econometric difficulties because of, among other things, joint production and non-linear output prices. The conditions under which the use of the household production function yields identifiable and unbiased estimates of the parameters of demand functions turn out to be quite restrictive. For a broad discussion of the theory and estimation of the household production function for wildlife recreation, the reader is referred to Bockstael and McConnell (1981).

A final comment relates to the problem of congestion. This problem occurs when the number of users of a recreation facility is 'too large'. Congestion may be interpreted as a kind of rationing and dealt with in the way discussed in Chapter 5. Alternatively, the stock of visitors, X say, is included as a separate argument in the utility functions. If X is reasonably small, it may have no or even a positive influence on utility because of the opportunities for social interaction. If the number of visitors is large, an increase in X may cause congestion and so decrease the marginal utility of a visit. Also, in an uncertain world, a household's decision whether or not to visit a particular site may be influenced by the household's expectations of the number of visitors. See the discussion on state dependent preferences in Chapter 10. In any case, in calculating willingness to pay measures, it is important to address the congestion issue. Several of the studies referred to in this chapter include congestion variables in the regression equations (see, for example, Brown and Mendelsohn, 1984; Cicchetti *et al.*, 1976; Vaughan and Russel, 1982, for details).

CHAPTER 8

Discrete choice models and environmental benefits

There are important situations in which consumers face a discrete rather than a continuous set of choices. For example, a household cannot simultaneously visit two different recreation sites. Quality changes, such as pollution or the development of new sites, may induce households to switch from trips to one area to trips to another. In order to cope with such discrete choice situations, the continuous choice models of the previous chapters must be modified.

To my knowledge, no general discrete choice theory is available for use in deriving consumer surplus measures. A few authors, notably Mäler (1974) and Small and Rosen (1981), have rigorously derived surplus measures for particular classes of discrete choices. Mäler considers a good which must be purchased in a given quantity or not at all. Small and Rosen concentrate on the case when two goods are mutually exclusive, but also briefly discuss other kinds of discrete choice situations. By contrast, Hau (1985) considers the case where the consumer does not know in advance which good he will choose, except up to a probability distribution. Recently, Hanemann (1984a) has developed a unified framework for formulating demand models which are suitable for empirical application.

This chapter concentrates on a case which is slightly different from those cases dealt with by the mentioned authors, but the analysis is much inspired by the work of Small and Rosen (1981). A household is assumed to have the option to visit a particular recreation site. This is the discrete part of the choice. However, if the household decides to visit the site, it is free to choose the on-site time subject to the budget and time constraints. Later, the option to choose among several different sites is introduced. Finally, we deal with the formulation and estimation of relationships that involve qualitative or binary variables.

126

1 *Behaviour functions when some goods are mutually exclusive*

The household consumes ordinary consumer goods, and divides its time between work and leisure. Leisure time in turn is split between visits to a recreation site and other leisure activities. A trip to the site requires inputs in the form of time and market goods, such as a car and gasoline. The trip is viewed as an all-or-nothing activity, i.e. the household either makes one trip or no trip at all. However, given a decision to make a trip, the household can freely choose the on-site time within the limits set by the total time available.

In order to produce a trip to the recreation site, time and, in general, market goods inputs are needed. This is represented by a production function

$$N = f(L, q) \tag{8.1}$$

where N is the number of trips, L is time taken for trips, and q is a composite market good input. In order to simplify the exposition, we will only consider the case where N take on values of zero or unity (represented by a delta δ below). In the former case $L = q = 0$, while in the latter case at least one input must take on a strictly positive value (and the isoquant is assumed to be strictly convex to the origin). For example, if the household walks to the recreation site, L is strictly positive while q may be equal to zero (although it is hard to visualize a successful trip without a 1974 Château La Mission Haut Brion or possibly a 1973 Dom Pérignon Moët et Chandon, depending on the specific form of the preference ordering). On the other hand, if the household travels by car, both L and q are strictly positive.

The decision problem of the household can be formulated in the following way. Assume that the household acts as if it maximizes a nicely behaved utility function

$$U = U(\mathbf{x}, \ell_0, \delta\ell_1, \mathbf{z}) \tag{8.2}$$

subject to

$$y + (T - \ell_0 - \delta\ell_1 - \delta L)w - \mathbf{px} - \delta P_\ell \ell_1 - \delta Pq(L, 1) = 0 \tag{8.3}$$

where all goods including leisure time are normal so that a lower price always implies more demand; $\mathbf{x}$ is a vector of consumer goods; $\mathbf{p}$ a vector of prices of such goods; δ is zero or unity; ℓ_1 is time at a recreation site; ℓ_0 is the time spent on other leisure activities; $\mathbf{z}$ is a vector of quality variables to be discussed later; y is a fixed income; T is total time; L is the time required for a trip to the recreation site; w is the wage rate; P_ℓ is a fee or price charged per unit of on-site time; q is a composite market good input to a trip to the site; P is the market price of this composite input; and equation (8.1) has been used to solve q as a function of the time on the trip, conditional on a decision to make a trip. In order to simplify the exposition, it is assumed that on-site time is a non-essential commodity having the property that the (conditional) demand is equal to zero if its price exceeds some finite level. For other possible assumptions, the reader is referred to Hanemann (1984a).

In this model, the benefits of the trip are an increasing function of on-site time. The characteristics of the site, such as the length of the downhill runs and the lifts available in the case of a ski site, are constants included in the vector $\mathbf{z}$. Hence, if the household is thought of as producing recreation, the only variable input, besides the decision on inputs in the travel production function, is on-site time. Moreover the satisfaction gained from recreation is assumed to be strictly increasing in time spent on site. There is, of course, a cost associated with additional on-site time, since other leisure activities and (or) working time must be reduced.

The formulation of the decision problem in (8.2) and (8.3) implies that a trip to the recreational site *per se* does not positively contribute to the utility of the household; the trip is only a necessary input in the production of recreation or on-site time. However, note that the household is charged a uniform price per unit of on-site time, an assumption which may seem a bit unrealistic but will turn out to be a useful analytical tool. In fact, this charge implies that the model does impute different values to different (marginal) uses of leisure time; see equations (8.4) below. A further generalization can be attained by imposing a quantity constraint on the number of working hours. This, i.e. underemployment, implies that the current wage overestimates the value of marginal leisure time. Another possibility, following Hanoch (1980), would be to distinguish between leisure on workdays and non-workday leisure. Such generalizations, however, seem to add few additional insights in the present context. Instead, they tend to add to the complexity and detract from the interest of the model. Furthermore, note that the household cannot choose among different recreation sites. However, such generalizations of the model will be considered later.

In order to simplify the exposition, we will consider two different maximization problems. First *assume* that $\delta = 1$ so that the household visits the recreation site. Then, the first-order conditions for utility maximization are written as

$$\frac{\partial U}{\partial \mathbf{x}} - \lambda \mathbf{p} = 0$$

$$\frac{\partial U}{\partial \ell_0} - \lambda w = 0$$

$$[\frac{\partial U}{\partial \ell_1} - \lambda(w + P_\ell)]\delta = 0 \tag{8.4}$$

$$-\lambda(w + P\frac{\partial q}{\partial L})\delta = 0$$

$$y + (T - \ell_0 - \delta\ell_1 - \delta L)w - \mathbf{p}\mathbf{x} - \delta P_\ell \ell_1 - \delta P q(L, 1) = 0$$

where it is assumed that the price–income vector is such that $\mathbf{x} \gg 0, \ell_0,$ $\ell_1, L > 0$, and λ denotes the Lagrange multiplier of the budget constraint.

Next, the maximization is repeated but now conditional on $\delta = 0$. The resulting system of first-order conditions for an interior solution consists of equations parallel to those contained in the two first and the final (with $\delta = 0$) lines of (8.4). Of course, the commodity bundle $(\mathbf{x}, \ell_0)$ associated with these new conditions need not coincide with the bundle associated with $\delta = 1$ in (8.4).

Solving these two equation systems yields two sets of behaviour functions conditional on $\delta = 0$ and $\delta = 1$ respectively

$$\left.\begin{array}{l} \mathbf{X}^c = \mathbf{X}^c(\mathbf{p}, w, y, \mathbf{z}) \\ (\delta\ell_1^c = \delta L^c = \delta q^c = 0) \end{array}\right\} \quad \text{for } \delta = 0 \tag{8.5}$$

$$\left.\begin{array}{l} \mathbf{X}^c = \mathbf{X}^c(\mathbf{p}, w, y, P_\ell, P, \mathbf{z}) \\ \ell_1^c = \ell_1^c(\mathbf{p}, w, y, P_\ell, P, \mathbf{z}) \\ L^c = L^c(w, P) \\ q^c = q^c(w, P) \end{array}\right\} \quad \text{for } \delta = 1 \tag{8.6}$$

where $\mathbf{X}^c = (\mathbf{x}^c, \ell_0^c, L_w^c)'$, superscript c denotes a conditional behaviour function, and $L_w^c = T - \delta\ell_1^c - \ell_0^c - \delta L^c$ is working time.

In the first case, the household does not undertake a trip to the recreation site. Then, the demand functions for goods, (other) leisure activities and work are independent of the prices of inputs needed for a visit to the recreation site. If a commodity is not purchased at all, changes in its price will not affect demand for the goods actually purchased.

On the other hand, if the household makes a trip to the site, all prices are included as arguments in the conditional behaviour functions. This is captured by the equations (8.6). It should be noted, however, that the optimal or cost minimizing input combination used to produce the single trip is determined by the price of time, w, and the price of the composite

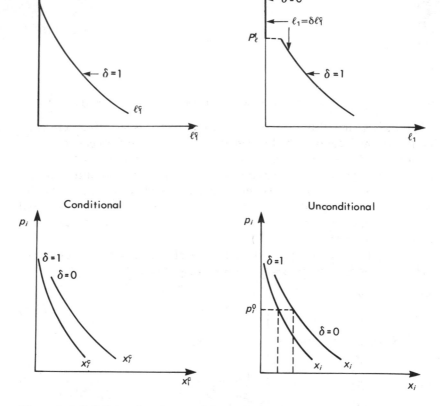

Figure 8.1 Conditional and unconditional demand curves for on-site time and a consumer good. (In drawing the unconditional curves it has been assumed that $\delta = f(P_\ell)$ such that $\delta = 0$ for $P_\ell > P_\ell^f$ and $\delta = 1$ for $P_\ell \leqslant P_\ell^f$)

market good input, P. The household selects a combination along the isoquant for $N = 1$, and the point of tangency between the isoquant and an isocost line identifies the least cost combination of the two inputs. This is seen by inverting the last but one equation in (8.4) for $\delta = 1$. The travel cost is like a lump sum tax on income conditional on $\delta = 1$. The household can escape the 'tax' by not consuming recreational services, though it then misses the benefits of such services. A utility maximizing household prefers the alternative corresponding to $\delta = 0$ if the travel cost exceeds the recreational benefits but switches to $\delta = 1$ if the price vector is changed so that the benefits exceed the cost.

It is important to note that *unconditional* behaviour functions can also be defined. For example, the unconditional demand function for on-site time is equal to $\delta \ell_1^c(\cdot) = \ell_1(\cdot)$. This function incorporates both the discrete choice itself, i.e. $\delta = 0$ or $\delta = 1$, and the on-site time ℓ_1^c demanded conditional on $\delta = 1$. Figure 8.1 indicates that discreteness introduces a point of discontinuity into (or a shift of) unconditional behaviour functions.

In order to illustrate these results, let us consider the following quasi-linear utility function:

$$U = \ell n \, \ell_0 + \delta \ell n \, (\ell_1 + 1) + x_1 \tag{8.2'}$$

Maximization of this utility function subject to the usual budget constraint yields the demand function $\ell_1^c = [1/(w + P_\ell)] - 1$ for time on site, conditional on $\delta = 1$. For example, if $w = 0.2$, the demand curve intersects the price axis at $P_\ell = 0.8$. In order to arrive at a decision whether to visit the recreation site, the household compares the maximal utility levels obtained for $\delta = 0$ and $\delta = 1$ respectively, and chooses the alternative that yields the highest level of satisfaction. The indirect conditional utility functions corresponding to the considered quasi-linear direct utility function can be written as

$$V = -\ell n \, w - \delta[\ell n(w + P_\ell) - (w + P_\ell - 1) + (wL + Pq)] + y + wT - 1 \tag{8.2''}$$

where $\delta = 0,1$. Suppose that $w = 0.2$, $y = 1$, $T = 24$, $L = 1$, and $Pq = 0.3$. It follows by means of straightforward calculations that the household visits the recreation site if the charge P_ℓ is below \$0.1 per hour, while it refrains from the visit if the charge is raised above approximately \$0.1 per hour. But note that if, for example, the price of petrol is increased so that Pq rises from \$0.3 to \$1, then the household will not visit the site, even if the charge P_l is abolished.

2 Critical price levels and corner solutions

The discrete choice, i.e. $\delta = 0$ or $\delta = 1$, is determined by the price–income vector. As is highlighted by the example presented above, there exists a critical entry fee or a reservation price P_ℓ^f per unit of on-site time which, given all other prices and exogenous income, induces the household to switch from $\delta = 0$ to $\delta = 1$. It is assumed throughout that the price–income vector $(\mathbf{p}, w, y, P)$ is such that δ switches from $\delta = 1$ to $\delta = 0$ for a strictly positive and finite value of P_ℓ. In order to examine more closely the properties of this critical price level it is useful to derive the (pseudo) expenditure function. Since there are two cases to consider, we obtain two *conditional* expenditure functions

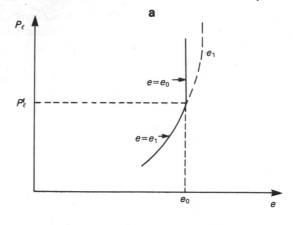

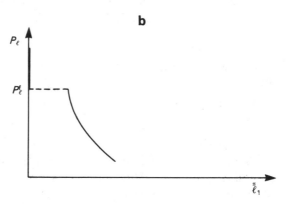

Figure 8.2 The expenditure function and unconditional demand for leisure time at the recreation site as functions of the price paid per time unit at the site

$$e_0(\mathbf{a}) = \mathbf{p}\tilde{\mathbf{x}}(\mathbf{a}) - w\check{L}_w(\mathbf{a}) \tag{8.7}$$

and

$$e_1(\mathbf{a}, P_\ell, P) = \mathbf{p}\tilde{\mathbf{x}}(\mathbf{a}, P_\ell, P) + P_\ell\tilde{\ell}_1(\mathbf{a}, P_\ell, P) + Pq(w, P) - w\check{L}_w(\mathbf{a}, P_\ell, P) \tag{8.8}$$

where subscripts 0 and 1 refer to $\tilde{\delta} = 0$ and $\tilde{\delta} = 1$ respectively, $\mathbf{a} = (\mathbf{p}, w, \bar{U}, \mathbf{z})$, $\bar{U}$ is the pre-specified utility level, a tilde denotes a *conditional compensated* behaviour function, and $\check{L}_w = T - \tilde{\ell}_0 - \tilde{\delta}\tilde{\ell}_1 - \tilde{\delta}\check{L}$. The behaviour functions in (8.7) and (8.8) are derived in the usual way by minimizing expenditure subject to the pre-specified utility level. The expenditure functions provide the exogenous income necessary to attain this utility level when the household is allowed to allocate its time between work and different leisure activities conditional on $\tilde{\delta} = 0$ and $\tilde{\delta} = 1$ respectively.

For any P_ℓ, assuming all other prices remain unchanged, the choice between $\tilde{\delta} = 0$ and $\tilde{\delta} = 1$ is made by comparing the corresponding minimal expenditures e_0 and e_1 required for reaching the specified utility level. Hence, we can define an overall or *unconditional* expenditure function as

$$e(\mathbf{a}, P_\ell, P) = \min \{e_0(\mathbf{a}), e_1(\mathbf{a}, P_\ell, P)\} \tag{8.9}$$

A graphical illustration of this result is found in Figure 8.2a. Given the assumptions introduced above, there is a finite price P_ℓ^f such that expenditure is left unaffected when switching from $\tilde{\delta} = 0$ to $\tilde{\delta} = 1$, i.e. when switching from no visit to one visit at the recreation site. In the numerical example of Section 1 this critical level is \$0.1. If P_ℓ is above the critical level, e_0 gives the least cost commodity bundle necessary to attain the specified level of utility, while e_1 gives the least cost combination if P_ℓ is below the critical level P_ℓ^f. This also illuminates the fact that the value $\tilde{\delta}$ takes on (zero or one) is determined by all prices and the income/utility level. Thus a change in say P_ℓ may cause $\tilde{\delta}$ to shift from $\tilde{\delta} = 0$ to $\tilde{\delta} = 1$ or vice versa. (The tilde is there to highlight the fact that the switch need not occur for the same critical price in the compensated as in the uncompensated case.)

The utility function (8.2) is well-behaved when $\delta = 0$ and $\delta = 1$ respectively. This implies that the conditional expenditure functions e_0 and e_1 and the associated conditional compensated behaviour functions are well defined and continuously differentiable. Hence, the unconditional expenditure function has the same convenient properties as in the previous chapters, except at those points for which $e_0 = e_1$. At such points, e is continuous (since $e_0 = e_1$), as can be seen from Figure 8.2a, and right and left differentiable. Hence, taking the partial derivative of the overall expenditure function with respect to P_ℓ yields

$$\frac{\partial e(\mathbf{a}, P_\ell, P)}{\partial P_\ell} = \tilde{\tilde{\ell}}_1(\mathbf{a}, P_\ell, P) \tag{8.10}$$

or

$$\frac{\partial e(\mathbf{a}, P_\ell, P)}{\partial P_\ell} = \left\{ \begin{array}{ll} \dfrac{\partial e_0(\mathbf{a})}{\partial P_\ell} = 0 & \text{for } \tilde{\delta} = 0 \\[2ex] \dfrac{\partial e_1(\mathbf{a}, P_\ell, P)}{\partial P_\ell} = \ell_1 & \text{for } \tilde{\delta} = 1 \end{array} \right\} \tag{8.11}$$

where a double tilde denotes the unconditional compensated demand function for on-site time, i.e. $\tilde{\tilde{\ell}}_1 = \tilde{\delta}\tilde{\ell}_1$. This unconditional compensated demand function, depicted in Figure 8.2b, incorporates both the discrete choice itself and the demand for on-site time conditional on that choice. At the point for which $e_0 = e_1$ the upper and lower expressions are interpreted as right and left derivatives respectively. Recall Figure 8.2a. since the price derivatives are bounded and piecewise continuous they are integrable. At the point for which $e_0 = e_1$ no change in expenditure arises from switching from not consuming to consuming recreation, i.e. integrating over this point of discontinuity does not affect expenditure (see the appendix to Chapter 6). Using the utility function (8.2′), the reader is invited to show that $e_0 = e_1$ (≈ 6.4) for $P_\ell = 0.1$. *Hint*: The expenditure function is obtained by simply replacing y by e in equation (8.2″)!

3 *Consumer surplus measures in the discrete choice case*

Using equation (8.10), the compensating variation measure for a fall in P_ℓ from P_ℓ^0 to P_ℓ^1 is defined as

$$CV_\ell = y^1 - y^0 + e(\mathbf{a}, P_\ell^0, P) - e(\mathbf{a}, P_\ell^1, P)$$

$$= \triangle y - \int_c \frac{\partial e(\mathbf{a}, P_\ell, P)}{\partial P_\ell} dP_\ell$$

$$= \triangle y - \int_c \tilde{\tilde{\ell}}_1(\mathbf{a}, P_\ell, P) dP_\ell \qquad (8.12)$$

where y^0 and y^1 denote initial and final exogenous incomes respectively, c denotes the path of integration, and the household's utility level is fixed at the initial level U^0. This measure gives the area to the left of the income compensated demand curve between initial and final prices (plus the change, if any, in exogenous income). From (8.11) and Figure 8.2a it is seen that $\tilde{\ell}_1 dP_\ell = 0$ for prices which exceed the critical level P_ℓ^f since $\delta = 0$ for such prices. It is interesting to note, however, that the techniques for deriving consumer surplus measures used in the previous chapters generalize to the case where there is discreteness.

The discreteness is caused by the travel cost. Loosely speaking, the household visits the recreation site if and only if the surplus gain of on-site time covers the fixed travel cost. In order to show this we first use the conditional expenditure functions to obtain

$$e_1(\mathbf{a}, P_\ell^f, P) = e_0(\mathbf{a}) = (e_0(\mathbf{a}) + C) - C = e_1(\mathbf{a}, P_\ell^*, P) - C \qquad (8.13)$$

where C is a sum of money which is equal to the travel cost, i.e. the sum of wage income lost when travelling to the site plus the cost of market goods inputs, and P_ℓ^* ($> P_\ell^f$) is an entrance feè sufficiently high that the *conditional* demand ℓ_1 for on-site time is zero. In the example discussed at the end of Section 1, $P_\ell^* = 0.8$ and $P_\ell^f = 0.1$.

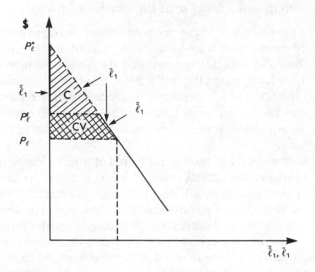

Figure 8.3 The allocation of on-site time as a function of fixed and variable costs

Next, consider the left-hand side term less the right-hand side terms in (8.13). The difference, which of course is equal to zero, can be written as

$$\int_c \frac{\partial e_1}{\partial P_\ell} \, dP_\ell - C = \int_c \tilde{\ell} \, dP_\ell - C = 0 \tag{8.14}$$

where c denotes the path of integration between P_ℓ^f and P_ℓ^*. This result, which is illustrated in Figure 8.3, confirms what one would expect, namely that the household decides to undertake a visit to the recreation site if and only if the associated increase in consumer surplus covers at least the fixed costs of the visit. The critical price P_ℓ^f is the watershed for which the consumer's surplus of on-site time just balances the fixed travel cost and hence makes the household indifferent between zero trips and one trip. If the actual price paid falls short of P_ℓ^f, a trip to the site adds to the consumer's surplus, as is illustrated by the area CV in Figure 8.3. This result can be checked for the utility function (8.2'). Since this utility function is quasi-linear, the ordinary and compensated demand functions coincide. Thus, integrating the ordinary conditional demand function for on-site time, as specified in Section 1, in the interval $0.8 to $0.1, yields a consumer surplus of $0.5, which exactly covers the transportation cost. If the actual charge is below (above) $0.1 per hour, the consumer gains (loses) from undertaking the trip.

4 *The critical price level and the choice of measure*

Following the procedure of the previous section, an equivalent variation measure of on-site time is easily derived. Accordingly this procedure is not repeated. The only difference is that the household now remains at its final utility level, not at the initial level. From previous chapters, it is clear that the CV and EV measures in general impute different money values to the unique change in utility. If the good under consideration is normal, the equivalent variation exceeds the compensating variation for a price change.

This latter property of money measures of utility change means that one would expect the critical price P_ℓ^f to be sensitive to the choice of measure. However, a price fall does not require compensation as long as the price exceeds P_ℓ^f since no on-site time is consumed. The unconditional ordinary and CV demand curves therefore coincide in this interval. However, this is not true for prices below P_ℓ^f unless income effects are zero.

This indicates that if the household consumes on-site time, i.e. $\delta = 1$, and the price rises while the utility level remains fixed, then the critical price for which δ switches from $\delta = 1$ to $\delta = 0$ need not be identical to the aforementioned level P_ℓ^f. Recall that P_ℓ^f was derived given that the household's utility level is fixed at a level corresponding to zero consumption of on-site time. Hence one would expect the two critical price levels to differ unless the EV and CV demand functions coincide; picture the conventional figure in which the EV demand curve falls outside the CV demand curve. This shows that the 'path-dependency' problem does not disappear just because choice is discrete.

5 *On the relevance of the travel costs method*

In the real world, the individual can often choose among several available recreation sites. At any point in time, however, these are mutually exclusive, since a household cannot simultaneously visit different sites. Suppose for simplicity, that there are only two sites which, from the point of view of the household, are perfect substitutes. However they differ with respect to travel costs, say $C_1 < C_2$. If the price–income vector is such that the household visits a site, it clearly chooses the low cost one. This means that the product of on-site time, $\ell_1 \cdot \ell_2$, at site 1 and site 2 is equal to zero at each point in time.

Next, suppose that the fee, $_1P_\ell$ paid per unit of on-site time at site 1 rises from zero to some strictly positive level while all other prices remain fixed. Three outcomes are possible. As an approximation, if $_1P_\ell \ell_1 + C_1 < C_2$, then the household continues to visit site 1, since this is still cheaper than switching to site 2. However, if $_1P_\ell$ becomes sufficiently high, then the sign of the above inequality is reversed and the household chooses to visit site 2 rather than site 1. Hence, differences in transportation costs can be used to measure differences in the consumer's valuation of the two recreation areas. This assumes, however, that the fee is below the critical level discussed at length in previous sections. If the actual unit price paid for on-site time exceeds the critical level, the household switches to zero consumption of on-site time.

More formally, the household now compares three conditional expenditure functions

$$e_0(\mathbf{a}) = \mathbf{p}\bar{\mathbf{x}}(\mathbf{a}) - w\bar{L}_w(\mathbf{a}) \tag{8.15}$$

$$e_i(\mathbf{a}, {_iP_\ell}, P) = \mathbf{p}\bar{\mathbf{x}}(\mathbf{a}, {_iP_\ell}, P) + {_iP_\ell}\bar{\ell}_i(\mathbf{a}, {_iP_\ell}, P) + Pq_i(w, P) - w\bar{L}_w(\mathbf{a}, {_iP_\ell}, P) \tag{8.16}$$

where $i = 1, 2$ refers to site i. The household may choose not to consume on-site time at all. This choice is made if e_0 gives the least expenditure to attain the specified utility level. Then, $\bar{\delta}_1 = \bar{\delta}_2 = 0$. If, on the other hand, e_1 and/or e_2 is smaller than e_0 the household will choose to visit the site for which expenditure is the least, so that either $\bar{\delta}_1 = 1$, $\bar{\delta}_2 = 0$ *or* $\bar{\delta}_1 = 0$, $\bar{\delta}_2 = 1$.

According to equation (8.14) in Section 3, the household visits a site provided the actual price P_ℓ^1 is below the critical level P_ℓ^f for which δ switches from $\bar{\delta} = 1$ to $\bar{\delta} = 0$. Assume that this condition holds. However, the household now chooses between two sites which are assumed to be perfect substitutes. Using equations similar to equation (8.14) it can be seen that the household visits site 1 if $C_1 < C_2$, i.e. if

$$\int_{c_1} \bar{\ell}_1 d_1 P_\ell - \int_{c_2} \bar{\ell}_2 d_2 P_\ell - (C_1 - C_2) = C_2 - C_1 > 0 \tag{8.17}$$

where $c_1 = (P_\ell^*, P_\ell^1)' = c_2$, P_ℓ^* is the price at which the compensated demand curves for on-site time at site 1 and 2, conditional on $\bar{\delta}_1 = 1$ and $\bar{\delta}_2 = 1$ respectively, intersect the price axis, and P_ℓ^1 is the price actually charged. The areas under the compensated conditional demand curves are of equal size since the 'commodities' are perfect substitutes by assumption and the actual price charged, $_iP_\ell^1 \geqslant 0$, is assumed to be the same for both sites. This result can be examined by replacing the second argument of the utility function (8.2′) by the argument $\ell n(\delta_1\ell_1 + \delta_2\ell_2 + 1)$. Apparently, the resulting conditional demand function for on-site time at site 2 is identical to the corresponding function for on-site time at site 1, as specified in Section 1. Thus, if the actual fee charged is the same at both sites and below \$0.1 per hour, the household will visit the low travel cost site.

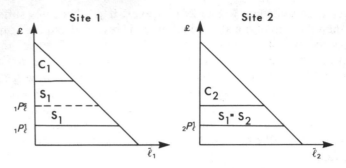

Figure 8.4 The consumer switches from visits to site 1 to visits to site 2 if $_1P_\ell >$ $_1P_\ell^s$ provided that $_1P_\ell^1 = {_2}P_\ell^1$ in the initial situation

Now, assume that $_1P_\ell$ is increased while $_2P_\ell = {_2}P_\ell^1$. From (8.17) it can be seen that there is a price $_1P_\ell^s$ charged for time at site 1 which turns the inequality (8.17) into an equality. If the actual price charged is above this level, the household switches from a trip to site 1 to a trip to site 2, assuming all other prices are fixed. Hence, as is illustrated in Figure 8.4, the area to the left of the conditional demand curve for on-site time at site 1 between the price $_1P_\ell^s$ and the lower, initial price $_1P_\ell^1 = {_2}P_\ell^1$ is equal to the difference in travel costs to the two sites. This implies that the *unconditional* demand $\bar{\ell}_1$ for on-site time at site 1 will switch to zero at $_1P_\ell^1 = {_1}P_\ell^s$ and not at the higher critical price P_ℓ^f which is relevant when the choice is between a trip to a site or no trip at all (provided, of course, that $_1P_\ell^s < P_\ell^f$). The area to the left of the unconditional or, equivalently, the conditional demand curve between $_1P_\ell^s$ and the (lower) price actually charged indicates the gain to the household when visiting site 1 rather than site 2. This area is denoted by S_1 in Figure 8.4.

Quality changes of the kind discussed in Section 5 of Chapter 6 (including changes in preferences) are easily generalized to the discrete choice case. Assume that on-site time at site 1 is a non-essential good and that

$$\ell\text{im}_{{_1}P_\ell\to\infty} \frac{\partial e(\mathbf{b}, {_1}P_\ell, z_\ell)}{\partial z_\ell} = 0 \qquad (8.18)$$

where $e(\cdot)$ is the unconditional expenditure function obtained from equations (8.15) and (8.16), $b = (\mathbf{p}, w, {_2}P_\ell, P)$, z_ℓ is the quality index of site 1, and all prices except $_1P_\ell$ remain fixed. The reader is invited to modify the utility function (8.2′) by multiplying ℓ_1 by z_ℓ and derive, for this particular utility function, the results presented in the remainder of this section.

Equation (8.18) states that if the price charged for time spent at site 1 is high enough to prevent the household visiting the site, then the quality of the site does not matter. Of course, the household may be interested in the preservation of a wilderness area even if it does not visit the area. However, this kind of existence value is not considered in this chapter.

Once again the unconditional expenditure function is differentiated with respect to z_ℓ but now the entry fee is held at some lower level $_1P_\ell^1$ for which the good is consumed, and (8.18) is subtracted to obtain

$$\frac{\partial e(\mathbf{b}, _1P_\ell^1, z_\ell)}{\partial z_\ell} - 0 = -\int_c \frac{\partial \bar{\bar{\ell}}_1(\mathbf{b}, _1P_\ell, z_\ell)}{\partial z_\ell} d_1P_\ell \qquad (8.19)$$

where $c = (\infty, _1P_\ell^1)'$. This expression states that the effect on total expenditure of a marginal change in the quality of site 1 can be obtained from market data. The effect on total expenditure equals the change in the area left of the compensated unconditional demand curve for site 1 as it shifts in response to a marginal shift in the quality of the site. (See the appendix to Chapter 6 for a detailed derivation of a similar expression.)

In order to obtain the effect of a discrete change in z_ℓ, say from z_ℓ^0 to z_ℓ^1, the approach used in deriving equation (A6.10) in the appendix to Chapter 6 is applied. After a few manipulations we obtain

$$CV_z = -\int_c [\bar{\bar{\ell}}_1(\mathbf{b}, _1P_\ell, z_\ell^0) - \bar{\bar{\ell}}_1(\mathbf{b}, _1P_\ell, z_\ell^1)] d_1P_\ell \qquad (8.20)$$

A deterioration in quality shifts both the demand curve to the left and lowers the price $_1P_\ell^s$ for which the household switches from a visit at site 1 to a visit at site 2.

Intuitively, if the loss in consumer surplus due to the deterioration in quality exceeds the cost difference $C_2 - C_1$ in equation (8.17) the household switches to site 2. Hence, if the evaluation of the first integral in (8.17), given the new lower quality of the site, indicates a reversal of the sign of (8.17), the household will not continue to visit site 1. In this case, the compensated unconditional demand for on-site time at site 1 will be equal to zero for all positive prices charged, assuming all other prices remain fixed. In less severe cases, e.g. pollution, unconditional demand may be positive for some prices[1] as is illustrated in Figure 8.5.

These discrete choice results lend some support to the Hotelling–Clawson–Knetsch travel cost method (for continuous choice) described in Chapter 7 (Clawson and Knetsch, 1966). In certain circumstances, the change in travel costs correctly measures the change in the consumer's surplus as a new recreation area is developed or an existing one is lost due to pollution. This assumes, however, that the two sites compared, from the point of view of the household, are perfect substitutes. If the sites differ in quality (even in the initial situation) there is no longer any simple

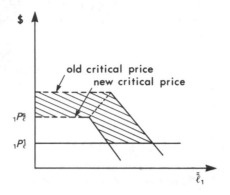

Figure 8.5 Loss of consumer's surplus (shaded area) as the quality of the site reduces

relationship between changes in transportation cost and changes in the consumer's surplus. For example, if site 1 is superior to site 2 from a quality point of view, the consumer may continue to visit site 1 even if the fee rises above $_1P_\ell^s$ in (8.17). Consequently, the loss of the consumer if, for example, site 1 is destroyed by pollution, exceeds the difference in transportation costs to site 1 and site 2.

In any case, it is important to note that results derived for situations in which consumers face a continuous set of choices cannot necessarily be generalized for discrete choice models. For example, Gramlich (1981, pp. 142–3) argues that the loss of a wilderness area through destruction is the usual consumer surplus triangle. That is, the area to the left of the demand curve for the site to be destroyed between the actual price charged and the price for which the curve intersects the price axis. This is a reasonable view if recreational services can be purchased in continuous quantities. On the other hand, if some decisions are mutually exclusive, inspection of Figures 8.3 and 8.4 shows that Gramlich's result must be interpreted with great care. In fact, the upper bound for the loss is given by the area CV in Figure 8.3. The lower bound is given by the change in travel costs, provided that recreation site exists which is a perfect substitute for the one under consideration (assuming that $\triangle C < S$), as is seen from Figure 8.4.

6 Econometric models

With regard to the application of the models considered in this chapter, it is important to note that the investigator cannot know with certainty if a particular household will consume on-site time or not. As Small and Rosen (1981) stressed, all that can be assigned is the probability that a good is purchased by a household. Even if the conditional demand functions are identical for all households, the critical price levels may differ across households due to differences in preferences.

Hence, it is useful to replace the choice index δ with a choice probability π. The fraction of the population which consumes the good under consideration can be viewed as a function of prices and income. In order to concentrate on the choice issue, assume that all consumers have identical conditional demand functions for on-site time but differ in their preferences between on-site time and other goods. This last assumption implies that not all households need switch from no visit to a visit at the same critical price level. The aggregate compensated demand for on-site time, assuming only one site is available, is written as

$$\tilde{\tilde{\ell}} = H\tilde{\pi}(\mathbf{a}, P_l)\,\tilde{\ell}_1(\mathbf{a}, P_\ell) \tag{8.21}$$

where H is the number of households, $\mathbf{a} = (\mathbf{p}, w, P, \mathbf{z}, \bar{U}^h)$, a tilde denotes a conditional compensated demand while a double tilde denotes an unconditional compensated demand function.

In (8.21) the fraction $\tilde{\pi}$ consuming on-site time is determined by the price–quality–utility vector. This implies that a change in a price or a quality attribute not only affects the conditional demand for on-site time, but also changes the critical price level for which the choice index δ switches from zero to unity or vice versa. As a consequence, the Slutsky equation for the aggregate demand function is more complicated than in the continuous goods case considered in Section 3 of Chapter 4. Small and Rosen (1981) have demonstrated that a Slutsky-like equation can be obtained

$$\frac{\partial \tilde{\tilde{\ell}}}{\partial P_\ell} = \frac{\partial \ell}{\partial P_\ell} + \ell[\frac{\partial \ell}{\partial Y} - (1-\pi)\,\frac{\partial \pi}{\partial Y}\,\frac{Y}{\pi}]/\pi \tag{8.22}$$

where ℓ is the unconditional ordinary or Marshallian aggregate demand function and $Y = Hy^h$ is aggregate income.

If π is constant with respect to changes in income, (8.22) is the usual aggregate Slutsky equation, except that the income effect is divided by $\pi < 1$. Hence, the income effect is larger than in the continuous case. In general, however, one would expect π to increase with income and thus augment the aggregate substitution effect of a price increase through the second term within brackets in (8.22). Hence, one must use caution in interpreting the aggregate effect of a price change in the discrete case. For instance, the own-price slope of the aggregate compensated demand function can no longer be inferred from estimates of the own-price and income slopes of the aggregate Marshallian demand function in the way used in the final section of Chapter 4.

Small and Rosen (1981), following McFadden (1973; 1976), have shown that the bulk of current empirical work on discrete choice is based on conditional stochastic indirect utility models of the form

$$V_i^h(p_i, y^h, z_i) = W^h(y^h) + W_i(p_i, y^h, z_i; \mathbf{J}^h) + \epsilon_i^h \tag{8.23}$$

for all goods i and households h. The function W_i is assumed to be identical for all households. The vector $\mathbf{J}$ contains observable characteristics of the household and ϵ_i^h is a random variable which is independent of the arguments of W_i. See Chapter 10 for definitions.

Assuming a joint probability distribution on $\{\epsilon_i\}$, the probability, conditional on prices etc., that utility is maximized by consuming on-site time is

$$\pi_\ell = \text{prob} \left[\epsilon_i - \epsilon_\ell < W_\ell - W_i, \text{ for all } i \neq \ell \right] \tag{8.24}$$

Intuitively, even if $V_\ell > V_i$ for all i, the problem is that this fact cannot be observed by the researcher. At best, the researcher has information on the magnitudes of W_ℓ and W_i. But knowledge of these magnitudes is not sufficient to determine the sign of the change in utility. Recall the presence of the random terms ϵ_ℓ and ϵ_i in (8.23). At best, we are able to calculate a probability that $V_\ell > V_i$, i.e. the probability that $\epsilon_i - \epsilon_\ell < W_\ell - W_i$ in (8.24). The latter requires that an assumption is made about the probability distribution. For example, assuming a cumulative normal distribution and a binary choice situation, we obtain

$$\left.\begin{aligned} \pi_\ell &= F(W_\ell - W_0) = F(\triangle W) \\ \pi_0 &= 1 - \pi_\ell \end{aligned}\right\} \tag{8.25}$$

where a subscript 0 denotes the second good, and F is the cumulative normal distribution function (see, for example Johnston, 1984; Maddala, 1984; Pindyck and Rubinfeld, 1976). Given specific forms for the observable part of the utility functions, the parameters of $\triangle W$ can be estimated from a sample of observed choices by maximizing the likelihood function associated with (8.25). The probability π_ℓ calculated from (8.25) can be interpreted as the fraction of consumers who will choose good ℓ. Moreover, the measure (8.21) can be computed for any price or quality change.[2] In order to illustrate the approach, the next section presents an empirical application.

7 *Estimating the value of a hunting permit from discrete response data*

In recent years, a few contingent market valuation studies have appeared involving discrete responses which are analysed by, for example, logit or probit techniques. The following example is adapted from Hanemann (1984d), who used data from the Bishop and Heberlein (1979) contingent valuation study of goose hunting in the Horicon Zone of East Central Wisconsin. A sample of hunters were asked if they would be willing to sell their hunting permits for a specified sum of money and, supposing they had not received their permits, if they would have been willing to pay a specified price to obtain one.

The above experiment was purely hypothetical, and no sales or purchases occurred. Bishop and Heberlein also performed a simulated market experiment in which they sent a real offer to a different sample of hunters. About 45 per cent of these actually sold their permits.

In contrast to most other studies, Bishop and Heberlein asked questions with yes or no answers, i.e. their approach involved discrete rather than continuous responses. The sample of hunters was divided into subsamples and each subsample of hunters was offered a specific amount of money ($1, $5, $10, $20, $30, $40, $50, $75, $100, $150, or $200). Bishop and Heberlein correlated the resulting yes and no responses with the amount of money offered to the individual using a logit model, and then derived an estimate of the value of a permit to an average hunter.

In his analysis of how the logit models should be formulated, Hanemann (1984d) assumed the following utility function:

$$V(\delta, y; \mathbf{J}) = W(\delta, y; \mathbf{J}) + \epsilon_\delta \qquad \delta = 0, 1 \qquad (8.26)$$

where $\delta = 1$ if the individual possesses a permit to hunt and $\delta = 0$ if he does not, y is income, $\mathbf{J}$ is a vector of observable attributes of the individual which might affect his preferences, and ϵ_0, ϵ_1 are independent and identically distributed (i.i.d.) random variables with zero means. The hunter is assumed to know his utility function, but it contains some unobservable components. These latter components generate the stochastic structure of the model.

Suppose the hunter is offered an amount of money C to forego hunting. The offer is accepted if

$$W(0, y + C; \mathbf{J}) + \epsilon_0 \geq W(1, y; \mathbf{J}) + \epsilon_1 \qquad (8.27)$$

i.e. if the sum of money C offered is so large that utility with C but without a permit to hunt is at least as high as utility with a permit but without C.

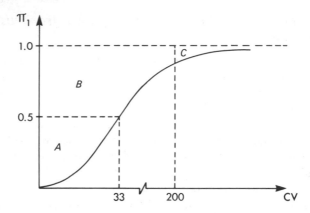

Figure 8.6 Illustration of different willingness to sell measures (the simulated market experiment), where
$$\bar{C}V_B = A + B + C$$
$$\bar{C}V_b = A + B$$

The individual hunter knows which choice maximizes utility, but the investigator does not. Hence for the latter, the response is a random variable, whose probability distribution is given by equation (8.24) with $\ell = 1$ and $i = 0$. Assuming a logit model, as Bishop and Heberlein, the willingness to sell probability can be written as

$$\pi_1 = F(\triangle W) = \frac{1}{1+e^{-\triangle W}} \tag{8.28}$$

where $F(\ )$ is the cumulative distribution function of $\epsilon_1 - \epsilon_0$, and $\triangle W = W(0, y, + C; \mathbf{J}) - W(1, y; \mathbf{J})$.

As noted by Hanemann, if a binary response model is to be interpreted as the outcome of a utility maximizing choice, then the argument of the cumulative distribution function must take the form of a utility difference. For example if $W = \alpha_i + \beta(y + \delta C)$, where $i = 0,1$, and the vector $\mathbf{J}$ is suppressed, then $\triangle W = (\alpha_0 - \alpha_1) + \beta C$. On the other hand, in the logit model employed by Bishop and Heberlein, $\triangle W = \alpha + \beta \ell n\, C$, a particular formula which no explicit utility model (8.27) can generate (Hanemann, 1984d, p. 334). In any case, note that the associated regression equation can be written as

$$\ell n(\frac{\pi_1}{1-\pi_1}) = \alpha + \beta \ell n\, C \tag{8.29}$$

The dependent variable is simply the logarithm of the odds that the hunting permit is sold. Equation (8.29) is obtained by rearranging the terms in (8.28) and taking logarithms, as is shown in, for example, Pindyck and Rubinfeld (1976, p. 248). The model was estimated using GLS (applying Cox's modification to the odds ratio, a modification described and discussed in, for example, Pindyck and Rubinfeld, 1976, p. 250). Hanemann (1984d) reestimated the model, using the maximum-likelihood method and obtained slightly larger absolute values for the coefficients than Bishop and Heberlein. For a comprehensive discussion of the advantages and disadvantages of various estimation techniques in the case of qualitative dependent variables, the reader is referred to Johnston (1984) and Maddala (1984).

Hanemann proceeds by deriving three different willingness to pay measures. We will not go into the details but only report Hanemann's application, which is illustrated in Figure 8.6. Suppose the hunter's level of satisfaction is held constant at the initial $(\delta = 1)$ level. Then, using Bishop and Heberlein's model $\triangle W = \alpha + \beta \ell n \, CV = 0$, i.e. $CV = \exp(-\alpha/\beta)$. Insertion of the estimates of α and β, reported by Bishop and Heberlein, yields point estimates of $CV_A = \$78$ for the hypothetical market experiment $(\alpha \approx -2.8, \beta \approx 0.64)$ and $CV_B = \$33$ for the simulated market experiment $(\alpha \approx -3.9, \beta \approx 1.11)$.

An alternative measure, suggested by Hanemann, is to employ the mean $\bar{C}V$ of the distribution of the random variable C. This measure can be written as

$$\bar{C}V = \int_c [1 - F(\triangle W)] dC = \int_c (1 + e^\alpha C^\beta)^{-1} dC \qquad (8.30)$$

where $c = (\infty, 0)'$, and $\triangle W = \alpha + \beta \ell n \, C$. Inserting the estimates of α and β yields, according to Hanemann, a point estimate $\bar{C}V_B = \$310$, while the integral in (8.30) does not converge for the hypothetical market experiment.

In order to interpret (8.30), let us consider the following expression:[3]

$$\int_0^\infty (1 - F(x)) dx = \int_0^\infty (1 - \int_0^x f(t) dt) dx$$

$$= \int_0^\infty dx \int_x^\infty dt f(t) = \int_0^\infty dt \int_0^t dx f(t)$$

$$= \int_0^\infty t f(t) dt \qquad (8.31)$$

where $x = C$, $f(x)$ is the probability density function, and $F(x)$ is the cumulative distribution function. If (8.31) is absolutely convergent, its value is called the expected value or the mathematical expectation of x. This explains that $\bar{C}V$ in (8.30) is interpreted, when it exists, as a mean value.

The money measure actually computed by Bishop and Heberlein

(1979) differed from (8.30) in that they truncated the measure at $C = \$200$. This produces $\bar{C}V_a = \$101$ and $\bar{C}V_b = \$63$, i.e. a truncation procedure may produce very poor approximations. Nevertheless, other authors (e.g. Seller *et al.*, 1985), who also calculate the measure (8.30) seem to truncate the measure. Moreover, as noted earlier, the model employed by Bishop and Heberlein, and used in deriving (8.30) since no other data were available, is not compatible with utility maximization. Thus, Hanemann's (1984d) study demonstrates that it is important to formulate logit models (and collect data) which are consistent with utility maximization, and to derive consumer surplus measures from the fitted models.

In closing, it should be mentioned that in the case of *continuous* responses, the appropriate approach is to estimate the money measure directly as a function of a set of independent variables (cf. Chapter 7). Nevertheless, suppose that we want to relate the measure, the CV say, to some functional form for the utility function $W(\cdot)$ in (8.26). Then we must insert the chosen function into (8.27) and solve the weak inequality (8.27) for CV, the amount of money that turns (8.27) into an equality. This procedure yields the function to be estimated. Once the equation is fitted to the data, the mean value of the dependent variable is obtained by calculating its expected value. This last step is mentioned simply because a glance at (8.27) shows that the disturbance term may enter the expression for CV in a complicated way (rather than additively, which is the usual assumption in econometrics).

CHAPTER 9

Consumer's surplus in an intertemporal context

Thus far we have dealt exclusively with consumer surplus measures in single-period models. This chapter opens a sequence of chapters that all deal with intertemporal problems. In developing the theory it is as well to discuss the simplest considerations first. For this reason the assumption that agents do not face any uncertainty is retained throughout the present chapter.

Section 1 extends the single-period model described in Chapter 3 to cover optimization for T-period horizons. Overall or lifetime consumer surplus measures are briefly discussed. Such overall measures, however, require huge amounts of information and may be difficult to calculate and estimate. Section 2, therefore, introduces so-called instantaneous consumer surplus measures, and investigates whether the present value of such instantaneous surpluses has the same sign as the lifetime utility change.

The prime attention in this book is focused on consumer surplus measures in atemporal and intertemporal models. However, in some applications, e.g. fishing and hunting, the size of the stock of a natural resource is of importance. Accordingly, the second part of this chapter focuses on models with renewable natural resources. In Section 3 the basic model developed in this chapter is modified so as to include a renewable resource. Section 4 presents a model used by Brown and Hammack (1972) and Hammack and Brown (1974) to analyse the optimal allocation of prairie wetlands in the north-central U.S. and Southern Canada. The main empirical results obtained by Brown and Hammack are reported in Section 5. An important question in studies of projects affecting several generations is how to compare welfare across generations. Therefore, the chapter ends with a brief presentation of different approaches for aggregation of intergenerational welfares.

147

1 *An intertemporal model*

We begin by considering a household with a T-period horizon which acts as if it maximizes a well-behaved utility function

$$U = U(\mathbf{x}^1, \ldots, \mathbf{x}^T) \tag{9.1}$$

subject to its lifetime budget constraint

$$y - \sum_{t=1}^{T} \alpha^t \mathbf{p}_c^t \mathbf{x}^t = 0 \tag{9.2}$$

where $\mathbf{x}^t = (x_{1t}, \ldots, x_{nt})$ is a row vector of goods consumed in the tth period, $\mathbf{p}_c^t = (p_{1t}^c, \ldots, p_{nt}^c)$ is the corresponding vector of prices in current terms, α^t is the present value in period 1 of one dollar in period t at the market rate of interest, and $y = \Sigma \alpha^t y_t$ is the sum of fixed incomes during T periods discounted to the initial period. As usual, primes that denote transposed vectors are suppressed.

Two remarks regarding the budget constraint (9.2) are in order. Firstly, the formulation implies that the household does not plan to leave its heirs assets or debts, although this can be incorporated trivially. Secondly, both borrowing and lending in any amount are allowed at the prevailing interest rate, i.e. capital markets are perfect.

Since the solution of this optimization problem parallels the solution of the optimization problem in Chapter 3 we will turn directly to the indirect utility function. This function is written as

$$V(\mathbf{p}, y) = U(x_{11}(p_{11}, \ldots, p_{nT}, y), \ldots, x_{nT}(p_{11}, \ldots, p_{nT}, y)) \tag{9.3}$$

where prices now are expressed as present values in order to simplify the notation, and $\mathbf{p}$ is a vector of order $1 \cdot (n \cdot T)$. From (9.3) it can be seen that the effects of changes in prices or income in this intertemporal model must be very similar to the effects obtained in the atemporal model investigated in Sections 1 and 2 of Chapter 3. In effect, the results concerning consumer surplus measures derived in Chapter 3 carry over to the intertemporal model, provided the word 'prices' is replaced by the phrase 'the present value of prices'.

Similarly, one may define the compensating variation (and, of course, the equivalent variation). As in the previous chapters, this measure can be derived from the expenditure function. Alternatively, using (9.3)

$$V(\mathbf{p}^b, y^b - \text{CV}) = V(\mathbf{p}^a, y^a) = \bar{V}^a \tag{9.4}$$

where superscript a (b) denotes initial (final) level values, and CV is the overall compensating variation, i.e. the present value of the lump sum income that can be taken from (must be given to) the individual while

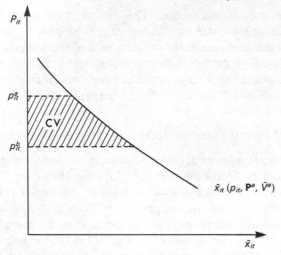

Figure 9.1 The compensating variation (CV) of a price fall in the intertemporal model

leaving him just as well off as he was before a fall (rise) in present value prices **p** and exogenous present value income y.

A graphical illustration of the case where only one price is changed is found in Figure 9.1. The area to the left of the compensated demand curve between the initial and final discounted prices corresponds to the compensating variation in income.

This result can be verified by differentiating the left-hand side of (9.4) with respect to p_{it} and CV, assuming that $\mathbf{p}^a = \mathbf{p}^b$, and noting that lifetime utility remains constant

$$\frac{\partial V}{\partial p_{it}} dp_{it} - \frac{\partial V}{\partial y} dCV = -\lambda \tilde{x}_{it} dp_{it} - \lambda dCV = 0 \qquad (9.5)$$

where $\tilde{x}_{it}(\mathbf{p}^a, \bar{V}^a) = x_{it}(\mathbf{p}^a, y^a)$ is a compensated demand function; it should be recalled that the household remains at the prespecified utility level according to (9.4). Rearranging and integrating between initial and final prices yields

$$CV \equiv \int_c dCV = -\int_c \tilde{x}_{it}(p_{it}, \mathbf{P}^a, \bar{V}^a) dp_{it} \qquad (9.6)$$

where $c = (p_{it}^b, p_{it}^a)'$, and $\mathbf{P}^a$ is a row vector whose elements are the $nT-1$ fixed prices. The right-hand side of (9.6) gives an area corresponding to the shaded area in Figure 9.1.

All of the results concerning path (in-)dependency of consumer surplus measures derived in Chapter 3 carry over to the simple intertemporal model used in this section. This means, for example, that the CV and EV measures are still path independent. Moreover, areas to the left of ordinary demand curves are proportional to the underlying change in utility if and only if the utility function is such that the marginal utility of income is constant with respect to the prices which change. For further details the reader is referred back to Chapters 3 and 4.

2 *Overall versus instantaneous surplus measures*

The consumer surplus measures discussed in the previous section may be called overall or lifetime measures. Suppose, however, that the consumer's surplus of a price change is, instead, calculated at each point in time, as would probably be the procedure in an empirical study because of the obvious problems entailed in calculating an overall or lifetime measure. Drawing on Blackorby *et al.* (1984), we ask whether the present value of these instantaneous consumer's surpluses has the same sign as the overall utility change.

Some restrictions will be placed on the utility function in this section. Following Blackorby *et al.* (1984), the utility function is assumed to be additively separable

$$U(\mathbf{x}) = \sum_{t=1}^{T} \gamma^t U_t(\mathbf{x}^t) \tag{9.7}$$

where γ^t is a discount factor for period t. It is necessary to assume that the utility function is separable in order to ensure that instantaneous preferences exist, a property which will be needed in this section. The utility function (9.7) represents a special case of separability. (It has been argued that (9.7) is not a very sensible form of modelling behaviour if the discount rate varies over time since the marginal rate of substitution between any two fixed time periods will change as one moves forward through time. This is inconsistent with the existence of a stable underlying preference structure; see Blackorby *et al.* (1973), Deaton and Muellbauer (1983), and Strotz (1956).)

The lifetime indirect utility function is defined as

$$V(\mathbf{p}, y) = \max_{\mathbf{x}} \{U(\mathbf{x}) \mid \mathbf{px} \leqslant y\} \tag{9.8}$$

where $\mathbf{p}, \mathbf{x}'$ are vectors of order $1 \cdot (nT)$, and the lifetime budget constraint corresponds to the one specified in equation (9.2).

Similarly, the instantaneous indirect utility functions are given by

$$V_t(\mathbf{p}^t, y_t) = \max_{\mathbf{x}^t} \{U_t(\mathbf{x}^t) \mid \mathbf{p}^t \mathbf{x}^t \leqslant y_t\} \quad \text{for all } t \tag{9.9}$$

Note that prices as well as income in (9.9) are expressed as present values in period 1. However, one could equally well multiply through by the scalar $1/\alpha^t$ to obtain prices and income in current terms. This is because the instantaneous demand functions and hence also the instantaneous indirect utility functions are homogeneous of degree zero in prices and income. Moreover, note that the household in (9.9), but not in (9.8), is prevented from borrowing and lending.

Using (9.8) and (9.9) it can be shown that

$$V(\mathbf{p}, y) \geqslant \Sigma \alpha^t V_t(\mathbf{p}^t, y_t) = F(\{V_t(\mathbf{p}^t, y_t)\}) \tag{9.10}$$

The lifetime utility maximization problem assumes that the household is free to borrow and lend any amount of money at the prevailing market rate of interest. The instantaneous indirect utility functions, on the other hand, assume that the household is constrained by its instantaneous income. Hence, the household is prevented from reallocating its consumption expenditures over time by borrowing and lending. In general, this means that the discounted value of the sum of instantaneous utility levels, i.e. the right-hand side of (9.10), falls short of the maximum lifetime utility level given by the left-hand expression in (9.10). However, if the sequence of y_t is chosen in such a way that saving, even if allowed, equals zero at each point in time, then (9.10) reduces to an equality. Hence

$$V(\mathbf{p}, y) = \max_{\{y_t\}} \{F(\{V_t(\mathbf{p}^t, y_t)\}) \mid \Sigma y_t \leqslant y\} \tag{9.11}$$

Overall (CV) and instantaneous (CV_t) present value compensating variations for a price change from $\mathbf{p}^a$ to $\mathbf{p}^b$ are defined as

$$\left.\begin{array}{l} V(\mathbf{p}^b, y - CV) = V(\mathbf{p}^a, y) = U^a \\[2mm] V_t(\mathbf{p}^{tb}, y_t - CV_t) = V_t(\mathbf{p}^{ta}, y_t) = U_t^a \end{array}\right\} \tag{9.12}$$

The overall compensating variation is the maximum amount of present value income or wealth that the household is willing to give up to secure the change. Similarly, the instantaneous compensating variation is the (present value) income in period t that can be taken from the household while leaving it just as well off as prior to the fall in (present value) prices in that period. However it should be remembered that the household in (9.12) is prevented, by assumption, from reallocating its consumption over time.

Now, assume that condition (9.11) holds for the initial price vector $\mathbf{p} = \mathbf{p}^a$. Then, since the household remains at the initial utility level according to (9.12), it must also be the case that

$$V(\mathbf{p}^b, y - CV) = F(\{V_t(\mathbf{p}^{tb}, y_t^* - CV_t)\}) \tag{9.13}$$

where an asterisk denotes an optimal income level according to (9.11). However, using (9.10) we obtain

$$V(\mathbf{p}^b, y - \Sigma CV_t) \geq F(\{V_t(\mathbf{p}^{tb}, y_t^* - CV_t)\}) \tag{9.14}$$

Even if the instantaneous incomes are chosen in an optimal way, the household may want to reallocate its consumption over time following the payment of CV_t. The left-hand expression, but not the right-hand expression, in (9.14) permits such reallocations. This explains the weak inequality sign.

Combining (9.13) and (9.14) it follows that $CV \geq \Sigma CV_t$. This indicates that ΣCV_t, the sum of discounted instantaneous compensating variations, can, but need not, have the same sign as the overall measure CV. However, if $\Sigma CV_t \geq 0$ then it must be the case that $CV \geq 0$. In this case, the discounted sum of instantaneous compensating variations ranks the alternatives in the same order as the overall measure.

The present value criterion does not work when $\Sigma CV_t < 0$. Even if the sum of discounted instantaneous compensating variations is negative, the overall compensating variation may be positive. In order to obtain a rule for project rejection, we use the equivalent variation instead, i.e. the minimum amount the household would accept in lieu of the change from $\mathbf{p}^a$ *to* $\mathbf{p}^b$. Overall (EV) and instantaneous (EV$_t$) equivalent variations are defined as

$$\left.\begin{array}{l} V(\mathbf{p}^b, y) = V(\mathbf{p}^a, y + EV) = U^b \\[2ex] V_t(\mathbf{p}^{tb}, y_t) = V_t(\mathbf{p}^{ta}, y_t + EV_t) = U_t^b \end{array}\right\} \tag{9.15}$$

where U^b and U_t^b denote the final utility levels.

Using equations similar to equations (9.13) and (9.14) reveals that $EV \leq \Sigma EV_t$. Hence, if the discounted sum of instantaneous equivalent variations is negative, then the overall equivalent variation must also be negative. This means that the sum of discounted instantaneous EVs can be used to check whether a project should be rejected.

In short, if the discounted sum of compensating variations (equivalent variations) is positive (negative), then lifetime welfare has increased (decreased). However, ambiguous results occur when the present value of compensating variations is negative and the present value of equivalent variations is positive. This is demonstrated by Blackorby *et al.* (1984). Nevertheless, in many cases the sum of the discounted consumer's surplus should be a useful concept. Assume that we have estimated compensated demand functions for one or more periods. Even if these demand functions, like the demand functions in the previous chapters, only reflect instantaneous utility maximization according to (9.9), some conclusions do emerge. Firstly, if the sum of the discounted instantaneous compensating variations associated with a project is positive, the project is certainly worthwhile. Secondly, if $\Sigma CV_t < 0$, compute the discounted sum of instantaneous equivalent variations. If this discounted sum is negative, the project must be rejected. Although there remains a zone of indeterminacy ($\Sigma CV_t < 0$ while $\Sigma EV_t > 0$), the discounted sum approach greatly simplifies the calculations in the many cases for which definite conclusions emerge.

3 *A model with renewable resources*

In some circumstances, households may be interested in the preservation of a natural resource. For example, some households may assign a value to the blue whales as living creatures in a natural environment. A household owning and harvesting a renewable resource must recognize that if it harvests more than the natural growth of the resource, then the resource will sooner or later be depleted. This latter phenomenon raises the question of the optimal stock of a natural resource. It is outside the scope of this book to deal at length with this issue. However, in calculating, for example, the willingness to pay of hunters, a problem which we will consider in the subsequent sections, the size of the stock of the species is of obvious interest. This is one reason for briefly dealing with this issue. The second reason is that we will deal, in a later chapter, with the benefits of preserving a resource in a risky world. The following discussion may serve as a background to that chapter.

Let us first consider a simple extension of the model presented in Section 1. Assume that the household owns and harvests a renewable resource. The harvest in period t plus what is left to period $t+1$ equals (cannot exceed) what was left over from the previous period plus the growth of the stock in period t

$$s_{t-1} + F_t(s_{t-1}) = h_t + s_t \tag{9.16}$$

where s_t is the stock at the end of period t, h_t is the harvest in period t, and $F_t(\cdot)$ represents the growth of the resource in period t as a function of the stock at the end of period $t-1$ with $\partial F_t/\partial s_{t-1} \gtreqless 0$ and $\partial^2 F_t/\partial s_{t-1}^2 < 0$. These properties of the growth function can be visualized by referring to Figure 9.2.

Assume that all markets, including the market for the renewable resource, are perfect, that no value is assigned to the stock of the resource *per se*, and that there are no harvesting costs. Accordingly, the household maximizes

$$L = U(\mathbf{x}) + \lambda[y + \sum_{t=1}^{T} p_{1t}h_t - \mathbf{px}] + \sum_{t=1}^{T} \mu_t[s_{t-1} + F_t(s_{t-1}) - h_t - s_t] \tag{9.17}$$

where $\mathbf{x}$ and $\mathbf{p}'$ are vectors of order $1 \times (n \times T)$, a subscript 1 denotes the

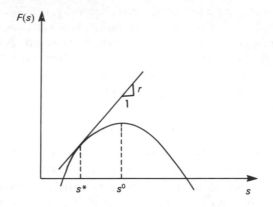

Figure 9.2 The growth function for a renewable resource

renewable resource so that x_{1t} denotes consumption of the resource in the tth period, and λ and μ_t are Lagrange multipliers. This formulation implies that the household sells (buys) $h_t - x_{1t}$ units of the resource in period t. Moreover, there is a constraint on the maximization problem over and above the budget constraint. The new constraint is the constraint on the level of harvest given by equation (9.16).

The terminal value of the stock discounted to the initial period is not included in (9.17). In order to maximize its total utility over an horizon containing T periods, the household must liquidate the stock at the end of period T. However, as T tends to infinity, the present value of this revenue tends to zero. This is why the terminal value discounted to the initial period is not included in expression (9.17) above; it should also be remembered that the management of a renewable resource is ultimately a long-run issue.

Taking partial derivatives of (9.17) with respect to x_{1t}, h_t and s_t, assuming interior solutions, yields

$$\left.\begin{aligned}
\frac{\partial L}{\partial x_{1t}} &= \frac{\partial U(\mathbf{x})}{\partial x_{1t}} - \lambda p_{1t} = 0 \\[2ex]
\frac{\partial L}{\partial h_t} &= \lambda p_{1t} - \mu_t = 0 \\[2ex]
\frac{\partial L}{\partial s_t} &= -\mu_t + \mu_{t+1}\left[1 + \frac{\partial F_{t+1}(s_t)}{\partial s_t}\right] = 0
\end{aligned}\right\} \quad (9.18)$$

In order to interpret these conditions, we focus on a steady-state situation, i.e. where the household harvests the growth in each period so that the stock of the resource remains constant over time. Moreover, this steady-state is taken to imply that the resource price is constant in current terms, i.e. the discounted price decreases over time: $p_{1t} = (1+r)p_{1t+1}$. Using the two last lines of (9.18) respectively for two consecutive periods yields

$$\left.\begin{array}{l} \mu_t = (1+r)\mu_{t+1} \\[2mm] \mu_t = [1+\dfrac{\partial F(s)}{\partial s}]\mu_{t+1} \end{array}\right\} \qquad (9.19)$$

The conditions in (9.19) imply that a utility maximizing household selects a stock such that marginal growth rate ($\partial F/\partial s$) equals the market rate of interest (r). This is a well-known result in the economics of renewable resources (see Clark, 1976; Dasgupta, 1982; Dasgupta and Heal, 1979; and Johansson and Löfgren, 1985).

The intuition behind this result is quite simple. If the household reduces the stock by one unit in period t it can earn a once and for all revenue which equals $p_{1t} \cdot 1$. On the other hand, the household loses all future revenues from the harvest of the natural growth of this unit of the stock. If the marginal growth of the resource ($\partial F(s)/\partial s$) falls short of the interest rate (r) it is profitable to decrease the stock, i.e. to transfer resources to the investment opportunity that gives the highest rate of return. If the marginal growth rate exceeds the market rate of interest, it pays to increase the stock of the resource. Hence, the optimal stock is the one for which the marginal growth rate equals the market rate of interest. As can be seen from Figure 9.2 this optimal stock s^* falls short of the stock s^0 which gives the maximum sustainable yield. It should be emphasized, however, that in more complicated models the optimal stock may exceed the maximum sustainable yield stock. For further information on such models, the reader is referred to Clark (1976), Herfindahl and Kneese (1974), Lecomber (1979), and Siebert (1982).

4 *The Brown–Hammack model for allocation of prairie wetlands*

The renewable resource model discussed in the previous section is a discrete time finite horizon model. Brown and Hammack (1972) have used a continuous time infinite horizon model to examine the optimal allocation of prairie wetlands in the north-central U.S. and Southern Canada.[1] If left in their natural state, these wetlands are essential to migratory waterfowl which are valued hunting objects. On the other hand, the farmers who own the land would prefer to drain the marshes and ponds and convert them to cropland. The Brown–Hammack model and its empirical results will be presented in this and the following section.

The benefits, of preserving the wetlands, are the aggregate consumer's surplus or the willingness to pay of waterfowl hunters while the costs are the opportunity costs or net value of the drained ponds in agricultural production. According to Brown and Hammack, the objective is to choose the bagged waterfowl kill and the number of ponds so as to maximize

$$\int_0^\infty [Hu(x_1(t), x_2(t)) - c(q(t))] e^{-rt} dt \tag{9.20}$$

where H is the number of hunters, $u(\cdot, \cdot)$ is the individual hunter valuation function, $x_1(t)$ is the bagged waterfowl kill at time t, $x_2(t)$ is consumption of other goods (net of goods used as inputs in hunting) at time t, $c(\cdot)$ is the pond cost function, $q(t)$ is the number of ponds at time t, and r is the discount rate.

Brown and Hammack employ a standard assumption in natural resource economics, namely that the utility function is additively separable (which is invariably the case with infinite horizon models). It is important to note, however, that the valuation functions (like the cost functions) are expressed in monetary units and not in 'utils'. Given x_2, the valuation function gives the hunter's willingness to pay for bagged waterfowl. This function is assumed to be concave in the number of waterfowl killed and bagged. Moreover, the valuation function is constant over time, and relates to the 'representative' hunter. The latter explains that we multiply the valuation function by the (constant) number of hunters. The linear or convex cost function in (9.20) indicates the net value of agricultural output forgone as a function of the number of ponds (not drained and converted).

The discount rate in (9.20) ought to reflect the individual's rate of time preference, i.e. the minimum premium the individual must receive before he will postpone a dollar's worth of consumption in one period. Assuming perfect capital markets, it is reasonable to set the rate of time preference equal to the market rate of interest r (see Dasgupta and Heal, 1979, chs 9–10).

It remains to describe the ecological system. The constraint on the waterfowl population is written as

$$\dot{s}(t) = -s(t) + a[I(s(t), q(t)) + bs(t) - cHx_1(t)] \tag{9.21}$$

where a dot denotes a partial derivative with respect to time, s is the number of mature birds, $I = I(\cdot, \cdot)$ is the number of immature, a is the survival fraction of the fall flight not killed by hunters from September to May, b is the survival fraction of adults from May to September, and c is an adjustment for unbagged kill.

Equation (9.21) describes the evolution over time of the waterfowl population. There is an outflow due to killing and other causes death, and an inflow of immature birds. Note that if the constants a, b, and c are all equal to one, the change over time of the population would simply equal the difference between the number of immature birds (the inflow) and the number killed and bagged by hunters (the outflow). In addition to (9.21), it must also hold that the initial population exceeds the threshold population and that, at any given moment in time, the resource stock and the harvest level cannot be negative.

In order to solve the problem raised by equations (9.20) and (9.21) we will use optimal control theory (see Pontryagin *et al.* 1962). The first step is to formulate the Hamiltonian function

$$L = [Hu(x_1, x_2) - c(q) + \mu(-s + aI(s, q) + abs - acHx_1)]e^{-rt} \quad (9.22)$$

where time indices are suppressed so as to simplify the notation, and μ is a costate variable. Among the necessary conditions for an 'interior' solution are

$$\left.\begin{array}{l} \dfrac{\partial L}{\partial x_1} = \dfrac{\partial u}{\partial x_1} - \mu ac = 0 \\[2ex] \dfrac{\partial L}{\partial q} = -\dfrac{\partial c}{\partial q} + \mu a\dfrac{\partial I}{\partial q} = 0 \\[2ex] \dfrac{\partial L}{\partial s} = -\dot{\mu} + r\mu = \mu\left(-1 + a\dfrac{\partial I}{\partial s} + ab\right) \end{array}\right\} \quad (9.23)$$

For purely expositional purposes, let us assume that the constants a, b, and c all equal one. Then, from the first line in (9.23), it can be seen that μ can be interpreted as the marginal value to hunters of waterfowl. A marginal increase in the number of ponds q creates not only a cost in the form of agricultural output forgone, but also a benefit in the form of an increased number of birds (immature) which are valued hunting objects. The second line of (9.23) tells us that the number of ponds should be increased to the point where the marginal cost is equal to the marginal revenue. In order to interpret the final line of (9.23), let us consider a steady state in which the marginal value of waterfowl is constant over time, i.e. $\dot{\mu} = 0$. It then follows that the optimal waterfowl stock is that for which the marginal growth rate $\partial I/\partial s$ is equal to the discount rate; it should be remembered that we have assumed that $a = b = c = 1$. This is exactly the result derived in Section 3.

5 *Estimation of the Brown–Hammack model*

Brown and Hammack made an attempt to estimate the model described in the previous section, and some of their results are reported below. For a detailed presentation the reader should consult Brown and Hammack (1972) and Hammack and Brown (1974). A good summary version of their work is found in Krutilla and Fisher (1975, ch. 9).

In order to obtain information on the hunter valuation function Brown and Hammack used the interview technique (the so-called Davis technique; see Davis, 1964). A sample of waterfowl hunters were questioned concerning the value each attached to hunting. The central question was as follows: 'About how much greater do you think your costs would have had to have been before you would have decided not to have gone hunting at all during that season?' (Hammack and Brown, 1974, p. 92). The resulting willingness to pay amounts were regressed on a number of independent variables to obtain

$$\ell n\, u = 1.5 + 0.4\ell n\, x_1 + 0.4\ell n\, y + 0.2\ell n\, A + 0.1\ell n\, B \quad R^2 = 0.22 \,(9.24)$$
$$\qquad\quad (12.9) \qquad\;\; (8.4) \qquad (4.4) \qquad (5.6)$$

where numbers in parentheses are t values, y is income, A is the number of seasons of waterfowl hunting, B is hunter costs for the season, and the number of observations is 1511. Taking the partial derivative with respect to x_1 and rearranging yields

$$\frac{\partial u}{\partial x_1} = 0.4 \frac{u}{x_1} \tag{9.25}$$

This expression indicates the valuation of a marginal unit of bagged kill and can be used to construct a (downward sloping) 'demand' curve for waterfowl kill. Note, however, that (9.25) is not defined for a zero hunting level; in fact, the underlying indifference surface does not intersect the $x_1=0$ hyperplane. Given the fact that the hunter is confronted with a sufficiently high (hypothetical) hunting cost to prevent him from hunting at all, it is not obvious why Hammack and Brown choose a functional form that is not consistent with such behaviour. Compare also equation (A6.16) in the Appendix to Chapter 6.

The growth function $I(s,q)$ was estimated using time series data running from 1955 to 1968. One (out of several different) estimated relationship is

$$\ell n\, I = 1.4 + 0.3\ell n\, s + 0.5\ell n\, q \qquad R^2 = 0.83 \tag{9.26}$$
$$\qquad\quad (1.6) \qquad\;\; (6.7)$$

where I is the number of immature birds in September, s is the

Table 9.1 *Economic optimal values and historical values*

| | Pond cost | | | Historical values |
	$4.76	$12	$17	
Breeders, s (millions)	33	15	11	8
Ponds, q (millions)	22	6	4	1
Marginal value of waterfowl, μ (dollars)	2	3	4	
Total kill, x_1 (millions)	15	7	5	4

Assumptions: $a = 0.84$, $b = 0.95$, $c = 1.25$, $r = 0.08$ and number of hunters, $H = 0.279$ million.
Source: Krutilla and Fisher (1975, p. 229).

continental breeding population in the preceding May, and q is the number of Canadian prairie ponds in July of the same year.

A number of results are reported in Table 9.1. The cost function $c(q)$ was not estimated. As can be seen from the table, Brown and Hammack assumed that the cost of a marginal pond is constant. Assumptions about the parameters are set out below the table.

It is interesting to note that the economically optimal level of breeding stock far exceeds the one actually observed, at least for reasonable pond cost levels. This result is probably due to the fact that the wetlands are privately owned, i.e. there is a market for wetlands, while there is no market for hunting. In other words, ponds cause a positive external effect which is not reflected in the maximization problems of the landowners.

The results can also be used to calculate the maximum sustainable yield stock of breeders. Differentiating (9.21) with respect to t, with q and x_1 fixed, and setting the resulting expression equal to zero yields

$$-1 + a\frac{\partial I}{\partial s} + ab = 0 \tag{9.27}$$

This expression can be solved to obtain the steady state stock that gives the highest possible sustainable level of kill. This level corresponds to point s^0 in Figure 9.2. Using the growth function given in (9.26) Brown and Hammack estimated the maximum sustainable yield stock to be 10 million for a pond value of 1.4 million. The corresponding figure for the value of kill is 6 million.

These maximum sustainable yield values are much lower than the economic optima reported in Table 9.1, at least for reasonable pond cost values. The reason is that the maximum sustainable yield values are calculated from the actual number of ponds. The economic optimal solution requires a much larger number of ponds; although a sufficiently high pond cost will reverse the result. Krutilla and Fisher (1975, pp. 231–3) point out that these results illustrate the problems with the biological, or maximum sustainable yield solution, i.e. how the decision maker is to choose the number of ponds. The (bio-)economic approach used by Brown and Hammack, on the other hand, indicates the optimal number of ponds, although this figure, like the rest of the results, must be interpreted with great care. Nevertheless, their approach is an interesting and promising one.

A final comment relates to the fact that the demand derived from the amenity services of a natural area may vary with time. Clearly, such factors as the degree of availability of substitute areas, as measured by cross-price elasticities and travel costs, and the rate of increase in real income, are of critical importance when forecasting demand. Recall the discussion in Chapter 8. Hammack and Brown do not consider such reasons for fluctuations in demand. The reader interested in practical methods used to forecast demand for scarce amenity resources is referred to Krutilla and Fisher (1975), who consider the case of a unique natural area, and Cuddington *et al.* (1981), who deal with the case where the resource in question is not unique but has recognized substitutes. Basically, Cuddington *et al.* multiply the present value of the consumer's surplus in year t by $(1+i)^t$ with i reflecting the rate of increase in real income. Moreover, the size of the surplus depends on the presence of substitute areas, as measured by a cross-price elasticity. Obviously such modifications may have quite an influence on the size of the present value of natural amenities. More generally, variations over time in benefits and/or costs highlight the fact that the decision *when* to undertake a project is of the utmost importance. We will consider this issue in a risky world in Chapter 11. The reader interested in the optimal timing of a reversible development project in situations without uncertainty is referred to Porter (1984).

6 *Aggregation of intergenerational welfares*

In a perfect market economy, the market rate of interest ought to provide a correct reflection of the rate of time preference of present consumers for consumption in the present rather than in the next period. It also indicates the value of using resources in investment projects. In the absence of a perfect market economy, it is well known that the social discount rate may exceed or fall short of the market rate of interest. For a discussion, as well as surveys of different methods for the practical determination of the social discount rate, the reader is referred to any textbook on welfare economics. We will, nevertheless, briefly consider one particular problem, namely the fact that the market rate of interest, even in a perfect market economy, need not accurately reflect society's regard for consumption by future generations.

A particularly important point concerns the fact that, in this chapter, the projects under consideration may affect several generations. It is especially this feature which causes problems in the evaluation of environmental programmes. This section, which draws heavily on Dasgupta and Heal (1979, ch. 9), reviews different frameworks for weighting different generations.

Probably the most influential doctrine is classical utilitarianism. By utilitarianism is meant 'the ethical theory, that the conduct which, under any given circumstances, is objectively right, is that which will produce the greatest amount of happiness on the whole; that is, taking into account all whose happiness is affected by the conduct' (Sidgwick, 1890, p. 409). According to this doctrine, utility is summed across all individuals in all generations without any discounting of future utilities. In point of fact, several utilitarians have found the discounting of future utilities morally objectionable (see, for example, Ramsey, 1928; Harrod, 1948, for discussions of this issue).

However, if there is a positive chance that life on earth will cease to exist, then one may find it defensible to discount future utilities at positive rates. For instance, if it is assumed that the probability π of survival is constant over time, then the probability that the world exists at date τ is $(\pi)^\tau$, which can be written as $(\pi)^\tau = 1/(1+r)^\tau$, where r is an appropriately chosen discount rate. Thus, it would seem to be a legitimate procedure to discount future utilities in a risky world, not because one is myopic, but because there is a positive chance that future generations will not exist. It does not make any sense to save or transfer consumption (resources) to generations that will not exist.

An alternative approach, associated with Harsanyi (1955) and Rawls (1972), is founded on the concept of social contracts. Suppose a particular individual does not know if he belongs to a relatively rich or poor generation. Instead he faces a subjective probability of being a member of any generation t. Accordingly, it is reasonable to choose between two intertemporal consumption programmes on the basis of the expected utility associated with the programmes. If the number of generations is finite, one possibility is to proceed as above. That is, to assume that the probability of doomsday follows a Poisson process so that the probability of survival at date τ is $(\pi)^\tau = (1+r)^{-\tau}$. Thus, there are formal similarities between this approach and the 'modified' utilitarian approach discussed previously. According to both approaches, future utilities are discounted at positive rates. There are, however, also important differences. In particular, the Harsanyi framework assumes that the choosing party satisfies the Neumann–Morgenstern axioms of expected utility (to be discussed in the next chapter). The utilitarian utility functions, on the other hand, are measures of the quantity of happiness of different generations (see Dasgupta and Heal, 1979, pp. 271–3, for a detailed discussion of this issue).

The third approach to the treatment of intergenerational welfare distribution introduces a social welfare function

$$W = W(U_1, \ldots, U_T) \tag{9.28}$$

where, for simplicity, there is only a single (representative) individual in each generation. This welfare function is usually assumed to be continuous and Paretian. The latter means that if two utility sequences have the property that $U_t^a \geqslant U_t^b$ for all t and the strict inequality holds for at least one t, then $W(U_1^a, \ldots, U_T^a) > W(U_1^b, \ldots, U_T^b)$. Moreover, (9.28) is assumed to obey the principle of equal treatment of different generations. Thus, if any two generations are interchanged in (9.28), welfare would be left unchanged.

However, there is no welfare function which is simultaneously continuous, Paretian, and satisfies the equal treatment principle, as is demonstrated in Dasgupta and Heal (1979, pp. 277–80). One way of getting round this problem is to dispense with the equal treatment principle. It is now possible to show that a continuous and Paretian welfare function can be written as

$$W = \sum_{t=1}^{\infty} U_t(1+r)^{-t+1} \tag{9.29}$$

provided the function satisfies the assumptions of independence and stationarity. Loosely speaking, the first assumption means that one treats the well-being of different generations independently of one another. The stationarity assumption means that in the evaluation of two utility sequences, the calendar date for the timing of the utility levels ought not to matter (see Dasgupta and Heal, 1979, pp. 278–80).

In closing, it is interesting to note that several frameworks are consistent with the additive separable form (9.29), with $r \geqslant 0$, which were employed in previous sections of this chapter. One need not appeal to a particular framework, such as the utilitarian one, in order to utilize the simple approach in (9.29). Naturally, it cannot be said that this approach is self-evident in intertemporal studies. On the contrary, the basic issue of the choice of principles for intergenerational aggregation remains unresolved.

CHAPTER 10

Welfare change measures in a risky world

There are many important situations in which prices, income or preferences are not known with certainty. For example, the waterfowl hunter of Chapter 9 cannot know for sure the number of waterfowl he will kill and bag during the next hunting season. Similarly, the recreationist of Chapter 8 may be uncertain as regards travel costs, entrance fees, and the weather at the site. In such cases it may seem reasonable to distinguish between risk, that refers to situations where probabilities are knowable, and uncertainty proper, which applies to situations where probabilities cannot even be defined. In this book, we will deal exclusively with the former class of situations, although the terms risk and uncertainty are used interchangeably.

Ordinary or compensated demand functions, obtained under certainty, imply very little about a household's attitudes towards risk. This is because the form of demand functions is an ordinal property, while risk aversion is a cardinal property of preferences. Moreover, while conventional demand theory begins with a quasi-concave direct utility function, risk analysis hinges on the stronger assumption of concavity or convexity. The first section of this chapter is devoted to exploring these different concepts.

In Section 2, the welfare change measures derived in previous chapters are modified so as to be able to cope with cases of uncertainty where some decisions must be made before prices are known. These issues are discussed in the context of a simple two-commodity model. Section 3 presents an empirical study involving a discrete choice situation as well as uncertain prices. In Section 4, we introduce the method of backward dynamic programming, which considers future optimal decisions as stochastic depending on new information that is accumulated along the way. In Section 5, this model is used to introduce a few concepts that have been the subject of much discussion among environmental econo-

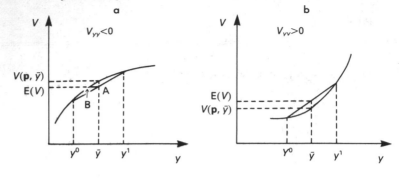

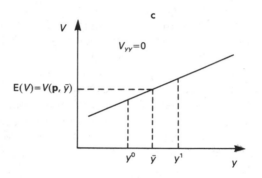

Figure 10.1 (a) A risk-averse, (b) a risk-loving, and (c) a risk-neutral household

mists: expected consumer's surplus, option price, and option value. In terms of the models used in this chapter, the debate concerns the money measure that ought to be used in situations involving changes in future demands which are viewed as random from the standpoint of the present.

1 *Risk measures and the properties of the utility function*

In order to illustrate the meaning of risk attitudes, it is useful to consider a household which faces an uncertain income. Taking partial derivatives with respect to income of a well-behaved indirect utility function $V(\mathbf{p},y)$ of the form considered in the previous chapters (further assumptions – in particular cardinality – are introduced below) yields

$$\left. \begin{aligned} \frac{\partial V}{\partial y} &= \lambda(\mathbf{p}, y) \\[2mm] \frac{\partial^2 V}{\partial y^2} &= \frac{\partial \lambda}{\partial y} = V_{yy} \end{aligned} \right\} \tag{10.1}$$

A household is said to be risk averse with respect to income risk if $V_{yy} < 0$. Conversely, the household is a risk lover if $V_{yy} > 0$, and risk neutral if the expression is equal to zero. Let us consider a Friedman–Savage (1948) diagram such as Figure 10.1 in which utility is depicted as an increasing function of income while all prices are held constant.

Figure 10.1a is drawn on the assumption that $V_{yy} < 0$. Assume that the household receives income y^0 with a probability of one-half, and income y^1 with a probability of one-half. Since the actual outcome is either y^0 or y^1, the expected utility is

$$E(V) = 0.5\,V(\mathbf{p}, y^0) + 0.5\,V(\mathbf{p}, y^1) \qquad (10.2)$$

where E is the expectations operator. However, the household clearly prefers to get the expected income $\bar{y}$ rather than the 'gamble', since

$$V(\mathbf{p}, \bar{y}) > E(V) = \Sigma_i \pi^i V(\mathbf{p}, y^i) \qquad (10.3)$$

where y^i occurs with probability π^i ($0 < \pi^i < 1$), and $\bar{y} = Ey^i$. Such behaviour, i.e. preferring the expected value of a gamble rather than the gamble, is called risk aversion. By moving horizontally to the left from point A towards point B in Figure 10.1a it can be seen that a risk averter is a person who would be willing to forego some part of his income to change a random prospect into a certain one.

Figure 10.1b pictures the case of a risk-loving household ($V_{yy} > 0$). In this case the straight line between y^0 and y^1 is above the corresponding segment of the utility function. Thus the household in Figure 10.1b may prefer a risky prospect to a certain one even if the former gives a lower expected income.

Finally, a risk-neutral household ($V_{yy} = 0$) has a utility function which is linear in income. Clearly, such a household will be indifferent between certain and risky prospects, as is seen from Figure 10.1c.

In the previous chapters it has been assumed that the direct utility function is strictly quasi-concave. The definition of risk attitudes, on the other hand, turns on the stronger assumption of concavity or convexity.

A function is quasi-concave for all commodity bundles $\mathbf{x}^0$, $\mathbf{x}^1$ over a region if

$$U(\pi\mathbf{x}^0 + (1-\pi)\mathbf{x}^1) \geqslant \min\,\{U(\mathbf{x}^0),\,U(\mathbf{x}^1)\} \qquad (10.4)$$

for all $0 \leqslant \pi \leqslant 1$. The function is strictly quasi-concave if the strict inequality holds for $0 < \pi < 1$.

A function is concave over a region if

$$U(\pi\mathbf{x}^0 + (1-\pi)\mathbf{x}^1) \geqslant \pi U(\mathbf{x}^0) + (1-\pi)U(\mathbf{x}^1) \qquad (10.5)$$

for all $0 \leqslant \pi \leqslant 1$, and strictly concave if the strict inequality holds for all

$0 < \pi < 1$. By reversing the signs of the inequalities in (10.4) and (10.5) we obtain definitions of quasi-convexity and convexity respectively. Referring back to Figure 10.1, it should be obvious that the measures of risk attitudes are founded on the concept of concavity/convexity, i.e. $V[\mathbf{p}, \mathrm{E}(y)] \underset{(<)}{\geq} \mathrm{E}[V(\mathbf{p}, y)]$ when the indirect utility function is strictly concave (convex) in income, a theorem often referred to as Jensen's inequality. Moreover, Hanoch (1977) has shown that risk aversion with respect to income implies and is implied by risk aversion with regard to quantity bundles. Hence, $V_{yy} < 0$ means that the direct utility function is strictly concave.

Measures of risk aversion are defined cardinally, whereas conventional demand theory assumes an ordinal utility function. The latter, i.e. ordinal measurability, means that if a function $U(\mathbf{x})$ is a suitable representation of the household's preference orderings, any other increasing function or monotonic transformation of $U(\mathbf{x})$, say $F(\mathbf{x}) = f(U(\mathbf{x}))$ with $\partial f/\partial U > 0$, will serve equally well. The signs of the first derivatives of an ordinal function are unchanged by a monotonic transformation, but signs of higher order derivatives, e.g. the sign of V_{yy}, can change (since no restriction can be placed upon $\partial^2 f/\partial U^2$).

If the utility function is weakly cardinal, any positive affine transformation of the function, say $G(\mathbf{x}) = a + bU(\mathbf{x})$ with $b > 0$, will serve equally well. Preferences are strongly cardinal if, in addition to being weakly cardinal, the ratio of two magnitudes of preference differences is also a meaningful magnitude of preference. The assumption of strongly cardinal preferences means that it is meaningful to say that $[U(\mathbf{x}^1) - U(\mathbf{x}^0)]/[U(\mathbf{x}^3) - U(\mathbf{x}^2)] = r$ means that a move from $\mathbf{x}^0$ to $\mathbf{x}^1$ is r times preferable to the move from $\mathbf{x}^2$ to $\mathbf{x}^3$ (see Morey, 1984, for details). Furthermore, note that the signs of the partial derivatives of any order, and hence the sign of V_{yy}, are unchanged by any positive affine transformation. In both the cardinal and the ordinal cases, the considered transformations leave the indifference map unchanged.

The magnitude of the second-order derivative V_{yy}, which was used as the risk indicator above, is not invariant under a linear transformation. This is readily verified by multiplying the (cardinal) utility function by a constant and taking the second-order derivative with respect to income. For this reason V_{yy} is not normally used as a measure of risk aversion. The best-known measure, the Arrow–Pratt coefficient of *absolute* risk aversion, is obtained by normalizing by V_y, and reversing the sign

$$R(y) = -(\frac{\partial^2 V}{\partial y^2})/(\frac{\partial V}{\partial y}) = -\frac{V_{yy}}{V_y} \tag{10.6}$$

Multiplying by income y yields the so-called Arrow–Pratt index of *relative* risk aversion

$$R^R(y) = -y\frac{V_{yy}}{V_y} \tag{10.7}$$

In a cardinal world, the signs of the partial derivatives of these measures with respect to income tell us whether risk aversion is increasing or decreasing when income is increased (see Arrow, 1971; Hey, 1979, 1981; Pratt, 1964).

In conclusion, it is important to emphasize that in analysis of expected utility, only the sub-utility indices $V(\mathbf{p}, y^i)$ need to be cardinally measurable. Expected utility, i.e. $E(V) = \Sigma \pi^i V(\mathbf{p}, y^i)$, on the other hand, is an ordinal concept, i.e. if $E(V)$ maximizes expected utility, so does $f[E(V)]$, where $f[\ ]$ is a monotonic increasing transformation. See Hirshleifer and Riley (1979), Jones-Lee (1976, ch. 3), and Neumann and Morgenstern (1947, ch. 1) for detailed analysis of the axioms underlying the expected utility hypothesis.

2 *Consumer's surplus under price uncertainty*

We now introduce the case where a household must decide upon quantities of commodities before the uncertainty about some prices is resolved. The analysis is performed in terms of a household consuming two (vectors of) normal commodities, x_1 and x_2, respectively. Prices of at least one commodity are random at the time that a decision on x_1 must be taken, but uncertainty is resolved before the decision on x_2 is taken. This last assumption is needed to ensure that the budget constraint is not violated. The fact that decisions are not taken at the same time means that prices are now present value prices, assuming perfect capital markets. However, for reasons which will become apparent, the price of the first commodity, but not the price of the second commodity, is assumed to be stochastic. This makes an interpretation of the model in intertemporal terms somewhat awkward. An explicit intertemporal model is introduced in Section 4.

The utility function of the household is written as

$$U = U(x_1, X_2) = U(x_1, \frac{y-p_1x_1}{p_2}) \tag{10.8}$$

where $X_2 = (y-p_1x_1)/p_2$ from the budget constraint. This and all other utility functions considered in the rest of this book are assumed to be cardinal and well-behaved.[1] For a detailed discussion of these assumptions and their implications the reader is referred to Drèze and Modigliani (1972) and Epstein (1975). Detailed comparative statics examinations of this and similar models can also be found in Block and Heineke (1975), Hey (1979), and Sandmo (1970).

Suppose that p_1 fluctuates randomly ($0 < p_1 < \infty$). If p_1 is a discrete variable, its expected value is a weighted average of all possible price levels. The expected value of a continuous variable is defined in a very similar fashion. In this latter case, we integrate for values of p_1 to obtain

$$E(p_1) = \int_c p_1 f(p_1) dp_1 = \bar{p}_1 \tag{10.9}$$

where the probability density function $f(p_1)$ is the household's subjective probability distribution on p_1, with finite moments of at least first and second order, c is the range of p_1, and a bar denotes an expected value. A simple and commonly used specification is: $p_1 = \bar{p}_1 + \beta\varepsilon$ with $E(\varepsilon) = 0$, where β is the standard deviation. A spread-preserving increase in the price may be represented by an increase in $\bar{p}_1$ and an increase in β may be used to represent a mean-preserving increase in the variability of the price.[2] This particular specification is implicitly employed in this chapter.

The (Neumann–Morgenstern) household is assumed to act as if it maximizes expected utility

$$E(U) = \int_c U(x_1, \frac{y - p_1 x_1}{p_2}) f(p_1) dp_1 \tag{10.10}$$

The problem that confronts the household is to choose the x_1 that will maximize this expression. The first-order condition for an interior solution is

$$E[U_1 - \frac{U_2 p_1}{p_2}] = 0 \tag{10.11}$$

where subscripts 1 and 2 denote partial derivatives with respect to x_1 and X_2 respectively. In principle, (10.11) can be solved to yield the resulting demand function for the first commodity

$$x_1 = x_1(\bar{p}_1, y, \phi) \tag{10.12}$$

where ϕ contains moments about the mean characterizing the stochastic properties of p_1.

Consumption of the second commodity, on the other hand, is a random variable defined by the budget constraint

$$X_2 = \frac{y - p_1 x_1(\bar{p}_1, p_2, y, \phi)}{p_2} = X_2(\bar{p}_1, p_1, p_2, y, \phi) \tag{10.13}$$

As long as the price of the first commodity fluctuates randomly, X_2 is also a random variable (but prices, etc, are assumed to be such that $X_2 > 0$). However, its expected value is obtained by integrating (10.13) over the range of p_1, i.e. replacing p_1 in the middle expression of (10.13) by its expected value $\bar{p}_1$.

Substituting (10.12) and (10.13) into (10.10) yields an indirect expected utility function

$$V = E[v(\bar{p}_1, p_1, p_2, y, \phi)]$$

$$= \int_c U[x_1(\bar{p}_1, p_2, y, \phi), X_2(\bar{p}, p_1, p_2, y, \phi)]f(p_1)dp_1 \qquad (10.14)$$

This function gives the maximum expected utility as a function of p_2 and y, which are known with certainty, and the stochastic properties of p_1. Taking partial derivatives of (10.14) with respect to (the mean of) prices and income yields

$$\left.\begin{array}{l} \dfrac{\partial V}{\partial \bar{p}_1} = -\dfrac{E(U_2)x_1(\bar{p}_1, p_2, y, \phi)}{p_2} \\[3mm] \dfrac{\partial V}{\partial p_2} = -\dfrac{E[U_2 \cdot X_2(\bar{p}_1, p_1, p_2, y, \phi)]}{p_2} \\[3mm] \dfrac{\partial V}{\partial y} = \dfrac{E(U_2)}{p_2} \end{array}\right\} \qquad (10.15)$$

This is shown in the appendix to this chapter. Note that the second line does not simplify to anything like the expression in the first line. This is because X_2, but not x_1, is a stochastic variable. We will return to this issue in Section 5.

Using (10.14) one can calculate the compensating variation CV of a *ceteris paribus* change in the mean price. This indicates the non-stochastic amount of money that the household is willing to pay, following a mean price fall, in order to return to the initial expected level of satisfaction

$$E[v(\bar{p}_1^b, \bar{p}_1^b+\varepsilon, p_2, y - CV, \phi)] = E[v(\bar{p}_1^a, \bar{p}_1^a+\varepsilon, p_2, y, \phi)] = \bar{V}^a \quad (10.16)$$

where a and b denote the initial and final mean prices respectively, and $\bar{p}_1^i + \varepsilon$ denotes the actual price in 'state' i, where $i = a,b$. For a marginal change in the mean, we obtain from (10.15) and (10.16)

$$- E(\tilde{U}_2)\,\tilde{x}_1 d\bar{p}_1 - E(\tilde{U}_2)\frac{\partial CV}{\partial \bar{p}_1}\,d\bar{p}_1 = 0 \qquad (10.17)$$

where a tilde, as usual, denotes a compensated function, and $x_1(\bar{p}_1, p_2, y - CV, \phi) = \tilde{x}_1(\bar{p}_1, p_2, \bar{V}^a, \phi)$. Note that both the compensated demand function and the marginal compensation are non-stochastic and thus 'factor out' of the expectation. Rearranging and integrating between initial and final mean prices yields

$$CV = -\int_c \tilde{x}_1(\bar{p}_1, p_2, \bar{V}^a, \phi)d\bar{p}_1 \qquad (10.18)$$

where $c = (\bar{p}_1^b, \bar{p}_1^a)'$, and $CV = \int_c(\partial CV/\partial \bar{p}_i)d\bar{p}_i$.

Thus, the compensating variation of a mean price change can be measured left of the compensated demand curve for x_1 corresponding to

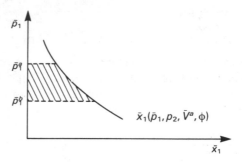

Figure 10.2 The compensating variation (shaded area) of a mean price change

the initial expected utility level. This is illustrated in Figure 10.2. Similarly, the equivalent variation of a subjective mean price change is obtained by fixing the utility level at its final expected value. In general, however, the CV and EV measures will not coincide, unless the underlying utility function is such that income effects are zero for the commodity under consideration. (Compare with the analysis in Chapter 4.)

The above analysis is concerned with a *ceteris paribus* mean price change. The same approach can be used to evaluate changes in higher moments of the probability distribution for p_1. Referring back to the particular specification discussed below equation (10.9), i.e. $p_1 = \bar{p}_1 + \beta\varepsilon$, an increase in β may be used to calculate CV and EV measures of a mean-preserving increase in the variability of the price. Moreover, income uncertainty is easily introduced into the model. It is a straightforward matter to show that x_1 will be a function of expected income $\bar{y}$, provided the uncertainty is revealed after a decision is taken on how much to consume of the commodity. In principle, the model can also be used to consider the effects of policies that affect future prices, i.e. p_2. However, such an investigation is delayed until Sections 4 and 5.

3 *Discrete choice under uncertainty: housing tenure*

In order to appreciate the results derived in the previous sections it is useful to illustrate them by means of an empirical study. Unfortunately, there seem to be no straightforward applications on the consumer surplus issue available. However, there is at least one study that examines a discrete choice situation similar to the one considered in Section 7 of Chapter 8, namely the choice, in a risky world, between owning and renting a house. In Chapter 8, the value of a hunting permit was estimated from discrete response data. The approach implicitly assumes that hunters know the value of a permit with certainty. Similarly, the standard approach to the choice between renting and owning assumes that households have perfect foresight in the sense that they know the true user cost of housing. However, it is highly unlikely that households are able to forecast the fluctuations in this user cost with certainty.

Recently, Rosen *et al.* (1984) have constructed and estimated a model of tenure choice that explicitly allows for the effects of uncertainty. As in Chapter 8, the individual makes his choice by comparing the outcomes of two sub-problems. Let $V(p_1, y)$ be the indirect utility function conditional on owning the house, and $V(p_2, y)$ the indirect utility function when renting is selected. The real cost p_1 of owner-occupation and the real renting price p_2 are both surrounded with uncertainty while income and the (*numéraire*) price of a composite good consumed by the household are known with certainty. The sub-utility functions are similar to those considered in Section 1, the difference being that Rosen *et al.* consider price risk instead of income risk.

An individual elects to own if

$$\triangle V = \mathrm{E}[V(p_1, y) - V(p_2, y)] > 0 \tag{10.19}$$

where the expectation is taken with respect to the joint distribution of prices (compare equation 10.27). Equation (10.19) simply states that the individual elects to own if the expected utility of owning exceeds the expected utility of renting. Taking second-order Taylor series expansions around the points $(\bar{p}_1, y)$ and $\bar{p}_2, y)$ respectively yields

$$\mathrm{E}[V(p_i, y)] = V(\bar{p}_i, y) + \frac{V_{i1}(\bar{p}_i, y)\sigma_i^2}{2} \qquad i = 1, 2 \tag{10.20}$$

where a bar denotes an expected price, $V_i \mathrm{E}(p_i - \bar{p}_i) = 0$, $V_{i1} = \partial^2 V / \partial \bar{p}_i^2$ and $\sigma_i^2 = \mathrm{E}(p_i - \bar{p}_i)^2$. Substituting (10.20) into (10.19) and proceeding in the same way as in Section 7 of Chapter 8, Rosen *et al.* suggest the following specification to be estimated (by OLS)

$$\ell n(\frac{\pi}{1 - \pi}) = \alpha + \beta_1 \bar{p}_1 + \beta_2 \bar{p}_2 + \beta_3 \sigma_1^2 + \beta_4 \sigma_2^2 + \beta_5 y + \varepsilon \tag{10.21}$$

where π is the aggregate proportion of home-owners. Thus, in this model, expected prices as well as forecast error variances affect the tenure decision, in sharp contrast to the perfect foresight discrete choice model considered in Chapter 8. It should also be noted that to the extent that the two underlying indirect utility functions are identical (up to an additive constant), expected prices and forecast error variances affect the tenure decision in a symmetrical fashion, i.e. $\beta_1 = -\beta_2$ and $\beta_3 = -\beta_4$. This assumption is employed by Rosen *et al.* when estimating (10.21).

Rosen *et al*. assume that as more information becomes available, individuals employ it when making forecasts, but continue to use old information as well. Basically, they assume (conditional) rational expectations, in contrast to adaptive expectations. According to the hypothesis of rational expectations, which has been proposed by the new classical economists, expectations are formed on the basis of all the available relevant information concerning the variable being predicted. As the originator of the concept, John Muth (1961), suggested, rational expectations are essentially the same as the predictions of the relevant economic theory. This is noted here because in future research on environmental economics, a field which is often concerned with 'long-run' issues, the modelling of expectations will probably be of the utmost importance.

After some preliminary analysis of the time series on prices, Rosen *et al*. (1984, pp 408–9) selected an autoregressive integrated moving-average (ARIMA) process to make forecasts in year τ:

$$p_{it} - p_{it-1} = \phi_i(\tau)(p_{it-1} - p_{it-2}) + \mu_t \qquad i = 1,2 \qquad (10.22)$$

where $t = 0, 1, \ldots, \tau-1$, $\phi_i(\tau)$ is the parameter to be estimated, and μ_t is a normally distributed white noise term. This equation is reestimated each year τ with observations from year 0 to $\tau-1$. The estimate of $\phi_i(\tau)$ can be used to solve (10.22) recursively to generate forecasts of the price p_i for as many future years from τ as desired. Rosen *et al*. assume that people form expectations not only for the current year but for the following four years, and base their tenure choice on the five-year average.

Equation (10.22) is also used to produce a series of forecast error variances. However, due to considerations of space, the tedious calculations are not reported here. Instead we turn directly to the results obtained when estimating (10.21) using annual U.S. data for 1956 to 1979, since the results provide a good idea of the interpretation of the model used by Rosen *et al*.

$$\ell n\left(\frac{\pi}{1-\pi}\right) = 0.125 - 4.75(\bar{p}_1 - \bar{p}_2) - 6.89(\sigma_1^2 - \sigma_2^2) + 2.04x \quad R^2 = 0.99$$
$$(10.21')$$

where x is per capita real consumption, the symmetry constraints $\beta_1 = -\beta_2$ and $\beta_3 = -\beta_4$ have been imposed, and all the β-coefficients are statistically significant at conventional levels. When the expected excess of the cost of owning over renting increases, the proportion of owner-occupiers decreases. Similarly, greater uncertainty in the price of owning reduces the proportion of home-owners. Finally, and also as expected, an increase in real consumption, which is used as a proxy for permanent income, increases the proportion of home-owners.

Athough the study reported here refers to the housing market, the approach taken by Rosen *et al.* is also certainly of great interest to environmental economists. For example, a decision whether or not to visit a recreation site may be influenced by expectations of the weather, the rate of congestion, and the size of the travel costs. Similarly, an individual may be uncertain about the true value of preserving a natural area or the value of obtaining a hunting permit, so that his reported willingness to pay is an expected consumer surplus measure. Apparently, in situations where individuals are unable to forecast variables with certainty, it may be quite misleading to use consumer surplus formulas that explicitly or implicitly are based on that particular assumption.

4 *Intertemporal models*

The approach used to derive consumer surplus measures in Section 2 is readily extendable to the multi-period case. Referring back to the T-period horizon model in Section 1 of Chapter 9, we select a *numéraire* commodity, e.g. x_n^T. As in Section 2 the budget constraint is then used to eliminate x_n^T from the utility function. If the household faces random prices, it maximizes the expected value of this T-period utility function.

However, this approach assumes that the subjective distribution of prices is constant over time, i.e. it ignores the possibility that decisions in later periods can be adjusted as more price information becomes available. On the other hand, the dynamic programming technique examined in this section, considers future optimal decisions to be stochastic depending on new information that the household accumulates over time.

In order to illustrate the principles of this technique, we will analyse a form of uncertainty which is probably closer to reality, in many situations, than those considered previously. Current prices are now known with certainty while future prices are random. For the sake of simplicity, let us suppose that the utility function is additively separable

$$U(\mathbf{x}) = \sum_{t=1}^{T} \gamma^t U_t(\mathbf{x}^t) \tag{10.23}$$

where γ^t is a discount factor for period t, and $\mathbf{x}^t = (x_{1t}, \ldots, x_{nt})$ is a vector of goods consumed in period t.

In order to analyse the utility maximization problem in a risky world, Bellman's (1957) technique of backwards induction is used. (A good presentation of this technique is found in Hey (1981, ch. 4).) As this name suggests, the household works backwards. The household decides an optimal strategy in the final period T. In the light of this strategy, the household then selects the optimal strategy in period $T-1$, and so on.

Assume that the household has arrived at the final period. The household's problem is to maximize

$$U_T = U_T(\mathbf{x}^T) \tag{10.24}$$

subject to the budget constraint

$$y_T + z_{T-1} - \mathbf{p}^T\mathbf{x}^T - z_T = 0 \tag{10.25}$$

where z_{T-1} is the amount of money saved and carried over to the final period, and z_T is the end-of-period stock of money. Since period T is the final period, it makes no sense to save, i.e. the optimal value of z_T is zero. For purely expositional reasons, the market rate of interest is set equal to zero in all periods.

An interior solution to the above final period maximization problem yields demand functions of the form

$$\mathbf{x}^T = \mathbf{x}^T(\mathbf{p}^T, y_T + z_{T-1}) \tag{10.26}$$

where z_{T-1} is a predetermined number when viewed from the final period.

The formulation of the maximization problem (10.24) subject to (10.25) implies that decisions are assumed to be taken *after* uncertainty about *current* prices is resolved. In many cases, this is probably a more realistic assumption than the one employed in Section 2, where households were assumed to buy a commodity before the uncertainty about its price was resolved. However, as viewed from period $T-1$ all final period prices may be uncertain, i.e. $p_{iT} = \bar{p}_{iT} + \varepsilon_{iT}$. Hence, the expected maximum value of final period utility, as viewed from period $T-1$, can be written as

$$V_T(z_{T-1}) = \mathrm{E}\{U_T[\mathbf{x}^T(\mathbf{p}^T, y_T + z_{T-1})]\} \tag{10.27}$$

where the expectation is taken with respect to the joint distribution of final period prices, i.e. there is a function $f(p_{1T}, \ldots, p_{nT})$ which gives the consumer's (subjective) probability distribution of final period prices. If some prices are known with certainty, then the distribution is degenerate in those dimensions.

The problem of the household in period $T-1$ is to choose a bundle of goods $\mathbf{x}^{T-1}$ and an end-of-period stock of money z_{T-1} so as to maximize expected utility over the two final periods

$$U_{T-1}(\mathbf{x}^{T-1}) + \gamma V_T(z_{T-1}) \tag{10.28}$$

subject to

$$y_{T-1} + z_{T-2} - \mathbf{p}^{T-1}\mathbf{x}^{T-1} - z_{T-1} = 0 \tag{10.29}$$

where z_{T-2} is the predetermined initial endowment of money, i.e. savings carried over from the preceding period.

The first-order conditions for an interior solution, if such a solution exists, to this maximization problem are

$$\frac{\partial U_{T-1}}{\partial \mathbf{x}^{T-1}} - \lambda_{T-1}\mathbf{p}^{T-1} = 0$$

$$\frac{\gamma \partial V_T}{\partial z_{T-1}} - \lambda_{T-1} = 0 \qquad \left.\right\} \qquad (10.30)$$

$$y_{T-1} + z_{T-2} - \mathbf{p}^{T-1}\mathbf{x}^{T-1} - z_{T-1} = 0$$

where λ_{T-1} is the Lagrange multiplier of the budget constraint (10.29).

Solving this equation system yields demand functions for goods and an end-of-period stock demand function for money

$$\mathbf{x}^{T-1} = \mathbf{x}^{T-1}(\mathbf{p}^{T-1}, y_{T-1} + z_{T-2})$$

$$z_{T-1} = z_{T-1}(\mathbf{p}^{T-1}, y_{T-1} + z_{T-2}) \qquad \left.\right\} \qquad (10.31)$$

where z_{T-2} is a predetermined number. See also (10.38) where the dependence on future expected prices is made explicit.

Moving back to period $T-2$, the expected value of the maximum final-two-period utility is obtained by substituting (10.31) into (10.28) and taking expectations with respect to the joint distribution of prices $\mathbf{p}^{T-1}$ in period $T-1$

$$V_{T-1}(z_{T-2}) = \mathrm{E}\{U_{T-1}[\mathbf{x}^{T-1}(\mathbf{p}^{T-1}, y_{T-1} + z_{T-2})] +$$
$$+ \gamma V_T[z_{T-1}(\mathbf{p}^{T-1}, y_{T-1} + z_{T-2})]\} \qquad (10.32)$$

Although the household's decisions are taken after the uncertainty about prices is resolved, utility is a random variable as long as future prices are random, i.e. utility will take on different values depending on the values taken by the future period prices.[3] Hence, the relevant concept is expected utility.

The household now continues to work back through the periods. In the first period, the problem of the household can be interpreted as if it maximizes (10.28) subject to (10.29) with time indices $T-1$ and $T-2$ replaced by 1 and 0 respectively. Hence, the expected maximum utility as viewed from the beginning of the first period is

$$V_1(z_0) = U_1[\mathbf{x}^1(\mathbf{p}^1, y_1 + z_0)] + \gamma V_2[z_1(\mathbf{p}^1, y_1 + z_0)] \qquad (10.33)$$

where $z_0 \geq 0$ is the initial endowment of money.

It should be emphasized that the function $V_2[\ \ ]$ in the expression (10.33) implicitly captures all future optimal decisions since it has been obtained by starting at the final period and then moving back period for period towards the present.

The model can now be used to discuss consumer surplus measures. Consider first a change in the price of the ith commodity in the first period. Differentiating (10.33) with respect to p_{i1} yields

$$\frac{\partial V_1}{\partial p_{i1}} = (\sum_{j=1}^{n} U_{j1} \frac{\partial x_{j1}}{\partial p_{i1}} + \gamma \frac{\partial V_2}{\partial z_1} \frac{\partial z_1}{\partial p_{i1}})$$

$$= \lambda_1 (\Sigma p_{j1} \frac{\partial x_{j1}}{\partial p_{i1}} + \frac{\partial z_1}{\partial p_{i1}}) \tag{10.34}$$

where the final expression has been obtained by employing first-order conditions parallel to those stated in (10.30). Using the budget constraint of the first period, it is readily seen that (10.34) can be written as

$$\frac{\partial V_1}{\partial p_{i1}} = -\lambda_1 x_{i1}(\mathbf{p}^1, y_1 + z_0) \tag{10.35}$$

Hence, the same procedure as used in previous chapters can be used to derive consumer surplus measures for changes in first period prices. This is also true for the CV and EV measures. For this reason, the reader is referred to Chapters 3 and 4, where detailed derivations can be found.

5 Expected consumer's surplus, option price and option value

We now turn to the case where policy changes affect future prices. This adds a new problem over and above those considered in the previous sections in designing a compensation scheme. This is because future decisions are random as viewed from today. In point of fact, since Weisbrod's (1964) article quoted in Chapter 1, there has been much debate among environmental economists regarding the appropriate money measure in such situations. A common interpretation of the Weisbrod quotation is that, when demand for, say, a park is uncertain, the expected consumer surplus will underestimate the constant maximum payment (option price) that the consumer is willing to make across states (Plummer and Hartman, 1985, p. 2). The difference, it is argued, arises because the option price, which is non-stochastic or state independent, measures both the value of retaining an option to consume the good *and* the expected value of actually consuming the good, i.e. the expected consumer surplus.

Thus, one would expect the difference between option price and expected consumer surplus, called option value, to be positive. Furthermore, if the option value is positive, one would know that the expected consumer surplus was an underestimate of the gain of, for example, preserving a national park. This would greatly simplify cost–benefit analysis in cases where an expected consumer surplus measure, but not option price or option value, is available (at least if the costs fall short of the expected benefits).

In order to illustrate the meaning of the concepts introduced above as well as to examine the sign of option value, we will use a two-period version of our dynamic programming model. First, substitute the right-hand side of (10.27) into (10.28) with $T = 2$, to obtain the first period maximization problem in the following form, i.e. maximize

$$U_1(\mathbf{x}^1) + \gamma E\{U_2[\mathbf{x}^2(\mathbf{p}^2, y_2 + z_1)]\} \tag{10.36}$$

subject to the first-period budget constraint

$$y_1 + z_0 - \mathbf{p}^1\mathbf{x}^1 - z_1 = 0 \tag{10.37}$$

where the expectation is taken with respect to the joint distribution of second-period prices. Note that (10.36) measures expected utility over both periods as a function of consumption $\mathbf{x}^1$ and saving z_1 in the first period, given that the consumption bundle $\mathbf{x}^2$ in the second period is optimally chosen.

Using the first-order conditions (10.30) for utility maximization, with $\partial V_2/\partial z_1$ replaced by $E(\partial U_2/\partial \mathbf{x}^2)\partial \mathbf{x}^2/\partial z_1$, yields first-period and second-period demand functions for goods of the form

$$
\left.
\begin{aligned}
\mathbf{x}^1 &= \mathbf{x}^1(\mathbf{p}^1, \bar{\mathbf{p}}^2, y_1, y_2, \phi) \\
\mathbf{x}^2 &= \mathbf{x}^2(\mathbf{p}^1, \mathbf{p}^2, \bar{\mathbf{p}}^2, y_1, y_2, \phi) = \mathbf{x}^2[\mathbf{p}^2, y_2 + z_1(\mathbf{p}^1, \bar{\mathbf{p}}^2, y_1, y_2, \phi)]
\end{aligned}
\right\} \tag{10.38}
$$

where a bar above second-period prices denotes expected values, and ϕ contains moments about the mean characterizing the stochastic properties of $\mathbf{p}^2$. Observe that $\mathbf{x}^2$ are stochastic as viewed from the first period. This is because second-period prices are random, i.e. $\mathbf{p}^2 = \bar{\mathbf{p}}^2 + \varepsilon^2$, although uncertainty is resolved before second-period decisions are taken.

Substitution of (10.38) into (10.36) yields an indirect expected utility function

$$V = U_1[\mathbf{x}^1(\mathbf{p}^1, \bar{\mathbf{p}}^2, y_1, y_2, \phi)] + \gamma E\{U_2[\mathbf{x}^2(\mathbf{p}^1, \mathbf{p}^2, \bar{\mathbf{p}}^2, y_1, y_2, \phi)]\} \tag{10.39}$$

where the expectation is taken with respect to the joint distribution of second-period prices. Taking partial derivatives of (10.39) and invoking

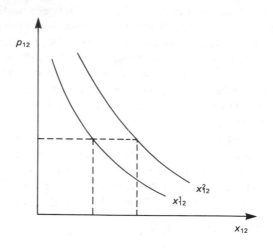

Figure 10.3 The optimal demand for commodity x_{12} is random as viewed from today, where $x_{12}^i = x_{12}^i$ ($\mathbf{p}^1$, p_{12}, $\bar{p}_{22}$, $\bar{p}_{22} + \varepsilon_i$, y_1, y_2, ϕ), $i=1, 2$ (in constructing the figure, p_{22}, but not p_{12}, is assumed to be random as viewed from today, and prices $p_{32}, \ldots, p_{n2}$ have been suppressed)

the envelope theorem, this yields, following certain calculations similar to those in the appendix,

$$\frac{\partial V}{\partial \mathbf{p}^1} = -\lambda_1 \mathbf{x}^1(\mathbf{p}^1, \bar{\mathbf{p}}^2, y_1, y_2, \phi)$$

$$\frac{\partial V}{\partial \bar{\mathbf{p}}^2} = -\gamma E[\lambda_2 \mathbf{x}^2(\mathbf{p}^1, \bar{\mathbf{p}}^2 + \varepsilon^2, \bar{\mathbf{p}}^2, y_1, y_2, \phi)]$$

$$\left.\frac{\partial V}{\partial y_1} = \lambda_1(\mathbf{p}^1, \bar{\mathbf{p}}^2, y_1, y_2, \phi) \right\} \qquad (10.40)$$

$$\frac{\partial V}{\partial y_2} = \gamma E[\lambda_2(\mathbf{p}^1, \bar{\mathbf{p}}^2 + \varepsilon^2, \bar{\mathbf{p}}^2, y_1, y_2, \phi)]$$

The first-period demand functions in the first line of (10.40) are the same as those given by (10.35), although the dependence on future (expected) prices and incomes is made explicit in (10.40).

The second line of (10.40) shows that future optimal demands are stochastic as viewed from today. Figure 10.3 depicts the case where the price of the considered commodity is known with certainty. Nevertheless, the demand for the commodity is uncertain as viewed from today due to uncertainty regarding the price of some other good. In order to illustrate the construction of compensation schemes in such situations, assume that the certain price of commodity x_{12} is changed. From the second line of (10.40), and using a well-known result from mathematical statistics, we have

$$\frac{\partial V}{\partial p_{12}} = -\gamma E(\lambda_2 x_{12}) = -\gamma E(\lambda_2)E(x_{12}) - \gamma\text{cov}(\lambda_2, x_{12}) \qquad (10.41)$$

where the expectation is taken with respect to the joint distribution of those second-period prices which are uncertain; at least one second-period price, but not p_{12}, is assumed to be random as viewed from today. Since x_{12}, like λ_2, is a stochastic variable, it does not factor out of the expectation in (10.41). In fact (10.41) illustrates that the expected value of the product of two random variables is equal to the product of their expectations plus their covariance, as is shown in any textbook on mathematical statistics (e.g. Hogg and Craig, 1978). Thus, it is not obvious how to construct a compensation scheme or money measure of utility change. There are, however, two principal candidates, namely stochastic and non-stochastic compensations respectively. In the present context, the stochastic compensation varies with the stochastic second-period prices, while the size of the non-stochastic compensation is independent of any random variations in prices.

In order to illustrate these concepts, let us assume that second-period income is adjusted in such a way that the consumer remains at his initial expected utility level following a change in p_{12}. Denote this (stochastic or non-stochastic as specified below) amount of money by S_ε. Using the second and final lines of (10.40), for a marginal price change we obtain

$$-\frac{\partial \bar{V}}{\partial p_{12}} = \gamma E(\lambda_2 x_{12}) + \gamma E(\lambda_2 S_\varepsilon') = 0 \qquad (10.42)$$

where a prime denotes a partial derivative with respect to p_{12}, and $S_\varepsilon = 0$ in the initial preprice-change situation.

Consider first a non-stochastic uniform marginal compensation. Since the compensation, denoted by $\text{OP}' = S_\varepsilon'$, is non-stochastic or 'state independent', it factors out of the expectation in (10.42). Using this fact, and rearranging the terms in (10.42), yields

$$\text{OP}' = -\frac{E(\lambda_2 x_{12})}{E(\lambda_2)} = -E(x_{12}) - \frac{\text{cov}(\lambda_2, x_{12})}{E(\lambda_2)} \qquad (10.43)$$

where the right-hand expression is obtained by using a result discussed below equation (10.41). The amount OP', which is often referred to as an option price, keeps the consumer at the same expected utility level when facing a lower/higher price p_{12} as was achieved at the initial level of p_{12}. Note that the amount OP' is paid/received regardless of the values the

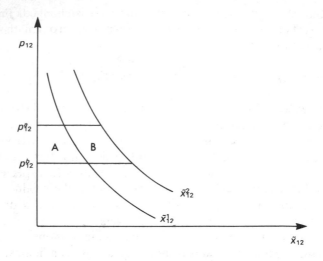

Figure 10.4 Compensating variations, area A or area A + B, depending on the value taken by the stochastic price p_{i2}, $i \neq 1$

stochastic second-period prices actually take on, i.e. it may turn out that the consumer gains or loses from having paid/received \$OP' depending on the realized values of $p_{22}, \ldots, p_{n2}$.

This latter fact hints at another possible compensation scheme, namely one that is constructed in such way that realized or ex post utility is unaffected by the considered change[4] in p_{12}. This amounts to replacing the compensation in (10.42) by compensations which are such that

$$-\frac{\partial \bar{V}}{\partial p_{12}} = \gamma E[\lambda_2 (x_{12} + CV'_\varepsilon)] = 0 \tag{10.44}$$

where CV'_ε is a stochastic marginal compensation, and $CV_\varepsilon = 0$ before the change in p_{12}. The amounts CV'_ε fluctuate with those prices that are random as viewed from today in such a way that the sum of the two terms within parentheses in (10.44) is equal to zero for each and every realization of the uncertain prices. This is illustrated in Figure 10.4 for a non-marginal change in p_{12}. Note that the integration between initial and final p_{12}-values is performed inside the expectations operator in (10.44), holding the utility level constant.

An expected compensating variation is obtained by multiplying each amount CV'_ε by the probability that the uncertain prices take on the associated values and summing all such weighted compensations. Thus, in the marginal price-change case, we have

$$E(x_{12}) = -E(CV'_\varepsilon) \tag{10.45}$$

In terms of Figure 10.4, the expected compensating variation is equal to π^1 times area A plus π^2 times area A+B, where π^i is the probability that $\tilde{x}_{12} = \tilde{x}^i_{12}$ and $i = 1,2$.

Option value is defined as the difference between option price and expected consumer surplus. A comparison of (10.43) and (10.45) shows that marginal option value OV' can be written as

$$OV' = OP' - E(CV'_\varepsilon) = \frac{\text{cov}(\lambda_2, x_{12})}{E(\lambda_2)} \tag{10.46}$$

Thus, the sign of option value is equal to the sign of the covariance between the marginal utility of second period income and the second period demand for the considered commodity. But note that this result holds only as an approximation in the discrete price change case since the expected demands in (10.43) and (10.45) refer to different compensation schemes and therefore need not net out in (10.46).

A useful result derived in Chavas and Bishop (1984) states that the sign of the covariance between two functions $f(\varepsilon)$ and $g(\varepsilon)$ is equal to the sign of the product of their derivatives with respect to ε. Applying this result to (10.46), one finds that option value may be of either sign, even if there is only a single stochastic second-period price. As is shown in Chavas and Bishop (1984), the sign of option value in (10.46) is equal to the sign of the product of the Arrow–Pratt index of relative risk aversion less the income elasticity of the demand for x_{12} times the partial derivative of x_{12} with respect to the uncertain price. Thus, risk aversion *per se* is not sufficient to determine the sign of option value.

Before commenting upon this result, two generalizations of the model and the above result should be mentioned. The model is easily extended in order to cover income uncertainty. Assume second-period income is uncertain about the mean value $\bar{y}_2$. Since, by assumption, second-period consumption is chosen after the consumer knows which state of the world has been realized, y_2 and $\bar{y}_2$ will appear in the behaviour functions (10.40) in a parallel manner to second-period prices. The second-period utility function may also contain a stochastic argument representing, say, the influence of the weather on the satisfaction derived from a trip to a recreation site. Once again, the realized and expected values respectively will appear in the behaviour functions (10.40) in the same way as second-period prices. These results mean that the sign of option value is also governed by (10.46) in the case of income uncertainty and/or state dependent preferences. Thus, regardless of the source of demand uncertainty, option value may generally be of either sign.

This result naturally raises a question regarding the money measure of utility change which would be appropriate in situations involving uncertainty. Unfortunately, there is no simple answer to this question, as will be demonstrated in Section 6 of Chapter 11. Here, only a few brief comments are made. Firstly, it should be observed from equation (10.42) that option price and expected compensating variation are just two out of possibly an infinite number of payment schemes; obviously, one can use (10.42) to construct various intermediate schemes. Secondly, both option price and expected compensating variation in (10.46) have the same sign as the underlying change in expected utility. However, in situations involving more complicated choices, the analysis performed in the next chapter demonstrates that expected consumer surplus measures are not necessarily valid indicators of the sign of the change in expected utility.

Appendix

In this appendix the properties of the indirect utility function (10.14) are derived. First, the expected utility function (10.10) is totally differentiated to obtain

$$E(dU) = E(U_1)dx_1 -$$

$$\frac{E(U_2 \cdot p_1)dx_1 + E(U_2)x_1 d\bar{p}_1 + E(U_2 \cdot (y - p_1 x_1))dp_2 - E(U_2)dy}{p_2} \quad \text{(A10.1)}$$

Next, using the fact that $E(U_1) = E(U_2 \cdot p_1)/p_2$ from the first order condition (10.11), and $X_2 = (y - p_1 x_1)p_2^{-1}$ from the budget constraint, (A10.1) simplifies to

$$E(dU) = - \frac{[E(U_2)x_1 d\bar{p}_1 + E(U_2 \cdot X_2)dp_2 - E(U_2)dy]}{p_2} \quad \text{(A10.2)}$$

This equation contains all the properties stated in equations (10.15) in Section 2.

CHAPTER 11

Money measures of the total value of environmental assets

A typical feature of many environmental resources is that they provide many different values. Following Boyle and Bishop (1985) one may distinguish between four more or less distinct values. First of all, there are consumptive use values such as fishing and hunting. Secondly, some resources provide non-consumptive use values. For example, some people enjoy bird watching, while others gain satisfaction from viewing wildlife. Thirdly, a resource may also provide services indirectly through books, movie pictures, television programmes, and so on. Finally people may derive satisfaction from the pure fact that a habitat or species exists.

In this chapter, the tools developed in the previous chapters are put together in an analysis of the total benefits of an environmental asset in a certain as well as in a risky world. Section 1 considers the total value of an environmental asset in a certain world. However, the future availability of a natural resource is frequently uncertain. Section 2 presents different willingness to pay measures that can be used to assess the value of having the supply of a resource stabilized at some arbitrary level. In some cases, a particular project may affect the random variations in the supply of an asset without achieving a certain future supply. Section 3 deals with this case, while Section 4 presents an empirical study concerned with many of the issues considered in this chapter. Then, in Section 5 we turn to decisions criteria in situations involving time as well as irreversible consequences. Section 6 contains a brief discussion of the choice of money measure in situations involving risks, and the chapter is rounded off by indicating a few possible directions for future research.

1 On the total value of a resource

If an environmental asset supplies just a single well-defined service, the associated benefits are generally quite easy to model. For example, if the service is traded in a perfect market, the money measures derived in Chapters 3 and 4 are useful, while a rationed service can be handled by methods assigned in Chapter 5. The benefits of a service which is a pure public good can be evaluated by the money measures presented in Chapter 6.

An environmental asset frequently provides several or all of these different kinds of services. Collecting the different cases, the compensating variation associated with a change in 'environmental quality' can be written as

$$V(\mathbf{p}^1, y^1 - \mathbf{P}^1\mathbf{q}^1 - CV, \mathbf{q}^1, \mathbf{z}^1) = V(\mathbf{p}^0, y^0 - \mathbf{P}^0\mathbf{q}^0, \mathbf{q}^0, \mathbf{z}^0) \qquad (11.1)$$

where a superscript 1 (0) denotes final (initial) values, $\mathbf{p}$ is a vector of non-negative prices of unrationed services provided by the considered asset, $\mathbf{q}$ is a vector of rationed services generated by the asset, $\mathbf{P}$ is a vector of prices of rationed services, $\mathbf{z}$ is a vector of public goods provided by the asset, and all prices referring to other commodities in the economy are suppressed. The overall compensating variation defined by (11.1) is the sum of money that makes the consumer as well off with a change in 'environmental quality' as he was before the change. The overall equivalent variation is easily defined by fixing utility at its final level instead of at its initial level.

Several comments to (11.1) are in order. Firstly, a change in the price vector $\mathbf{p}$ covers all kinds of consumptive, non-consumptive, and indirect uses of the asset that are traded in perfect markets. Services that are priced below their market clearing levels and hence are rationed are included in the $\mathbf{q}$-vector. Secondly, the existence value of the asset is included in the $\mathbf{z}$-vector and is therefore treated as a pure public good, a fact that is commented upon below. Furthermore, some non-consumptive uses such as bird watching, and indirect uses, e.g. watching a television programme on blue whales, may be thought of as public goods. Thirdly, a change in income y is included in (11.1) since, for example, if a park is closed and its trees cut down, the income of the considered household may be affected. This is particularly the case when the household owns the land.

In evaluating (11.1), it should be noted that the overall compensating variation is equal to the sum of the changes in compensating variations in the 'markets' where prices, quantity constraints or the supply of public goods change. This assumes, however, that each change is evaluated subject to all previously considered changes holding utility throughout at its initial level, just as was done in Chapters 3–6. See also the appendix to Chapter 6 for a line integral (almost) corresponding to the money measure in (11.1). The practical implication of this result is that one cannot simply ask a respondent about his willingness to pay for the opportunity to fish in a polluted lake that is cleaned up, then ask about his willingness to pay for the scenic beauty provided by the restored lake, and sum these amounts and hope to obtain the total value of the lake. Instead, one may proceed by asking for the maximum willingness to pay for fishing, disregarding any scenic values. Next, the respondent is asked of his maximum willingness to pay for the scenic values provided by the lake, subject to the change in fishing. This 'order of integration', just like the reverse or any intermediate 'order of integration', yields the overall compensating variation. Alternatively, one may simply ask of the total willingness to pay for the improvement in fishing *and* scenic beauty. Using results derived in the appendix to Chapter 6, it is possible to show that this total willingness to pay, which corresponds to the compensating variation in (11.1), has the same sign as the underlying change in utility. However, as usual and contrary to the EV-measure, the CV-measure cannot be used to compare or rank different changes in 'environmental quality'.

In the welfare change measure (11.1), existence value is included as a separate argument. In general, existence value is motivated by some kind of altruistic behaviour. Boyle and Bishop (1985, p. 13), following Bishop and Heberlein (1984), suggest five altruistic motives for existence values.

(i) *Bequest motives*. As Krutilla (1967) argued many years ago, it would appear quite rational to will an endowment of natural amenities as well as private goods and money to one's heirs. The fact that future generations are so often mentioned in debates over natural resources is one indication that their well-being, including their endowments of natural resources, is taken seriously by some present members of society.

(ii) *Benevolence toward relatives and friends*. Giving gifts to friends and relatives may be even more common than making bequests of them. Why should such goals not extend to the availability of natural resources?

(iii) *Sympathy for people and animals*. Even if one does not plan to personally enjoy a resource or do so vicariously through friends and relatives, he or she may still feel sympathy for people adversely affected by environmental deterioration and want to help them. Particularly for living creatures, sympathy may extend beyond humans. The same emotions that lead us to nurse a baby bird or stop to aid a run-over cat or dog may well induce us to pay something to maintain animal populations and ecosystems.

(iv) *Environmental linkages*. A better term probably exists here. What we are driving at is the belief that while specific environmental damage such as acidification of Adirondack lakes does not affect one directly, it is symptomatic of more widespread forces that must be stopped before resources of direct importance are also affected. To some extent this may reflect a simple 'you've-got-to-stop-'em-somewhere' philosophy. It may also reflect the view that if 'we' support 'them' in maintaining the environment, 'they' will support us.

(v) *Environmental responsibility*. The opinion is often expressed that those who damage the environment should pay for mitigating or avoiding future damage. In the acid rain case, there may be a prevalent feeling that if 'my' use of electricity is causing damage to ecosystems elsewhere, then 'I' should pick up part of the costs reducing the damage. (Boyle and Bishop 1985, p. 13.)

Given that an existence value is admitted, this value is often modelled by including the stock of the resource as an argument in the utility functions (see Dasgupta, 1982, ch. 5, for a discussion of this issue). In the case of assets such as air and water, one may instead use visibility measures and water quality indexes respectively. The use of such measures highlights the fact that existence is not normally treated as a binary variable. Rather, it is generally assumed that the marginal existence value is positive but a decreasing function of the size of the stock of the resource (but it is not obvious that this holds for all kinds of 'resources', e.g. mosquito).

Suppose that z_i in (11.1) denotes the current level of the stock of a renewable resource. By taking the partial derivative of the left-hand side of (11.1) with respect to z_i, one obtains the marginal compensating variation or the marginal existence value associated with a small change in z_i. However, as was demonstrated in Chapter 9, there is a close correspondence between the size of the stock of a renewable resource and the size of the steady-state harvest of the resource. In fact, the steady-state harvest is equal to the natural growth of the resource. Therefore, it may be difficult to isolate a pure marginal existence value, beyond, possibly, the short run, i.e. in the long-run most, if not all, elements of the vectors $\mathbf{p}$, $\mathbf{q}$ and $\mathbf{z}$ may be functions of z_i.

These results also highlight that the total value of a resource is difficult to define, even within the simple framework employed in this section. As a first approximation, one may choose a $\mathbf{p}^1$-vector in (11.1) such that the corresponding demands are all equal to zero, conditional on $\mathbf{q}^1 = \mathbf{z}^1 = 0$. The resulting compensating variation is a measure of the total value of the current supply of services of the resource. However, a priori, there is no reason to believe that the current stock of the resource is the optimal one, or even that the current harvest level is a steady-state harvest level. Therefore, one may instead formulate a generalized version of the dynamic model discussed in Chapter 9. In particular, the simple utility function employed in that chapter is replaced by one that covers multiple uses of the resource. Such a model may be used to derive the optimal stock as well as the optimal levels of flow consumptions of the resource. The solution can also be used to calculate a money measure of the total value of the resource. However, this is still an incomplete or partial valuation, since the model neglects any general equilibrium repercussions. We will resist all temptations to try to formulate such models in this book. For some attempts to model multiple use of a resource in a dynamic context, the interested reader is referred to Johansson and Löfgren (1985).

2 *Uncertain supply of an environmental asset*

A concept which has received considerable attention in the literature is Bishop's (1982) supply-side option value. In the case discussed in Section 5 of Chapter 10 uncertainty arises because of uncertainty about 'demand-side' factors such as preferences and income. In many circumstances, however, uncertainty pertains to the environment, or the supply side. The household will demand the good, such as a visit to a natural park, at its current price, but is uncertain about whether the park will be available.

In this section, the analysis of the value of an environmental asset is extended to the case of a risky world. In the option value literature, analyses are usually based on static models, as opposed to the intertemporal models employed in Chapter 10. In order to simplify the analysis, we will follow this tradition here, and use a simple variation of the model of Section 1. The (Neumann–Morgenstern) household is assumed to consume an environmental asset Q and a composite good which serves as the *numéraire*. The smooth indirect utility function of the household is written as $V(y, Q^i)$. There are n states of the world[1] and the probability that state i occurs is denoted by π^i. The analysis is restricted to uncertainty with regard to Q, but the model is easily extended to cover income uncertainty and/or state dependent preferences, i.e. demand-side uncertainty. The reader interested in such analysis is referred to Freeman (1984a), Graham (1981), and Schmalensee (1972), but see also Section 6.

Suppose that there is an opportunity to stabilize the supply of the environmental asset at some level $\bar{Q}$. This level is assumed to be no higher than the highest level attained in the stochastic case. For example, there is perhaps a positive probability that Q, the population of water-fowl say, takes on an extremely high value. A priori, there seems to be no particular reason to believe that 'supply' is always stabilized at this highest attainable level, although this is the special case generally considered in the literature on supply-side option value. The expected gain in going from a stochastic Q to $\bar{Q}$ can be written as

$$\Delta V = V(y,\bar{Q}) - E[V(y,Q^i)] \tag{11.2}$$

where the expectation is taken with respect to the distribution of Q. The household gains from the stabilization if (11.2) has a positive sign, while it loses from the stabiliziation if (11.2) has a negative sign. In particular, a risk-loving household does not view the stabilization with the same eyes as a strongly risk-averse household.

We will consider two different money measures of the utility change in (11.2), namely option price and expected consumer surplus, since these are the measures generally employed in empirical studies. Consider first option price. This is a state-independent payment, denoted OP, which makes the household indifferent between having and not having Q stabilized

$$V(y-\text{OP},\bar{Q}) = E[V(y,Q^i)] \tag{11.3}$$

This expression defines the compensating option price, i.e. the amount the household is willing to pay ahead of time to ensure that Q is stabilized at $Q=\bar{Q}$. Alternatively, one can base the definition on the equivalent variation measure. In any case, substitution of (11.3) into (11.2) immediately reveals that the sign of ΔV is equal to the sign of OP, i.e. OP is a sign-preserving money measure.

Alternatively, one can define the compensating variation, which is the consumer surplus measure used in this chapter, in state i if the supply of the environmental asset is stabilized

$$V(y-\text{CV}^i,\bar{Q}) = V(y,Q^i) \qquad \forall i \tag{11.4}$$

The compensating variation is the amount of income that can be taken from/must be given to the household while leaving it just as well off when consuming $\bar{Q}$ units as when consuming Q^i units of the asset. This compensating variation varies between states since the 'no-stabili-zation' case supply of the asset is state-dependent. Substitution of (11.4) into (11.2), making second-order Taylor series expansions around y, yields

$$\Delta V = E[V(y,\bar{Q}) - V(y-\text{CV}^i,\bar{Q})] \approx [E(\text{CV}^i) - \frac{V_{yy}E(\text{CV}^i)^2}{V_y}]V_y \tag{11.5}$$

where subscripts y denote partial derivatives with respect to income evaluated at $(y, \bar{Q})$, and $E(CV^i)$ is the expected compensating variation.

Two important observations follow from (11.5). Firstly, the expected compensating variation depends only on the ordinal properties of the utility function. In order to see this, suppose the utility function is subjected to a monotone increasing transformation. This transformation affects the Arrow–Pratt index of absolute risk aversion V_{yy}/V_y in (11.5), but leaves the expected compensating variation unchanged. The latter is easily checked by subjecting (11.4) to a monotone transformation. These results highlight Hanoch's (1977) warning, mentioned in the introduction to Chapter 10, that demand functions, obtained under certainty, imply very little with regard to a household's attitudes towards risk. Option price, on the other hand, is sensitive to the cardinal properties of the sub-utility functions since it refers to a particular level of expected utility, as can be seen from (11.3). Secondly, since, depending on the attitudes towards risk, expected utility may increase or decrease following a stabilization of Q, one may suspect that expected consumer surplus measures, such as the one in (11.5), may have the wrong sign. Indeed, in the context of price stabilization, Helms (1985) proves that expected consumer surplus measures may rank changes wrongly. Intuitively, the final term within brackets in (11.5) may have the same sign as $E(CV^i)$ and be so large that the change in expected welfare and the expected compensating variation are of opposite signs. Moreover, just as was the case under certainty, (expected) compensating variation measures cannot be used to rank several different projects.

Supply-side uncertainty, as defined by Bishop (1982), is a special case of the general case considered above. Bishop considers two states, namely, $Q^1 = \bar{Q}$ and $Q^2 = 0$, where, as before, $\bar{Q}$ denotes the proposed level of stabilization. In the absence of 'stabilization', the supply is Q^i with probability π^i for $i = 1, 2$. In this special case, the expected compensating variation is easily seen to be a sign-preserving measure of utility change. Using (11.3) and (11.5) one obtains

$$\triangle V = \pi^2[V(y, \bar{Q}) - V(y - CV^2, \bar{Q})] = V(y, \bar{Q}) - V(y - OP, \bar{Q}) \quad (11.6)$$

Obviously, the sign of the welfare change in (11.6) must equal the sign of CV^2 and hence the sign of the expected compensating variation $\pi^2 CV^2$, provided utility is increasing in income. Equation (11.6) also illustrates in a simple way that option price is a sign-preserving money measure of the change in expected utility.

Bishop (1982) proceeds by defining a supply-side option value

$$OV = OP - E(CV^i) \quad (11.7)$$

This option value OV is easily proved to be positive for a risk-averse household, zero for a risk-neutral household, and negative for a risk-loving household. (Hint: perform second-order Taylor series expansions of (11.6), or consult Bishop (1982) for a proof.) This is an important relation, which has been elaborated upon by Freeman (1984a) and Smith (1984) who try to provide an analytical bound for option value, useful in empirical investigations. Nevertheless, it should be recalled that Bishop's measure is derived subject to the assumption that $Q^1 = \bar{Q}$ and $Q^2 = 0$. In more complicated choice situations, it may simply be meaningless to define an option value due to the aforementioned deficiencies of expected consumer surplus measures.

3 *Access value*

Thus far, the value of preserving an environmental asset has been considered in the context of stabilizing supply. Frequently, however, one would expect a policy to affect the probability of a particular event without ensuring a certain outcome. For example, in the hunting study reported in the next section, hunters are bidding on an increased probability of a future suply of endangered animal species. This is the case since a hunter cannot be expected to believe that the considered 'project' ensures with certainty that the hunter will obtain a hunting permit. Thus, using a term due to Galagher and Smith (1985), the project leads to a change in access conditions for an asset whose availability is uncertain.

An access value can be defined by using two different probability distributions for the asset. The change in expected utility associated with a shift in the probability distribution can be written as

$$\triangle V = E_1[V(y,Q_1^i)] - E_0[V(y,Q_0^i)] \tag{11.8}$$

where a subscript refers to a particular probability distribution, and Q_1^i and Q_0^i are assumed to be independently distributed. Performing second-order Taylor series expansions around $(y,\bar{Q}_1)$ and $(y,\bar{Q}_0)$ respectively, just as in equation (10.20) in the previous chapter, gives an idea of the forces that are involved. The expected values $\bar{Q}_1$ and $\bar{Q}_0$, as well as the variations around the expected values affect the sign of (11.8). Expected utility increases if the considered project increases the expected access to the asset, *ceteris paribus*, or reduces the variability of the supply of the resource, *ceteris paribus*. The latter result, however, assumes that the household is risk averse with respect to supply (or price) risk, as can be seen from equation (10.20).

Applying the definition of access value to Bishop's (1982) supply-side model, an access option price ΛP, i.e. an ex ante state independent uniform payment, can be defined as

$$\sum_{i=1}^{2} \Pi^i V(y-\text{AP}, Q^i) = \pi^1 V(y,Q^1) + \pi^2 V(y-\text{CV}^2,Q^1) \tag{11.9}$$

where Π^1 is the probability of having access to the asset given that the option is purchased, $\Pi^2 = 1 - \Pi^1$, π^i denotes the corresponding probabilities if the option is not purchased, and equation (11.4) has been used to obtain the final term on the right-hand side of (11.9). Note that if Π^1 is equal to one, then (11.9) reduces to the usual definition of supply-side option price. In the general case, however, it is the expected future availability of the asset upon which the household is bidding. An attempt to estimate AP will be the core of the empirical study summed up in the next section.

A few comments regarding money measures of access values are in order. Firstly access option price is a sign-preserving money measure of utility change. This is seen by substituting the following definition of AP

$$E_1[V(y-\text{AP},Q_1^i)] = E_0[V(y,Q_0^i)] \tag{11.10}$$

into equation (11.8), noting that utility, by assumption, is increasing in income. Straightforward calculations confirm that AP in (11.9) is an increasing function of the probability of having access to the resource. Expected consumer surplus change measures,[2] on the other hand, may fail to correctly rank any two distributions, neither of which are stabilized, as is shown in Helms (1984); recall also the discussion in Section 2 dealing with a special case of the more general case considered here. However, in the simple case considered in equation (11.9), the change in expected compensating variation is simply $(\pi^2 - \Pi^2)\text{CV}^2$, a measure which, just like the underlying change in expected utility, has a positive sign if the considered project has a positive impact on the probability of gaining access to the resource. Nevertheless, as is shown in Freeman (1985), even in this simple case it is impossible to determine the sign of access option value, defined as access option price less the increase in expected consumer surplus, without invoking very restrictive assumptions regarding the properties of the utility function. Thirdly, the analysis performed in this and the previous section, can be given an intertemporal interpretation. For example, referring to equation (11.3), the considered project is now interpreted as a more or less permanent stabilization of the supply of the asset when the alternative is that the supply varies randomly from period to period.

4 *Estimating option prices for wildlife resources*

Little research has been devoted to the empirical estimation of option price. However, in recent years a few attempts have been made to estimate option and/or access price. Brookshire *et al.* (1983), Greenley *et al.* (1981), and Walsh *et al.* (1978) constitute interesting initial efforts in this direction.

This section briefly summarizes the Brookshire *et al.* (1983) study. The focus of their study was on uncertainty of supply. Two wildlife populations, grizzly bears and bighorn sheep in Wyoming, whose future availability is uncertain were selected for analysis.

Approximately 3,000 bighorn-sheep and grizzly-bear survey instruments were mailed to Wyoming hunters (but only 25–30 per cent of these were returned). The respondent was informed that under existing conditions, the probability of any individual obtaining a hunting licence in a year was 10 per cent for bighorn sheep and zero for grizzly bears. A contingent market was established in that new hunting areas were proposed which would be made available for hunting either five or fifteen years in the future (since respondents could not be expected to believe that making a payment this year would immediately result in a larger stock). Exclusion from the market was prescribed since payment each and every year was necessary to qualify the respondent to enter a draw for licences in the future. The method of payment was specified as a grizzly bear or bighorn sheep stamp. The respondent was asked how much he was willing to pay annually for a specified time horizon at four alternative probabilities of future supply. The expected probability of future licence availability is the 'good' for which respondents are bidding. If the probability of licence availability is a 25 per cent chance of future availability, then the individual's bid will represent a Hicksian compensated measure of welfare associated with this chance of future licence availability, i.e. it represents the (compensated) access option price, which is associated with a 0.25 probability of future supply.

The respondent was also questioned as to whether, if a licence was obtained, he would definitely or only possibly hunt the species in question. This allows an analysis of the influence of uncertain demand on the stated access option price.

Figure 11.1 plots the estimated mean values for the access option prices related to the alternative probabilities of future supply. One would expect access option price to be an increasing function of the probability of future availability. This can be checked by using equation (11.9) to calculate the sign of $\partial AP/\partial \Pi^1$. Such a pattern is, in fact, also present in Figure 11.1, i.e. the mean bids for the option to hunt grizzly bears or

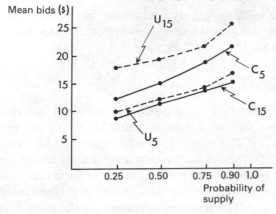

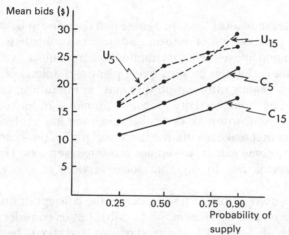

Figure 11.1 (a) Mean grizzly and (b) bighorn bids for certain (C) and uncertain (U) hunting demands for alternative time horizons (5 and 15 years)
Source: Brookshire *et al.* (1983, pp. 8–9)

bighorn sheep both increase as the probability of future availability increases.

One final observation should be made concerning the Brookshire *et al.* (1983) study. A respondent who is certain not to be a hunter may still be willing to pay for the existence of grizzly bears or bighorn sheep or for the option to observe wildlife resources. Therefore, the non-hunter was directed to answer a set of questions concerned with payments to preserve grizzly bears or bighorn sheep. The mean bids for observer access prices are in the range of $20 for both grizzly bears and bighorn sheep. The estimated existence values show more variation, with $24 mean existence value for grizzly bears in the five-year sample and $15 in the fifteen year sample, while the sheephorn results are significantly lower at about $7.

5 *Quasi-option value*

A different concept of option value than the one dealt with thus far in this chapter has been advanced independently by Arrow and Fisher (1974) and Henry (1974). This concept, labelled quasi-option value by Arrow and Fisher (1974), focuses on the intertemporal aspects of development problems (cf. Chapter 10). In particular, it is stressed that environmental decisions concerning the development of resources often involve irreversible consequences. This imposes constraints on the range of subsequent actions.

Fisher and Hanemann (1983, p. 3) note that there are at least two ways in which the preservation of natural resources can contribute to human welfare (over and above their contribution to non-material welfare, such as scenic values). Firstly, by preserving plant and animal populations, one conserves genetic information that may, in the future, be useful in some form of economic activity. Secondly, removal of any one species can cause a system to break down because each has evolved a set of characteristics that make it a unique functional part of the system. It may be possible, to some extent, to replace ecosystem services. However, in general, it seems fair to say that some services of ecosystems are non-substitutable.

The model used in this section to derive the concept of quasi-option value was developed by Hanemann (1984b). Let us consider a planner who has to decide how much of a tract of wild land should be developed in each of two periods, where the first period represents 'today' and the second period represents the uncertain future. It is assumed that development is a binary choice, i.e. either develop fully during a period or do not develop at all. Moreover, any development is irreversible. Let the net benefits of any development program be

$$U = U_1(d_1) + U_2(d, d_2; \theta) \tag{11.11}$$

where $d_t \geqslant 0$ is the amount of land developed in period t ($t = 1, 2$) $d = d_1 + d_2 \leqslant 1$, θ is a random variable, and $\partial U_t / \partial d_t$, $\partial U_2 / \partial d > 0$. Benefits are here measured in 'utils', but they could as well be measured in money. It should also be noted that the discount factor is suppressed in (11.11) in order to simplify notation.

Two scenarios are introduced regarding the behaviour of uncertainty over time. In the first case, no more information about θ becomes available over time. This corresponds to the case considered in Section 2 of Chapter 10, where the household was assumed to choose a vector of actions before the uncertainty about prices was resolved. The second scenario to be considered assumes that the specific value of θ is known at the beginning of period 2. It now makes sense to defer a decision on d_2 to the second period. This corresponds to the case considered in Section 5 of Chapter 10, where the household chose quantities after the uncertainty about prices was resolved.

It should be emphasized that learning[3] here is independent of the amount of land developed in the first period. What has been learned in the first period is exogenous to the model and due to such activities as research. We will discuss subsequently the case in which undertaking some development provides desirable information on the consequences of irreversible development.

The planner (or the household) aims at maximizing the expected benefits over both periods. In the first scenario considered, all development decisions must be taken before uncertainty is resolved. Hence, the planner maximizes

$$\bar{U}(d_1) = U_1(d_1) + \max_{d_2} \left[E\{U_2(d, d_2; \theta)\} \right] \tag{11.12}$$

In order to interpret this expression, and referring back to the method of backward induction used in Section 5 of Chapter 10, we can work backwards. Firstly, the optimal development strategy in the second period is decided, i.e. $d_2 = 0$ or $d_2 = 1$ is chosen, subject to d_1 which is a predetermined number ($d_1 = 0$ or $d_1 = 1$), and subject to $d \leqslant 1$. Then we move back to the first period. The problem is now to choose d_1 in such a way as to maximize total expected benefits over both periods. This is captured by (11.12), and the maximum value of the expression is denoted $\bar{U}(\bar{d}_1)$, where $\bar{d}_1$ maximizes (11.12) subject to $d_1 = 0$ or $d_1 = 1$. Note, however, that since nothing further is learned about the value of θ by the second period, the decision maker could equally well choose both d_1 and d_2 in the first period (instead of sequentially as above).

Since the choice is between no development and full development, the planner has only to compare $\bar{U}(0)$ and $\bar{U}(1)$. Hence, he chooses not to develop if $\bar{U}(0) \geqslant U(1)$, and to develop if $\bar{U}(0) < U(1)$.

Turning now to the second scenario, the planner learns the value of the random variable θ by the second period. The decision is now to maximize

$$\bar{U}(d_1) = U_1(d_1) + E\{\max_{d_2} U_2(d, d_2; \theta)\} \tag{11.13}$$

where the decision on d_2 can be taken after the uncertainty is resolved, but subject to the amount developed in the first period, i.e. $d_1 = 0$ or $d_1 = 1$, and $d_1 + d_2 \leqslant 1$. The aim of the planner is then to choose d_1 in order to maximize (11.13), given that the amount of development in the second period is optimally chosen. Call this optimal first period amount of development $\bar{\bar{d}}_1$. This amount is found by comparing $\bar{U}(0)$ and $\bar{U}(1)$ in (11.13). Clearly, it is optimal to refrain from development in the first period if $\bar{U}(0) \geq \bar{U}(1)$, and vice versa.

Now, we are ready to define quasi-option value, QV, as

$$QV = \bar{\bar{U}}(0) - \bar{U}(0) \geq 0 \tag{11.14}$$

This expression gives the increase in expected benefits of not developing the area in the first period, when the planner can wait to determine d_2 after uncertainty is resolved instead of taking a decision before uncertainty is resolved. The difference between the two terms in (11.14) is known as the expected value of perfect information (conditional on $d_1 = 0$). The sign of (11.14), which in general is strictly positive, can be determined by invoking a theorem originally developed by Marschac (see Hey, 1981, pp. 87–9).

It is possible to correct the inefficiency which follows if decision makers ignore the possibility of improved information by introducing a tax on development. This tax τ should be such that

$$\bar{U}(0) - [\bar{U}(1) - \tau] = \bar{\bar{U}}(0) - \bar{\bar{U}}(1) \tag{11.15}$$

where $\bar{U}(1) = \bar{\bar{U}}(1)$, since, with full development in the first period, new information available by the second period makes no difference. Thus, the tax on development in (11.15) is equal to the quasi-option value defined by equation (11.14).

In closing, three remarks regarding the above analysis are in order. Firstly, Hanemann (1982) has shown that the result $\bar{\bar{d}}_1 \leq \bar{d}_1$ does not follow in the general case where d_1 can take any value in the interval $[0, 1]$. Nevertheless, of course, the value of information is still there. Secondly, development *per se* may provide information, i.e. the problem may allow for active learning in the sense that the amount and types of information gained depend upon the action taken in the first period. This has been stressed by Freeman (1984b) and Miller and Lad (1984). Moreover, as is the case in the Viscusi and Zeckhauser's (1976) analysis, some development can provide information regarding whether development is in fact irreversible. These results mean that development decisions involving a quasi-option are not necessarily more conservationist than decisions without the quasi-option (see also Lohmander, 984, for a similar discussion). Thirdly, the reader interested in interpretations of quasi-option value in terms of expected consumer surplus and option values is referred to Hanemann (1984b) and Mäler (1984). The latter author also deals with the aggregation of option and quasi-option values among individuals.

6 *Some concluding remarks on the choice of money measure in a risky world*

The results concerning the sign of option value are rather devastating. If option value was always positive, at least for a risk-averse household, one could argue that the expected consumer surplus of, for example, preserving a national park, underestimates the true gain. However, as the results of this and the previous chapter make clear, no such simple rule holds.

Ulph (1982) has shown that the kind of option value considered here is due to a distinction between ex ante and ex post welfare; option price is an ex ante measure while expected consumer surplus is an ex post measure. Ulph (1982) holds that even if one were interested in ex ante welfare judgements, there may be situations where one wishes to use ex post compensation measures. For example, a project which is expected to be profitable may actually cause the death of a lot of people and hence result in an outcome that is rather bad. In such situations there is no reason to believe that a uniform ex ante measure, i.e. option price, necessarily leads to the same decision as an ex post compensation measure. Nor is it entirely obvious which welfare change measure is the appropriate one in such situations (see Hammond, 1981, Ulph, 1982, for further discussion of this issue).

The concept of option value is often interpreted as a risk-aversion premium. This interpretation may seem reasonable when viewed in the light of the above distinction between ex ante and ex post welfare, and the discussion of ordinal versus cardinal properties of money measures in Section 2. However, the sign of option value is in general ambiguous, even in the case of risk-averse households. Hanemann (1984b) has shown that even if the individual's utility depends solely on his income, option value (due to income uncertainty) is not strictly the same as a risk premium. Turning to multivariate utility functions, Karni (1983) has shown that there is no longer any simple correspondence between the concavity of the utility function in income and a positive risk premium.

Moreover, option price and expected consumer surplus are just two out of possibly an infinite number of money measures of a unique change in expected utility. To see this, it is useful to consider a simple model with income uncertainty. Following Graham (1981), the willingness-to-pay function associated with a certain change in the supply of Q from Q^0 to Q^1 is defined by the relationship

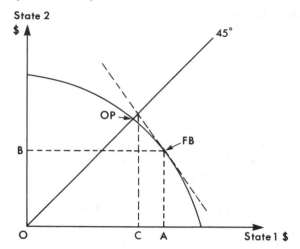

Figure 11.2 Collecting a maximum certain payment OC

$$E[V(y_h^i - S_h^i, Q^1)] = E[V(y_h^i, Q^0)] \qquad \forall h \qquad (11.16)$$

where S_h^i is the payment collected from household h in state i, and the expectation is taken with respect to the distribution of income. For example, both a state-independent payment and expected compensating variation preserve the equality in (11.16). Obviously, however, there are possibly an infinity of other such payment schemes.

Graham (1981) suggests that one should collect the maximum aggregate certain payment subject to (11.16). If this amount of money exceeds the certain costs of the project, then the project is obviously worthwhile whatever state of the world happens to occur. In a single-household context, where risk necessarily must be 'collective', this maximum state-independent payment is equal to option price. This result generalizes to a multi-household society, provided all individuals are similar and everyone experiences the same state of the world, i.e. risk is collective.

At the other extreme, risks are insurable on an individual basis. Suppose that individuals are alike but that $\pi^i H$ individuals experience state i, where $\pi^i < 1$. Consider the two-states case illustrated in Figure 11.2, which is due to Graham (1981). The slope of the willingness-to-pay locus depicted in the figure is obtained by differentiating the left-hand expression in (11.16) (see Graham, 1981, pp. 717–18 for details). By assumption, the probability is π^1 that an individual experiences state 1 and $\pi^2 = 1 - \pi^1$ that he experiences state 2. The maximum aggregate sure payment the society can collect is equal to

$$H(\pi^1 OA + \pi^2 OB) = H \cdot OC \qquad (11.17)$$

Thus, by collecting \$OA from each of those π^1 per cent households which experience state 1 and \$OB from each of those π^2 per cent who experience state 2, society can collect a certain payment corresponding to \$$H \cdot OC$. Note that the point FB in the figure denotes the 'fair bet' associated with fair insurance in the insurance literature. The tangent to the willingness-to-pay locus at this point yields alternative payment combinations with the same expected value; the slope of the tangent is equal to $-\pi^1/\pi^2$. Thus, expected values are of interest if the situation involves individual-insurable risks (regardless of whether markets for contingent dollar claims actually exist or not). It is important to stress, however, that option price and the expected compensating variation are lower bounds for the expected value of the fair bet. The latter amount of money can be viewed as obtained by maximizing $E(S_h^i)$ subject to (11.16). This procedure equates the marginal utility of income between all states of nature. The first-order conditions for an interior optimum are $\pi^i = \psi \pi^i \partial V/\partial S_h^i$ for all i, where ψ is a Lagrange multiplier. Substitution of these conditions into the expression for the willingness-to-pay function, assuming two states of the world, yields

$$\frac{dS_h^2}{dS_h^1} = -\frac{\pi^1 (\partial V/\partial S_h^1)}{\pi^2 (\partial V/\partial S_h^2)} = -\frac{\pi^1}{\pi^2} \qquad \forall h \qquad (11.18)$$

at the optimum, i.e. at FB in Figure 11.2. The calculation of option price and the expected compensating variation, on the other hand, are based on 'actual' incomes, implying that the possibility of extracting additional payments by equating the marginal utility of income between states is not exploited (although, if fair insurance is available, individuals continuously adjust in order to equate marginal utilities of income between states).

Graham (1981, p. 716) concludes that option price is the appropriate money measure in situations involving identical individuals and collective risk, while expected value calculations are appropriate in situations involving similar individuals and individual risks. Therefore, with the exception of the former case, and possibly option price and expected consumer surplus measures as lower bounds in the other extreme case, there does not seem to be any simple rules of thumb that could be used in empirical investigations. Obviously, it is not an easy task to try to estimate complete willingness-to-pay loci, which can be used to calculate aggregate certain payments in various situations. There are also the problems of ex ante versus ex post utility and the failure of expected consumer surplus measures always to rank correctly alternative regimes.

In addition, most of the literature on option value employ models of atemporal risk, while the considered problems often involve temporal risk, just as the models of Chapter 10 and Section 5 of the present chapter. Therefore, conclusions drawn from the models employed in the option value literature do not necessarily generalize to more realistic and complicated decision problems. On the other hand, modelling temporal risk is a difficult task, and the models easily become too complicated and data consuming to be able to be used in empirical investigations.

In closing, it is important to stress that the ambiguous sign of option value does not mean that the underlying change in expected utility is ambiguous. On the contrary, in all of the cases considered, the change in expected utility is unique.[4] The problems appear when one tries to express the utility change in terms of a money measure. The willingness-to-pay loci employed above indicate that a utility change may be expressed in terms of an infinite number of money measures. Hence it seems unlikely that the controversies about which money measure to use can be solved solely by invoking purely theoretical considerations. The choice of measure must, in general, be made on other grounds, such as the possibility of obtaining sufficient information to calculate one or other measure. Nevertheless, analyses of the relationship between different money measures may be of considerable help in such situations, i.e. such analyses may indicate whether or not the chosen measure over- or under-estimates the true gain from a particular project. The reader interested in further discussion of decision criteria in situations involving risk is referred to Arrow (1964), Arrow and Lind (1970), and Hirschleifer (1965).

7 *On directions for future research*

The results derived and discussed in this book show that much of the confusion prevailing a decade or so ago regarding the properties of money measures of utility change has been removed. For example, the conditions under which ordinary and various compensated money measures provide a correct ranking of utility changes has been explored. Moreover, appropriate money measures of simultaneous changes in prices, quantity constraints, and the provision of public goods are now available. There are also numerous empirical studies that seek to compare the properties of different empirical methods for estimations of money measures.

In spite of these extensions, much remains to be done. This book is rounded off by indicating a few possible directions, for future research. Firstly, Chapter 8 indicates that situations involving discrete choices are both common and important in environmental economics. Undoubtedly, existing models can be refined and extended so as to be able to deal with more complicated choice situations than is presently the case. In particular, most, if not all, available studies within the field consider binary responses while many real world decisions involve more than two possible responses. Similarly, the econometrics of discrete choices is developing rapidly. In future empirical investigations, it seems probable that the simple logit and probit models currently employed will be replaced by more general econometrical approaches.

Another important feature of choices highlighted in this book is that they are often taken before the agent knows for sure what prices, incomes, and so on, will prevail. Even if the agent knows the prevailing levels of these variables, he cannot be sure of their future values. This general uncertainty regarding the future will affect today's decisions. It is an important task for future research to integrate uncertainty in a way that is suitable for empirical studies. For example, the implications of uncertainty with regards to the formulation of questionnaires remains unclear. Similarly, it remains to integrate discrete choices and uncertainty regarding prices, incomes, and preferences. The empirical study of the housing market presented in Chapter 10, clearly indicates that forecasts of prices and variances are of extreme importance for the individual's decision making in a risky world. Similarly, the analysis performed in this chapter shows that demand functions obtained under certainty imply very little with regard to an individual's attitudes towards risk.

The literature dealing with supply-side option value generally compares a situation where a resource is available at its present level of quality to a situation where the resource is not available at all. The more general and interesting case, however, seems to be the one where a particular project affects the probability distribution, e.g. reduces the chance of bad outcomes and increases the chance of favourable outcomes. As noted in Section 3 of this chapter, ordinary as well as compensated expected consumer surplus change measures may fail to correctly rank such changes. This implies that questions about the willingness to pay, originally formulated for a riskless world, must be used with great caution in situations involving risk. Option price measures, on the other hand, provide a correct ranking of changes in expected utility. Nevertheless, the recent discussion between Mitchell and Carson (1985) and Greenley et al. (1985) highlights that it is quite easy to misspecify the questions and that the outcome may be quite complicated to interpret. Their discussion also underscores the importance of carefully deriving money measures when there are several uses of an asset before constructing a survey instrument. Otherwise, the chance of asking the questions in the wrong order and invoking wrong 'subject to' constraints is high (compare Section 1 of this chapter).

A final extension to be mentioned is the combination of expected utility maximization and hedonic housing value analysis. A recent study by Brookshire *et al.* (1985) demonstrates that the expected utility hypothesis may be a reasonable description of the behaviour of individuals who face a low-probability, high-loss natural hazard event. They show that the property value markets for Los Angeles and San Francisco convey hedonic price differentials to consumers that correspond closely to expected earthquake damages for particular homes located in relatively hazardous areas. This approach is an interesting and promising one and can probably also be used for examinations of the reliability of the survey technique in situations involving uncertainty. Moreover, the approach may provide further insight regarding the appropriate treatment of risk in social cost–benefit analysis. Although there is a considerable literature on this issue (e.g. Arrow, 1964; Arrow and Lind, 1970; Hirschleifer, 1965) there are still few applications to environmental problems.

Notes

1. Introduction

1 For a recent and comprehensive survey of the literature the reader is referred to Ekelund and Hébert (1985).
2 See Bailey (1954), Friedman (1949), and McKenzie (1983) for discussions of alternative interpretations of the Marshallian case.

2. Some basic concepts

1 Loosely speaking, continuous means that no gaps exist in the ordering while increasing means that more is preferred to less.
2 $X = \{x|x \geq 0\}$, i.e. the set of all x such that x is non-negative.
3 See Section 1 of Chapter 4 for a definition of a non-essential good.

3. The concept of consumer surplus

1 However, in an ordinal world, only the signs of S and $\triangle U$ matter. See the discussion below equation (3.21) and also Section 1 of Chapter 4.
2 Assuming, of course, that at least one price and/or income is fixed since all of the conditions stated in (3.7) cannot hold simultaneously.

4. Topics in the theory of consumer surplus measures

1 See the Slutsky equation (2.11) in Chapter 2.
2 If income elasticities change signs in the considered path, the indicated relationship between the different money measures need not hold; in fact, the three measures could coincide.
3 A comparison of EV in (4.1) and $EV_1 = e(\mathbf{p}^0, U^2) - e(\mathbf{p}^0, U^0)$ establishes this claim.
4 The money measures CV, EV and S are not affected since the demand functions (and hence also the conditions for path independency of the money measures) are unaffected by monotone transformations.
5 Under quasi-homotheticity, the income expansion paths are straight lines but need not go through the origin. The well-known Stone–Geary utility function, associated with the linear expenditure system, provides an example of this case (see Geary, 1949/50; Stone, 1954).

5. Consumer surplus measures in quantity-constrained regimes

1 Any subscripts denoting effective or quantity-constrained functions, as opposed to the notional or unconstrained functions of Chapters 3 and 4, are omitted in order to

simplify the notation. Similarly, primes denoting transposed vectors and matrices are suppressed.

2 If two or more demands are rationed, the argument becomes more complicated since a change in q_1 will affect the virtual prices of other rationed goods. This interaction must be accounted for when considering (changes in) several constraints.

3 This is the case at least where there is just a single *initial* vector of prices, quantity constraints and income. See the appendix to Chapter 6.

6. Public goods and externalities in consumption

1 For more information on the definitions of public goods (and mixed goods which fall between the polar cases of purely public and purely private goods) and external effects see McGuire and Aaron (1969), Milleron (1972), Musgrave (1959), Mäler (1974), Ng (1979), Samuelson (1954; 1955; 1969), and Strotz (1958). For recent surveys of the environment in economics and externalities, respectively, the reader is referred to Fisher and Peterson (1976) and Mishan (1971).

2 The path independency conditions are easily obtained from those stated in the appendix to Chapter 5.

3 In order to show this, we use equation (A6.2) in the appendix to this chapter. Set z^0 equal to a decision to preserve both parks, z^1 equal to a decision to preserve only the first park, and z^2 equal to a decision to preserve the second, but not the first park. The result then follows directly. Moreover, using (A6.1) with $U^2 = U^1 < U^0$, it can easily be shown that the EV measure ranks the alternatives correctly. However, see the appendix for a case where the EV measure, but not the CV measure, fails to rank bundles correctly.

7. How to overcome the problem of preference revelation; practical methodologies

1 See for example Bohm (1972; 1977; 1979; 1984), Clarke (1971), Kurz (1974), Malinvaud (1971), Sinden (1974), and the survey in Schulze *et al.* (1981).

2 Average poor air quality corresponds to 12.38 pphm/day, average fair to 9.55 pphm/day, and average good to 6.9 pphm/day.

3 A translog utility function is written as
$$\ell n\, U = \Sigma_i\, \alpha_i\, \ell n\, x_i + (\Sigma_i\, \Sigma_j\, \beta_{ij}\, \ell n\, x_i\, \ell n\, x_j)\frac{1}{2}$$
where $i, j = 1, \ldots, n$.

4 Bojö (1985) uses standardized estimates of travel costs rather than questionnaire results.

8. Discrete choice models and environmental benefits

1 It is important to note that the critical price levels derived in this section are not, in general, constant with respect to the choice of money measure. See the discussion in Section 4. Also, great care must be shown in using the CV measure for multi-site comparisons. Recall the discussion in Section 4 of Chapter 6.

2 For detailed derivations as well as extensions the reader is referred to Small and Rosen (1981) and, in particular, Hanemann (1984a). Amemiya (1981) presents a survey of the literature on qualitative response models. Recent interesting contributions include the generalized extreme value model and the distribution-free maximum likelihood method, see Small (1982) and Cosslett (1983) respectively, and also Maddala (1984). An application of discrete choice models to outdoor recreation is given by Lundin (1975).

3 See Lindley (1969, p. 59).

9. Consumer's surplus in an intertemporal context

1 Hammack and Brown (1974, pp. 78–83) also formulate a discrete-time, infinite-horizon model, however, the economic interpretation of the continuous time approach is easier to understand because of its notational simplicity.

10. Welfare change measures in a risky world

1 The utility function is assumed to be strongly quasi-concave, i.e. we do not rule out risk loving. See the definition of a well-behaved utility function in Section 1 of Chapter 2. (As was demonstrated in Section 1, $V_{yy} \leqslant 0$ if the utility function is concave.)

2 For different risk measures see Diamond and Stiglitz (1974) and Rothschild and Stiglitz (1970; 1971).

3 It is assumed that $E(\varepsilon_i^t) = 0$ and $E(\varepsilon_i^t \varepsilon_j^\tau) = 0$ for all commodities i, j $(i \neq j)$ and all periods t, τ $(t \neq \tau)$. Moreover, all prices and incomes are assumed to be strictly positive and finite.

4 A problem is to design compensation schemes that preserve incentives. See Just *et al.* (1982, pp. 355–6) for a discussion of this moral hazard problem.

11. Money measures of the total value of environmental assets

1 A state of world or nature is a description of the world so complete that, if true and known, the consequence of every action would be known (Arrow, 1971, p. 45).

2 Expected compensating variation, expected equivalent variation, and the expectation of the uncompensated money measure.

3 According to the subjectivist or Bayesian theory of the foundation of probability, there is no need for individual probability beliefs to coincide with either each other or some outside 'objective' standard. Proponents of the rational expectations hypothesis, on the other hand, argue that without some way of inferring what an agent's subjective view of the future is, the Bayesian hypothesis is of no help in understanding the agent's behaviour. For discussion on this point, see Lucas (1977), Sheffrin (1984), Swamy *et al.* (1982), and Zellner (1985).

4 For a critique of the expected utility theory of rationality the reader is referred to Allais and Hagen (1979).

Bibliography

Allais, M. and Hagen, O. (eds.) (1979) *Expected Utility Hypothesis and the Allais Paradox*. Reidel, Dordrecht.

Amemiya, T. (1981) Qualitative response models: A survey. *Journal of Economic Literature* 19, 1483–536.

Arrow, K. J. (1951) *Social Choice and Individual Values*. John Wiley & Sons, New York.

(1964) The role of securities in the optimal allocation of risk-bearing. *Review of Economic Studies* 31, 91–6.

(1971) *Essays in the Theory of Risk-bearing*. North-Holland, Amsterdam.

Arrow, K. J. and Fisher, A. C. (1974) Environmental preservation, uncertainty, and irreversibility. *Quarterly Journal of Economics* 88, 312–19.

Arrow, K. J. and Lind, R. (1970) Uncertainty and the evaluation of public investment decisions. *American Economic Review* 60, 364–78.

Bailey, M. J. (1954) The Marshallian demand curve. *Journal of Political Economy* 63, 255–61.

Barten, A. P. and Böhm, V. (1982) Consumer theory. In Arrow, K. J. and Intriligator, M. D. (eds.), *Handbook of Mathematical Economics*, vol. II. North-Holland, Amsterdam.

Bellman, R. (1957) *Dynamic Programming*. Princeton University Press, Princeton.

Benassy, J. P. (1982) *The Economics of Market Disequilibrium*. Academic Press, New York.

Bergson, A. (1938) A reformulation of certain aspects of welfare economics. *Quarterly Journal of Economics* 52, 310–34.

Bishop, R. C. (1982) Option value: An exposition and extension. *Land Economics* 58, 1–15.

Bishop, R. C. and Heberlein, T. A. (1979) Measuring values of extra-market goods: Are indirect measures biased? *American Journal of Agricultural Economics* 61, 926–30.

(1984) Contingent valuation methods and ecosystem damages from acid rain.

University of Wisconsin-Madison, Dept. of Agricultural Economics. Staff Paper No. 217.

Blackley, P., Follain, J. R. Jr and Ondrich, J. (1984) Box–Cox estimation of hedonic models: How serious is the iterative OLS variance bias? *Review of Economics and Statistics* 66, 348–53.

Blackorby, C., Donaldson, D. and Moloney, D. (1984) Consumer's surplus and welfare change in a simple dynamic model. *Review of Economic Studies* 51, 171–6.

Blackorby, C., Nissen, D., Primont, D. and Russell, R. R. (1973) Consistent intertemporal decision making. *Review of Economic Studies* 40, 239–48.

Blackorby, C., Primont, D. and Russell, R. R. (1978) *Duality, Separability, and Functional Structure: Theory and Economic Applications*. North-Holland, New York.

Block, M. K. and Heineke, J. M. (1975) Factor allocations under uncertainty: An extension. *Southern Economic Journal* 41, 526–30.

Boadway, R. W. (1974) The welfare foundations of cost-benefit analysis. *Economic Journal* 84, 926–39.

(1975) Cost-benefit rules in general equilibrium. *Review of Economic Studies* 42, 361–73.

Boadway, R. W. and Bruce, N. (1984) *Welfare Economics*. Basil Blackwell, Oxford.

Bockstael, N. E. and McConnel, K. E. (1981) Theory and estimation of the household production function for wildlife recreation. *Journal of Environmental Economics and Management* 8, 199–214.

Bohm, P. (1972) Estimating demand for public goods: An experiment. *European Economic Review* 3, 111–30.

(1975) Option demand and consumer's surplus: Comment. *American Economic Review* 65, 733–6.

(1977) Estimating access values. In Wingo, L. and Evans, A. (eds.), *Public Economics and the Quality of Life*. Johns Hopkins University Press, Baltimore.

(1979) Estimating willingness to pay: Why and how? *Scandinavian Journal of Economics* 81, 142–53.

(1984) Revealing demand for an actual public good. *Journal of Public Economics* 24, 135–51.

Bojö, J. (with the collaboration of Hultkrantz, L.) (1985) *A Cost–benefit Analysis of Forestry in Mountainous Areas: The Case of Valadalen*. Stockholm School of Economics, Stockholm (in Swedish).

Bös, D., Genser, B. and Holzmann, R. (1982) On the quality of publicly supplied goods. *Economica* 49, 289–96.

Bowden, R. J. (1978) *The Econometrics of Disequilibrium*. North-Holland, Amsterdam.

(1984) A note on the 'bottom-up' approach to measuring compensating variations. *Metroeconomica* 36, 65–76.

Bowen, H. R. (1943) The interpretation of voting in the allocation of economic resources. *Quarterly Journal of Economics* 58, 27–48.

Bowes, M. D. and Loomis, J. B. (1980) A note on the use of travel cost models with unequal zonal populations. *Land Economics* 56, 465–70.

(1982) A note on the use of travel cost models with unequal zonal populations: Reply. *Land Economics* 58, 408–10.

Box, G. E. P. and Cox, D. R. (1964) An analysis of transformations. *Journal of the Royal Statistical Society* 26 (Series B), 211–52.

Boyle, K. J. and Bishop, R. C. (1985) The total value of wildlife resources: Conceptual and empirical issues. Invited paper, Association of Environmental and Resource Economists Workshop on Recreational Demand Modeling, Boulder, Colorado, 17–18 May 1985.

Boyle, K. J., Bishop, R. C. and Welsh, M. P. (1985) Starting point bias in contingent valuation bidding games. *Land Economics* 61, 188–94.

Bradford, D. and Hildebrandt, G. (1977) Observable public good preferences. *Journal of Public Economics* 8, 111–31.

Brookshire, D. S., D'Arge, R. C., Schulze, W. D. and Thayer, M. A. (1981) Experiments in valuing public goods. In Smith, K. V. (ed.), *Advances in Applied Microeconomics*, vol. 1. JAI Press, Greenwich, Connecticut.

Brookshire, D. S., Eubanks, L. S. and Randall, A. (1983) Estimating option prices and existence values for wildlife resources. *Land Economics* 59, 1–15.

Brookshire, D. S., Thayer, M. A., Schulze, W. D. and d'Arge, R. C. (1982) Valuing public goods: A comparison of survey and hedonic approaches. *American Economic Review* 72, 165–77.

Brookshire, D. S., Thayer, M. A., Tschirhart, J. and Schulze, W. D. (1985) A test of the expected utility model: Evidence from earthquake risks. *Journal of Political Economy* 93, 369–89.

Brown, G. M. Jr. and Hammack, J. (1972) A preliminary investigation of the economics of migratory waterfowl. In Krutilla, J. V. (ed.), *Natural Environments: Studies in Theoretical and Applied Analysis*. Johns Hopkins University Press, Baltimore.

Brown, G. Jr and Mendelsohn, R. (1984) The hedonic travel cost method. *Review of Economics and Statistics* 66, 427–33.

Brown, J. N. and Rosen, H. S. (1982) On the estimation of structural hedonic price models. *Econometrica* 50, 765–8.

Burns, M. E. (1973) A note on the concept and measure of consumer surplus. *American Economic Review* 63, 335–44.

Burt, O. R. and Brewer, D. (1971) Estimation of net social benefits from outdoor recreation. *Econometrica* 39, 813–27.

Caulkins, P. P., Bishop, R. C. and Bouwes, N. W. (1985) Omitted cross-price variable biases in the linear travel cost model: Correcting common misperceptions. *Land Economics* 61, 182–7.

Cesario, F. J. (1976) Value of time in recreation benefit studies. *Land Economics* 55, 32–41.

Chavas, J.-P. and Bishop, R. C. (1984) *Ex-ante Consumer Welfare Evaluation in Cost–Benefit Analysis*. Department of Agricultural Economics, University of Wisconsin, Madison.

Chipman, J. S. and Moore, J. C. (1980) Compensating variation, consumer's surplus, and welfare. *American Economic Review* 70, 933–49.

Christensen, J. B. and Price, C. (1982) A note on the use of travel cost models with unequal zonal populations: Comment. *Land Economics* 58, 395–9.

Cicchetti, C. J. and Freeman, A. M. III (1971) Option demand and consumer surplus: Further comment. *Quarterly Journal of Economics* 85, 528–39.

Cicchetti, C. J. and Smith, K. V. (1976) The measurement of individual congestion costs: An economic application to wilderness recreation. In Lin, S. A. Y. (ed.) *Theory and Measurement of Economic Externalities*. Academic Press, New York.

Cicchetti, C. J., Fisher, A. C. and Smith, V. K. (1976) An econometric evaluation of a generalized consumer surplus measure: The Mineral King issue. *Econometrica* 44, 1259–76.

Clark, C. W. (1976) *Mathematical Bioeconomics: The Optimal Management of Renewable Resources*. John Wiley & Sons, New York.

Clarke, E. (1971) Multipart pricing of public goods. *Public Choice* 8, 19–33.

Clawson, M. (1959) *Methods of Measuring Demand for and Value of Outdoor Recreation*. Reprint 10, Resources for the Future, Washington, D.C.

Clawson, M. and Knetsch, J. L. (1966) *Economics of Outdoor Recreation*. Johns Hopkins University Press, Baltimore.

Cornes, R. and Albon, R. (1981) Evaluation of welfare change in quantity-constrained regimes. *Economic Record* 57, 186–90.

Cornwall, R. R. (1984) *Introduction to the Use of General Equilibrium Analysis*. North-Holland, Amsterdam.

Cosslett, S. R. (1983) Distribution-free maximum likelihood estimator of the binary choice model. *Econometrica* 51, 765–82.

Courant, R. and John, F. (1965) *Introduction to Calculus and Analysis*, vol. 1. John Wiley & Sons (Wiley-Interscience), New York.

(1974) *Introduction to Calculus and Analysis*, vol. 2. John Wiley & Sons (Wiley-Interscience), New York.

Cuddington, J. T., Johansson, P.-O. and Löfgren, K. G. (1984) *Disequilibrium Macroeconomics in Open Economies*. Basil Blackwell, Oxford.

Cuddington, J. T., Johnson, F. R. and Knetsch, J. L. (1981) Valuing amenity resources in the presence of substitutes. *Land Economics* 57, 526–35.

Cummings, R. G., Brookshire, D. S. and Schultze, W. D. (1986) *Valuing Public Goods: The Contingent Valuation Method*. Rowman and Allanheld Publishers, Totowa, N.J.

Dasgupta, P. S. (1982) *The Control of Resources*. Basil Blackwell, Oxford.

Dasgupta, P. S. and Heal, G. M. (1979) *Economic Theory and Exhaustible Resources*. James Nisbet/Cambridge University Press, Oxford.

Davis, R. K. (1964) The value of big game hunting in a private forest. In Transactions of the twenty-ninth North American wildlife conference. Wildlife Management Institute, Washington, D.C.

Deaton, A. and Muellbauer, J. (1983) *Economics and Consumer Behavior*. Cambridge University Press, New York.

Deyak, T. A. and Smith, K. V. (1978) Congestion and participation in outdoor recreation: A household production function approach. *Journal of Environmental Economics and Management* 5, 63–80.

Diamond, P. A. and McFadden, D. (1974) some uses of the expenditure function in public finance. *Journal of Public Economics* 3, 3–22.

Diamond, P. A. and Stiglitz, J. E. (1974) Increases in risk and in risk aversion. *Journal of Economic Theory* 8, 337–60.

Diewert, W. E. (1982) Duality approaches to microeconomic theory. In Arrow, K. J. and Intriligator, M. D. (eds.), *Handbook of Mathematical Economics*, vol. II. North-Holland, Amsterdam.

Dixit, A. K. and Weller, P. A. (1979) The three consumer's surpluses. *Economica* 46, 125–35.

Domencich, T. A. and McFadden, D. (1975) *Urban Travel Demand. A Behavioral Analysis*. North-Holland, Amsterdam.

Drèze, J. H. and Modigliani, F. (1972) Consumption decisions under uncertainty. *Journal of Economic Theory* 5, 308–35.

Dupuit, J. (1844) De la mesure de l'utilité des travaux publics. Annales des Ponts et Chaussées. Translated by R. H. Barback in *International Economic Papers* 17 (1952), 83–110, Macmillan, New York.

Ekelund, R. B. Jr and Hébert, R. F. (1985) Consumer surplus: the first hundred years. *History of Political Economy* 17, 419–54.

Epstein, L. (1975) A disaggregate analysis of consumer choice under uncertainty. *Econometrica* 43, 877–92.

Fisher, A. C. and Hanemann, M. W. (1983) *Endangered Species: The Economics of Irreversible Damage*. Department of Agricultural and Resource Economics, University of California, Berkeley.

Fisher, A. C. and Peterson, F. M. (1976) The environment in economics: A survey. *Journal of Economic Literature* 14, 1–33.

Fleming, W. H. (1965) *Functions of Several Variables*. Addison-Wesley, Reading, Mass.

Freeman, A. M. III (1979a) *The Benefits of Environmental Improvement. Theory and Practice*. Johns Hopkins University Press, Baltimore.

(1979b) Hedonic prices, property values and measuring environmental benefits: A survey of the issues. *Scandinavian Journal of Economics* 81, 154–73.

(1984a) The sign and size of option value. *Land Economics* 60, 1–13.

(1984b) The quasi-option value of irreversible development. *Journal of Environmental Economics and Management* 11, 292–5.

(1985) Supply uncertainty, option price, and option value. *Land Economics* 61, 176–81.

Friedman, M. (1949) The Marshallian demand curve. *Journal of Political Economy* 57, 463–95.

Friedman, M. and Savage, L. J. (1948) The utility analysis of choices involving risk. *Journal of Political Economy* 56, 279–304.

Gallagher, D. R. and Smith, K. V. (1985) Measuring values for environmental resources under uncertainty. *Journal of Environmental Economics and Management* 12, 132–43.

Geary, R. C. (1949/50) A note on a constant utility index of the cost of living. *Review of Economic Studies* 18, 65–6.

Gerking, S. D. and Weirick, W. N. (1983) Compensating differences and interregional wage differentials. *Review of Economics and Statistics* 65, 483–7.

Graham, D. A. (1981) Cost–benefit analysis under uncertainty. *American Economic Review* 71, 715–25.

(1984) Cost–benefit analysis under uncertainty: Reply. *American Economic Review* 74, 1100–2.

Gramlich, E. M. (1981) *Benefit–cost Analysis of Government Programs.* Prentice-Hall, Englewood Cliffs, N.J.

Greenley, D. A., Walsh, R. G. and Young, R. A. (1981) Option value: Empirical evidence from a case study of recreation and water quality. *Quarterly Journal of Economics* 95, 657–73.

(1985) Option value: Empirical evidence from a case study of recreation and water quality: Reply. *Quarterly Journal of Economics* 100, 292–9.

Griliches, Z. (ed.) (1971) *Price Indexes and Quality Change.* Harvard University Press, Cambridge, Mass.

Halvorsen, R. A. and Pollakowski, H. O. (1981) Choice of functional form for hedonic price equations. *Journal of Urban Economics* 10, 37–49.

Hammack, J. and Brown, G. M. Jr (1974) *Waterfowl and Wetlands: Toward Bioeconomic Analysis.* Johns Hopkins University Press, Baltimore.

Hammond, P. J. (1981) Ex ante and ex post welfare optimality under uncertainty. *Economica* 48, 235–50.

Hanemann, M. W. (1982) *Information and the Concept of Option Value.* Department of Agricultural and Resource Economics, University of California, Berkeley.

(1984a) Discrete/continuous models of consumer demand. *Econometrica* 52, 541–61.

(1984b) *On Reconciling Different Concepts of Option Value.* Department of Agricultural and Resource Economics, University of California, Berkeley.

(1984c) Entropy as a measure of consensus in the evaluation of recreation site quality. *Journal of Environmental Economics and Management* 18, 241–51.

(1984d) Welfare evaluations in contingent valuation experiments with discrete responses. *American Journal of Agricultural Economics* 66, 332–41.

Hanoch, G. (1977) Risk aversion and consumer preferences. *Econometrica* 45, 413–26.

(1980) Hours and weeks in the theory of labor supply. In Smith, J. P. (ed.), *Female Labor Supply: Theory and Estimation.* Princeton University Press, Princeton.

Harberger, A. C. (1971) Three basic postulates for applied welfare economics: An interpretive essay. *Journal of Economic Literature* 9, 785–97.

Harrison, D. Jr and Rubinfeld, O. L. (1978) Hedonic housing prices and the demand for clean air. *Journal of Environmental Economics and Management* 5, 81–102.

Harrod, R. F. (1948) *Towards a Dynamic Economy*. Macmillan, London.

Harsanyi, J. (1955) Cardinal welfare, individualistic ethics, and interpersonal comparison of welfare. *Journal of Political Economy* 63, 309–21.

Hau, T. D. (1985) A Hicksian approach to cost–benefit analysis with discrete-choice models. *Economica* 52, 479–90.

Hause, J. C. (1975) The theory of welfare cost measurement. *Journal of Political Economy* 83, 1145–82.

Hausman, J. A. (1981) Exact consumer's surplus and deadweight loss. *American Economic Review* 71, 662–76.

Helms, J. L. (1984) Comparing stochastic price regimes: The limitations of expected surplus measures. *Economics Letters* 14, 173–8.

(1985) Expected consumer's surplus and the welfare effects of price stabilization. *International Economic Review* 26, 603–17.

Henderson, A. (1940/1) Consumer's surplus and the compensating variation. *Review of Economic Studies* 8, 117–21.

Henry, C. (1974) Option values in the economics of irreplaceable assets. *Review of Economic Studies Symposium on Economics of Exhaustible Resources*, 89–104.

Herfindahl, O. C. and Kneese, A. V. (1974) *Economic Theory of Natural Resources*. C. E. Merrill Publishing Company, Columbus.

Hey, J. D. (1979) *Uncertainty in Microeconomics*. Martin Robertson, Oxford.

(1981) *Economics in Disequilibrium*. Martin Robertson, Oxford.

Hicks, J. R. (1939) The foundations of welfare economics. *Economic Journal* 49, 696–712.

(1940/1) The rehabilitation of consumers' surplus. *Review of Economic Studies* 8, 108–15.

(1943) The four consumer's surpluses. *Review of Economic Studies* 11, 31–41.

(1945/6) The generalized theory of consumer's surplus. *Review of Economic Studies* 13, 68–73.

(1946) *Value and Capital*. Clarendon Press, Oxford.

Hirshleifer, J. (1965) The investment decision under uncertainty: Choice-theoretic approaches. *Quarterly Journal of Economics* 79, 509–36.

Hirshleifer, J. and Riley, J. G. (1979) the analytics of uncertainty and information – An expository survey. *Journal of Economic Literature* 17, 1375–421.

Hof, J. G. and King, D. A. (1982) On the necessity of simultaneous recreation demand equation estimation. *Land Economics* 58, 547–52.

Hogg, R. V. and Craig, A. T. (1978) *Introduction to Mathematical Statistics*, 4th edn, Macmillan, New York.

Hori, H. (1975) Revealed preference for public goods. *American Economic Review* 65, 978–91.

Hotelling, H. (1938) The general welfare in relation to problems of taxation and of railway and utility rates. *Econometrica* 6, 242–69.

(1947) Unpublished letter to Director of National Park Service.

Howard, D. (1977) Rationing, quantity constraints, and consumption theory. *Econometrica* 45, 399–412.

Hurwics, L. and Uzawa, H. (1971) On the integrability of demand functions. In Chipman, J. S., Hurwics, L., Richter, M. K. and Sonnenschein, H. F. (eds.), *Preferences, Utility and Demand*. Harcourt Brace Jovanovich, New York.

Hylland, A. and Strand, J. (1983) *Valuation of Reduced Air Pollution in the Grenland Area*. Department of Economics, University of Oslo, Norway (in Norwegian).

Johansson, P.-O. and Löfgren, K. G. (1985) *The Economics of Forestry and Natural Resources*. Basil Blackwell, Oxford.

Johnson, F. R., Krutilla, J. V., Bowes, M. D. and Wilman, E. A. (1983) *Estimating the impacts of forest management on recreation benefits. Part I: Methodology. Part II: Application with reference to the White Mountain National Forest* (by Johnson, F. R. and Krutilla, J. V.). Multiple Use Forestry Project, Resources for the Future, Washington, D.C.

Johnston, J. (1984) *Econometric Methods*, 3rd edn, McGraw-Hill, Tokyo.

Jones-Lee, M. W. (1976) *The Value of Life*. Martin Robertson, Oxford.

Just, R. E., Hueth, D. L. and Schmitz, A. (1982) *Applied Welfare Economics and Public Policy*. Prentice Hall, Englewood Cliffs, N.J.

Kaldor, N. (1939) Welfare propositions of economics and interpersonal comparisons of utility. *Economic Journal* 49, 549–52.

Kannai, Y. (1977) Concavifiability and constructions of concave utility functions. *Journal of Mathematical Economics* 4, 1–56.

Karni, E. (1983) On the correspondence between multivariate risk aversion and risk aversion with state-dependent preferences. *Journal of Economic Theory* 30, 230–42.

Katzner, D. W. (1970) *Static Demand Theory*. Macmillan, London.

Knetsch, J. L. and Davis, R. K. (1966) Comparisons of methods for recreation evaluation. In Kneese, A. V. and Smith, S. C. (eds.) *Water Research*. The Johns Hopkins University Press, Baltimore.

Knetsch, J. L. and Sinden, J. A. (1984) Willingness to pay and compensation demanded: Experimental evidence of an unexpected disparity in measures of value. *Quarterly Journal of Economics* 99, 507–21.

Krutilla, J. A. (1967) Conservation reconsidered. *American Economic Review* 57, 777–86.

Krutilla, J. V. and Fisher, A. C. (1975) *The Economics of Natural Environments: Studies in the Valuation of Commodity and Amenity Resources*. Johns Hopkins University Press, Baltimore.

Kurz, M. (1974) An experimental approach to the determination of the demand for public goods. *Journal of Public Economics* 3, 329–48.

Laffont, J.-J. (ed.) (1979) *Aggregation and Revelation of Preferences*. North-Holland, Amsterdam.

Lancaster, K. J. (1966) A new approach to consumer theory. *Journal of Political Economy* 74, 132–57.

Lau, L. J. (1969) Duality and the structure of utility functions. *Journal of Economic Theory* 1, 374–96.

Lecomber, R. (1979) *The Economics of Natural Resources*. Macmillan, London.

Lindley, D. V. (1969) *Introduction to Probability and Statistics. Part 1: Probability*. Cambridge University Press, Cambridge.

Lohmander, P. (1984) Diversification in the natural resource enterprise, option values and improved industrial coordination. Department of Forest Economics, Swedish University of Agricultural Sciences. Working Paper No. 40.

Lucas, R. E. Jr (1977) Understanding business cycles. In Brunner, K. and Meltzner, A. (eds.), *Stabilization of the Domestic and International Economy*. Carnegie-Rochester Conference Series in Public Policy. North-Holland, Amsterdam.

Lundin, S. A. G. (1975) A conditional logit analysis of the demand for outdoor recreation. Unpublished Ph.D. dissertation, University of California, Berkeley.

McFadden, D. (1973) Conditional logit analysis of qualitative choice behavior. In Zacembka, P. (ed.), *Frontiers of Econometrics*. Academic Press, New York.

(1976) Quantal choice analysis: A survey. *Annals of Economic and Social Measurement* 5, 363–90.

McGuire, M. C. and Aaron, H. (1969) Efficiency and equity in the optimal supply of a public good. *Review of Economics and Statistics* 51, 31–9.

Mackay, R. J. and Whitney, G. A. (1980) The comparative statics of quantity constraints and conditional demands: Theory and applications. *Econometrica* 48, 1727–44.

McKenzie, G. W. (1983) *Measuring Economic Welfare: New Methods*. Cambridge University Press, Cambridge.

McKenzie, G. W. and Pearce, I. F. (1982) Welfare measurement – A synthesis. *American Economic Review* 72, 669–82.

McMillan, M. L. (1979) Estimates of households' preferences for environmental quality and other housing characteristics from a system of demand equations. *Scandinavian Journal of Economics* 81, 174–87.

Maddala, G. S. (1984) *Limited-dependent and Qualitative Variables in Econometrics*. Cambridge University Press, New York.

Mäler, K.-G. (1971) A method of estimating social benefits from pollution control. *Swedish Journal of Economics* 73, 121–33.

(1974) *Environmental Economics. A Theoretical Inquiry*. Johns Hopkins University Press, Baltimore.

(1977) A note on the use of property values in estimating marginal willingness to pay for environmental quality. *Journal of Environmental Economics and Management* 4, 355–69.

(1981) A note on the possibility of calculating demand for a public good from information on individual behaviour. Research paper 6209, Stockholm School of Economics, Stockholm.

(1984) *Risk, Uncertainty and the Environment*. Stockholm School of Economics, Stockholm.

Malinvaud, E. (1971) A planning approach to the public good problem. *Swedish Journal of Economics* 73, 96–117.

Marshall, A. (1920) *Principles of Economics*, 8th edn, Macmillan, London.

Massell, B. F. (1969) Price stabilization and welfare. *Quarterly Journal of Economics* 83, 284–98.

Mendelsohn, R. and Strang, W. J. (1984) Cost–benefit analysis under uncertainty: Comment. *American Economic Review* 74, 1096–9.

Miller, J. R. and Lad, F. (1984) Flexibility, learning, and irreversibility in environmental decisions: A Bayesian analysis. *Journal of Environmental Economics and Management* 11, 161–72.

Milleron, J.-C. (1972) Theory of value with public goods: A survey article. *Journal of Economic Theory* 5, 419–77.

Mishan, E. J. (1971) The postwar literature on externalities: An interpretative essay. *Journal of Economic Literature* 9, 1–28.

(1976) The use of compensating and equivalent variation in cost–benefit analysis. *Economica* 43, 185–97.

Mitchell, R. C. and Carson, R. T. (1985) Option value: Empirical evidence from a case study of recreation and water quality: Comment. *Quarterly Journal of Economics* 100, 291–4.

Morey, E. R. (1981) The demand for site-specific recreational activities: A characteristics approach. *Journal of Environmental Economics and Management* 8, 345–71.

(1984) Confuser surplus. *American Economic Review* 74, 163–73.

Musgrave, R. A. (1959) *Theory of Public Finance*. McGraw-Hill Kogakuska, Tokyo.

Muth, J. F. (1961) Rational expectations and the theory of price movements. *Econometrica* 29, 315–35.

Neary, J. P. and Roberts, K. W. S. (1980) The theory of household behaviour under rationing. *European Economic Review* 13, 25–42.

Neumann, J. von and Morgenstern, O. (1947) *Theory of Games and Economic Behavior*, 2nd edn, Princeton University Press, Princeton, N.J.

Ng, Y.-K. (1979) *Welfare Economics. Introduction and Development of Basic Concepts*. Macmillan, London.

(1982) Beyond optimality: The necessity of interpersonal cardinal utilities in distributional judgements and social choice. *Zeitschrift für Nationalökonomie* 42, 207–33.

Patinkin, D. (1963) Demand curves and consumer's surplus. In Christ, C. F. *et al.*

216   *Bibliography*

(eds), *Measurement in Economics, Studies in Mathematical Economics and Econometrics in Memory of Yehuda Grunfeld.* Stanford University Press, Stanford.

Pearse, P. H. (1968) A new approach to the evaluation of non-priced recreational resources. *Land Economics* 44, 87–99.

Pindyck, R. S. and Rubinfeld, D. L. (1976) *Econometric Models and Economic Forecasts.* McGraw-Hill Kogakusha, Tokyo.

Plummer, M. L. and Hartman, R. C. (1985) Option value: A general approach. Mimeo.

Polinsky, A. M. and Rubinfeld, D. L. (1975) Property values and the benefits of environmental improvements: Theory and measurement. Discussion Paper No. 404, Harvard Institute of Economic Research, Cambridge, Mass.

Pontryagin, L. S., Boltyanski, V. S., Gamkrelidze, R. V. and Mishchenko, E. F. (1962) *The Mathematical Theory of Optimal Processes.* John Wiley & Sons (Wiley-Interscience), New York.

Porter, R. C. (1984) The optimal timing of an exhaustible, reversible wilderness development project. *Land Economics* 60, 247–54.

Pratt, J. W. (1964) Risk aversion in the small and in the large. *Econometrica* 32, 122–36.

Quandt, R. E. Bibliography of rationing and disequilibrium models. Unpublished.

Ramsey, F. (1928) A mathematical theory of saving. *Economic Journal* 38, 543–59.

Randall, A. and Stoll, J. R. (1980) Consumer's surplus in commodity space. *American Economic Review* 70, 449–55.

Randall, A., Ives, B. and Eastman, C. (1974) Bidding games for valuation of aesthetic environmental improvements. *Journal of Environmental Economics and Management* 1, 132–49.

Rawls, J. (1972) *A Theory of Justice.* Clarendon Press, Oxford.

Rogerson, W. P. (1980) Aggregate expected consumer surplus as a welfare index with an application to price stabilization. *Econometrica* 48, 423–36.

Rosen, S. (1974) Hedonic prices and implicit markets: Product differentiation in pure competition. *Journal of Political Economy* 82, 34–55.

Rosen, H. S., Rosen K. T. and Holtz-Eakin, D. (1984) Housing tenure, uncertainty, and taxation. *Review of Economics and Statistics* 66, 405–16.

Rothbarth, E. (1940–1) The measurement of changes in real income under conditions of rationing. *Review of Economic Studies* 8, 100–7.

Rothschild, M. and Stiglitz, J. E. (1970) Increasing risk. I: A definition. *Journal of Economic Theory* 2, 225–43.

(1971) Increasing risk. II: Its economic consequences. *Journal of Economic Theory* 3, 66–84.

Rowe, R., D'Arge, R. C. and Brookshire, D. S. (1980) An experiment on the economic value of visibility. *Journal of Environmental Economics and Management* 7, 1–19.

Roy, R. (1942) *De l'Utilité, Contribution à la Théorie des Choix*. Hermann, Paris.

Samuelson, P. A. (1942) Constancy of the marginal utility of income. In Lange, O., McIntyre, F. and Yntema, T. O. (eds), *Studies in Mathematical Economics and Econometrics in Memory of Henry Schultz*. University of Chicago Press, Chicago.
    (1947) *Foundations of Economic Analysis*. Harvard University Press, Cambridge, Mass.
    (1950) The problem of integrability in utility theory. *Economica* 30, 355–85.
    (1954) The pure theory of public expenditure. *Review of Economics and Statistics* 36, 387–9.
    (1955) Diagrammatic exposition of a theory of public expenditure. *Review of Economics and Statistics* 37, 350–6.
    (1969) Pure theory of public expenditure and taxation. In Margolis, J. and Guitton, H. (eds.), *Public Economics*. Macmillan, London
    (1972) The consumer does benefit from feasible price stability. *Quarterly Journal of Economics* 86, 476–93.
Sandmo, A. (1970) The effect of uncertainty on saving decisions. *Review of Economic Studies* 37, 353–60.
Schmalensee, R. (1972) Option demand and consumer's surplus: Valuing price changes under uncertainty. *American Economic Review* 62, 813–24.
Schulze, W. D., D'Arge, R. C. and Brookshire, D. S. (1981) Valuing environmental commodities: Some recent experiments. *Land Economics* 57, 151–72.
Scitovsky, T. (1941) A note on welfare propositions in economics. *Review of Economic Studies* 9, 77–88.
Seade, J. (1978) Consumer's surplus and linearity of Engel curves. *Economic Journal* 88, 511–23.
Seller, C., Stoll, J. R. and Chavas, J.-P. (1985) Validation of empirical measures of welfare change: A comparison of nonmarket techniques. *Land Economics* 61, 156–75.
Shapiro, P. and Smith, T. (1981) Preferences for non-market goods revealed through market demands. In Smith, K. V. (ed.), *Advances in Applied Microeconomics* vol. 1. JAI Press, Greenwich, Connecticut.
Sheffrin, S. M. (1984) *Rational Expectations*. Cambridge Surveys of Economic Literature. Cambridge University Press, New York.
Sidgwick, H. (1890) *The Methods of Ethics*. Macmillan, London.
Siebert, H. (1982) Nature as a life support system. Renewable resources and environmental disruption. *Zeitschrift für Nationalökonomie* 42, 133–42.
Silberberg, E. (1972) Duality and the many consumer's surpluses. *American Economic Review* 62, 942–52.
    (1978) *The Structure of Economics: A Mathematical Analysis*. McGraw-Hill, New York.
Silverman, R. A. (1969) *Modern Calculus and Analytic Geometry*. Macmillan, New York.
Sinden, J. A. (1974) A utility approach to the valuation of recreational and

aesthetic experiences. *American Journal of Agricultural Economics* 56, 61–72.

Small, K. A. (1982) *Ordered Logit: A Discrete Choice Model with Proximate Covariance among Alternatives.* Department of Economics, Princeton University.

Small, K. A. and Rosen, S. (1981) Applied welfare economics with discrete choice models. *Econometrica* 49, 105–30.

Smith, B. and Stephen, F. H. (1975) Cost–benefit analysis and compensation criteria: A note. *Economic Journal* 85, 902–5.

Smith, K. V. (1984) A bound for option value. *Land Economics* 60, 292–6.

Smith, K. V. and Desvousges, W. H. (1985) The generalized travel cost model and water quality benefits: A reconsideration. *Southern Economic Journal* 52, 371–81.

Spitzer, J. J. (1982) A primer on Box–Cox estimation. *Review of Economics and Statistics* 64, 307–13.

Stahl, D. O. II (1983a) Quasi-homothetic preferences, the generalized Divisia quantity index, and aggregation. *Economica* 50, 87–93.

(1983b) A note on the consumer surplus path-of-integration problem. *Economica* 50, 95–8.

(1983c) On cost–benefit analysis with quality attributes. *Zeitschrift für Nationalökonomie* 43, 273–87.

(1984) Monotonic variations of consumer surplus and comparative performance results. *Southern Economic Journal* 51, 503–20.

Stiglitz, J. E. (1969) Behavior towards risk with many commodities. *Econometrica* 37, 660–7.

Stone, R. (1954) Linear expenditure systems and demand analysis: An application to the pattern of British demand. *Economic Journal* 64, 511–27.

Strotz, R. H. (1956) Myopia and inconsistency in dynamic utility maximization. *Review of Economic Studies* 23, 165–80.

(1958) Two propositions related to public goods. *Review of Economics and Statistics* 40, 329–31.

Swamy, P. A. V. B., Barth, J. R. and Tinsley, P. A. (1982) The rational expectations approach to economic modelling. *Journal of Economic Dynamics and Control* 4, 125–48.

Tobin, J. and Houthakker, H. S. (1950/1) The effects of rationing on demand elasticities. *Review of Economic Studies* 18, 140–53.

Turnovsky, S. J., Shalit, H. and Schmitz, A. (1980) Consumer's surplus, price instability, and consumer welfare. *Econometrica* 48, 135–52.

Ulph, A. (1982) The role of ex ante and ex post decisions in the valuation of life. *Journal of Public Economics* 18, 265–76.

Varian, H. R. (1978) *Microeconomic Analysis.* W. W. Norton & Company, New York. (Second edn 1984).

Vartia, Y. O. (1983) Efficient methods of measuring welfare change and compensated income in terms of ordinary demand functions. *Econometrica* 51, 79–98.

Vaughan, W. J. and Russell, C. S. (1982) Valuing a fishing day: An application of a systematic varying parameter model. *Land Economics* 58, 450–63.

Vaughan, W. J., Russell, C. S. and Hazilla, M. (1982) A note on the use of travel cost models with unequal zonal populations: Comment. *Land Economics* 58, 400–7.

Viscusi, W. K. and Zeckhauser, R. J. (1976) Environmental policy choice under uncertainty. *Journal of Environmental Economics and Management* 3, 97–112.

Walsh, R. G., Greenley, D. A., Young, R. A. Mckean, J. R. and Prato, A. A. (1978) *Option Values, Preservation Values and Recreational Benefits of Improved Water Quality: A Case Study of the South Platte River Basin, Colorado.* Department of Economics, Colorado State University, Fort Collins.

Waugh, F. W. (1944) Does the consumer benefit from price instability. *Quarterly Journal of Economics* 58, 602–14.

Weisbrod, B. A. (1964) Collective-consumption services of individual-consumption goods. *Quarterly Journal of Economics* 78, 471–7.

Weymark, J. A. (1985) Money-metric utility functions. *International Economic Review* 26, 219–32.

White, F. C. and Ziemer, R. F. (1983) Disequilibrium prices and economic surplus in the U.S. fed beef market. *Canadian Journal of Agricultural Economics* 31, 197–204.

Widder, D. V. (1961) *Advanced Calculus*, 2nd edn, Prentice-Hall, Englewood Cliffs, N.J.

Willig, R. D. (1973) Consumer's surplus: A rigorous cookbook. Technical report No. 98, Institute for Mathematical Studies in the Social Sciences, Stanford.

(1976) Consumer's surplus without apology. *American Economic Review* 66, 589–97.

(1978) Incremental consumer's surplus and hedonic price adjustment. *Journal of Economic Theory* 17, 227–53.

Zabalza, A. (1982) Compensating and equivivalent variations, and the deadweight loss of taxation. *Economica* 49, 355–9.

Zellner, A. (1985) Bayesian econometrics. *Econometrica* 53, 253–69.

Index

220